Understanding Economic Inequality

To Daria, 100 percent

Understanding Economic Inequality
Bigger Pies and Just Deserts

Todd A. Knoop

David Joyce Professor of Economics and Business, Cornell College, USA

Edward Elgar
PUBLISHING

Cheltenham, UK • Northampton, MA, USA

Published by
Edward Elgar Publishing Limited
The Lypiatts
15 Lansdown Road
Cheltenham
Glos GL50 2JA
UK

Edward Elgar Publishing, Inc.
William Pratt House
9 Dewey Court
Northampton
Massachusetts 01060
USA

A catalogue record for this book
is available from the British Library

Library of Congress Control Number: 2019951900

This book is available electronically in the **Elgar**online
Economics subject collection
DOI 10.4337/9781788971607

ISBN 978 1 78897 159 1 (cased)
ISBN 978 1 78897 160 7 (eBook)

Printed and bound by CPI Group (UK) Ltd, Croydon, CR0 4YY

Contents

Preface

> It was the best of times, it was the worst of times, it was the age of wisdom, it was the age of foolishness, it was the epoch of belief, it was the epoch of incredulity, it was the season of Light, it was the season of Darkness, it was the spring of hope, it was the winter of despair, we had everything before us, we had nothing before us, we were all going direct to Heaven, we were all going direct the other way—in short, the period was so far like the present period, that some of its noisiest authorities insisted on its being received, for good or for evil, in the superlative degree of comparison only.
>
> *Tale of Two Cities*, Charles Dickens

We are living in a new age of economic inequality; a new age that is reminiscent of past ages, but also a new age that is better than it ever has been before. Over the last 25 years, nearly two billion people across the globe have risen out of poverty, poverty rates in the US and other developed countries have declined, and income levels have risen worldwide (albeit slower than before for most of the rich world). Yet economic dissatisfaction—driven by the persistent fear felt by many that they are "falling behind"—is higher than at any point since the 1930s. This is because of rising inequality. To pick just one fact to illustrate how much inequality has increased, in the US the top 1 percent earn twice the amount of income as the poorest 50 percent of the population. Read that sentence again. It means that those in the top 1 percent have average incomes that are 100 times what the bottom half of the US population earns.

Any history of the twenty-first century would be incomplete without discussing the "99 percent versus the 1 percent". Many political leaders have referred to inequality as the crucial issue of our time, and inequality is now dominating our civic conversations in ways that it has never done before. The proportion of articles in *The New York Times* mentioning economic inequality increased by a factor of ten between 2009 and 2016.[1] Recent elections on both sides of the Atlantic, in both the northern and southern hemispheres, from both the right and the left of the political spectrum, have been driven by the fears and frustrations associated with economic dislocation and the increasing disparity between those racing ahead and those who are running in place but falling further behind. There is growing recognition that increasing disparities in income and wealth pose a serious threat to entrepreneurship, democracy, social mobility, public health, education, and our civil society.

The fact that you are reading this book means that you too have been caught up in these discussions and share the same fears about inequality that most of your fellow Earthlings share—the anxiety associated with economic uncertainty is one rare thing that is more evenly owned by everyone in this time of polarization. The objective of this book is to bring an economist's eye and a mind broadened by insights from philosophy, sociology, psychology, and political science to examine questions related to why economic inequality is growing today and why this is so important for our economics and for our society. Why does inequality matter? How has it changed over time? What is driving it? How does it differ across people and places? What policies can be adopted to moderate it? These are seemingly simple yet extremely complicated questions. The good news is that many of our brightest minds are paying attention: inequality has risen to the forefront of the research agendas of many of the best scholars in sociology, political science, philosophy, and in economics. The last decade has brought with it more groundbreaking research into the causes and consequences of inequality—both theoretical and empirical—than the previous 50 years combined. My focus in this book is to serve as translator and facilitator—organizing and repackaging some of this groundbreaking research into a form that it is accessible to the rest of us who want to understand our world, our society, our politics, our paychecks, and our neighbor's paychecks better.

Let me begin this book on economic inequality by possibly surprising you: until recently, economics has not really had much to say about inequality. Let me explain why this was, and why economists today are finally recognizing the importance of inequality long after the public was paying attention to it.

Economics is primarily the study of who gains and who gains more. In many ways, economics is the most optimistic of the academic disciplines. Its primary focus is on understanding where improvements in quality of life come from and how to get more of them. Economics generally focuses on mutually beneficial trades, not zero-sum outcomes where one person gains only when someone else loses. It tends to be most interested in growth and development, not decay and retreat. In contrast to its well-known moniker as the "dismal science", economics is the study of progress as much as it is the study of scarce resources, incentives, and trade. And the fact that our overall quality of life—by whatever measure you choose to use—has risen so dramatically over time and across the globe is a testament to the fact that while there have been periodic episodes of reversal, the greater arc of history is one of progress.

What drives improvements in people's quality of life? The primary focus of economics has been on advocating for efficiency and increasing productivity (output per worker hour) as the best means of improving the quality of life for everyone. The idea is that if people can become more productive and efficient, they will produce more with whatever resources they have. Greater production will expand the resources available to everyone in society, improving our general quality of life. In other words, by expanding the size of the proverbial pie, most people (although no guarantee that all people) will be left with more to eat than they would if the pie was small, regardless of the fact that everyone's slice may not be the same.

This iron link between productivity and well-being can be traced back to Adam Smith. The impetus for Smith's *The Wealth of Nations* was Smith's curiosity about why the quality of life was so much higher in England than in France in the mid-1700s. Smith placed the focus squarely on productivity. According to Smith's "invisible hand" theory, it is the efficiency gains from specialization amplified by the power of markets to share these gains far and wide that drive increases in productivity over time and that generate higher standards of living for society. Specialization is crucial to growth because it allows each individual to develop particular skills and tools that increase their productivity at specific activities. But markets are also necessary because they allow us to trade the narrow range of goods that we are good at producing for an infinite variety of goods that we are not so good at producing, granting each of us the best of both worlds—variety and volume—that improve our quality of life. While Smith's ideas on specialization and trade are simple, they are also powerful; after 250 years, they remain the most succinct explanation of the fundamental sources of improvements in our material conditions. Because of the predictive power of Smith's theories, and of the many other economists that came after him, efficiency has regularly been treated as synonymous with well-being by many economists.

A few of the founding fathers of economics did think about the role that distribution, not just efficiency, plays in determining our quality of life. Thomas Malthus worried about population growth among the lower classes and how this could depress their incomes below subsistence levels, leading to widespread famine. David Ricardo worried about how economic growth could raise the rental rate on land to levels that were unsustainable over time. The windfall for rentiers would consign tenant farmers to higher and higher levels of debt, eventually exposing everyone to the dangers of default and financial collapse. And there was Karl Marx, who believed that profits entirely flow to the rich owners of capital—profits that are generated only by depressing wages and consigning workers to subsistence levels of income. However, these economic worrywarts have never been the mainstream voices in economics, in part because their discussions of inequality were couched within dour economic models of economic collapse that are incongruous with the overall historical arc of economic progress. The dire predictions of their models have contaminated the study of inequality with the one idea that is abhorred in economics: pessimism.

As a result, until recently, economists have never really given income distribution the attention that it deserves. Inequality has generally been a second-order concern to efficiency, despite the fact that even the most ardent free-market economists recognize that the unequal distribution of resources has costs (as well as possibly benefits) that should be considered when studying economic behavior. The predominant viewpoint in economics is well captured by the Nobel Prize winning economist Robert Lucas, who sees less danger in inequality than he does in people worrying too much about inequality:

> Of the tendencies that are harmful to sound economics, the most seductive, and in my opinion the most poisonous, is to focus on the questions of distribution ... The potential for improving the lives of poor people by finding different ways of distributing current production is nothing compared to the apparently limitless potential of increasing production.[2]

You might say that Lucas ascribes to the invisible hand theory of pie-making: if you make the pie bigger, the market will figure out a way to make sure that most people will get a larger piece than they had before.

Consider two specific examples of how economists have often purposefully ignored the impact of inequality. The first is the widespread use of representative agent models in economics, where groups of people are assumed to be just the same median person, multiplied. Representative agent models significantly simplify economic analysis, but at the cost of pretending that inequality doesn't matter because everyone is basically the same. Second, economists sometimes evaluate the welfare impacts of policy using the "Pareto efficient" standard, meaning that one policy cannot be superior to another unless every single person is made better off by it. Any policy that redistributes income from one person to another is destined to fail the Pareto standard, even a policy that benefits everyone at a slight expense to a single individual. Using the Pareto efficient standard to evaluate policy places a heavy hand on the scale in favor of policies that emphasize overall efficiency and ignore how any gains from these policies are distributed.

However, the study of economics in the real world recognizes few Pareto efficient outcomes where everyone wins but no one loses. By too often focusing on scenarios where macroeconomic outcomes are emphasized and distributional effects are glossed over, economists have reduced their public standing in the debate over economic inequality and weakened their influence. The impact of this on the study of economics generally—and on the study of inequality specifically—has not been good. By failing to give inequality the consideration that it deserves, economists have ceded much of the study of economic inequality and the notion of what constitutes "fairness" to other disciplines: political science, philosophy, sociology, and psychology chief among them. This is not to say that these disciplines have nothing to say on this topic—in fact, they have a great deal to say, and I will attempt to present some of what we have learned from these disciplines regarding what fairness means and what it looks like in the real world. But by assuming that fairness has more to do with politics and philosophy than economics, economists have allowed muddled thinking and mistaken conclusions about inequality to persist in our public debates. All economists must recognize that fairness can be an important outcome for society in and of itself, and must think more carefully about what economic fairness looks like both in theory and in practice.

There is another, and in my mind more important, reason why inequality must move to the forefront of economics. It is because understanding inequality is key to understanding how economics actually works. In the real world—not the world of most theoretical economists—it is not our *absolute* standing that often determines our behavior, but it is our *relative* status. Inequality is not just the outcome of economic interactions, but it fundamentally influences economic decision-making because of our psychology and the complex social and institutional environments within which we interact with each other.

Traditional economics has assumed that there is a simple tradeoff between efficiency and equity: to have efficiency, we must accept a certain level of inequality. However, if there is one thing I hope to accomplish in this book, it is to convince you that if the only thing you know about the economics of inequality is the efficiency/equity tradeoff, then your knowledge of economics is dangerously simplistic. In fact, efficiency and equity often go hand-in-hand. Belief in a strict efficiency/equity tradeoff is based upon a worldview that ignores many of the major developments in economic thinking over the last three decades. Some of these new developments (which we will talk about in much greater detail later) include: the power of networks in generating new ideas; the importance of psychology and behavioral economics in decision-making; the significance of social norms and status; the crucial roles of social capital and trust; the market failures created by information externalities; the importance of coordination failure and historical path dependence; the impact of financial market failures and macroeconomic instability; the political economy of democratic capitalism; and the primacy of economic institutions.

In this book, I hope to convince you that there is no simple tradeoff between efficiency and equity, but a virtuous/vicious circle can exist between the two where more equality can actually increase efficiency and productivity, while higher levels of inequality can actually reduce productivity. In such a world, inequality is no longer just a matter of second-order importance, but of first-order significance equal to that of efficiency. Studying inequality is not at the periphery of economics, but at its core.

In a counter to Robert Lucas, another Nobel Prize winning economist, Robert Solow, captures this new thinking in the following quote:

> Heterogeneity is the essence of a modern economy. In real life we worry about the relations between managers and shareowners, between venture capitalists and

entrepreneurs, you name it … We know for a fact that heterogeneous agents have different and sometimes conflicting goals, different information, different capacities to process it, different expectations, different beliefs about how the economy works. [Traditional economic] models exclude all this landscape.[3]

To put this another way, modern economics recognizes that there is more than a little truth to the quip by H. L. Mencken that a wealthy person is anyone with an "income that is at least $100 more a year than the income of one's wife's sister's husband".[4]

Let me give you a brief introduction to the ways that the relationship between efficiency and equality is more complicated than it is often portrayed in an introductory economics course. Consider the way that wages are set within an economy. Classical economic models assume that everyone's wages reflect their own marginal productivity, meaning the amount of output that they alone produce. As a result, the Classical assumption is that inequality simply reflects the fact that some workers are more productive than others. But in the real world, how does a firm know a single worker's productivity? Most people work in groups, where the productivity of one worker is dependent upon the productivity of their teammates, of the business strategies they may or may not have a hand in drafting, on the capital and technology that the firm has available to use, and even on social norms within the firm. This is true if you are the lowest level worker in the company hierarchy, and even more true if you are the CEO of a company. As a practical matter, there is no such thing as individual productivity for most jobs, yet many Classical economists act like there is. If wage differences do not reflect large differences in individual productivity, the Classical explanation of income inequality falls apart.

Likewise, even if the productivity of individual workers could be measured, do wages always reflect that productivity? There are good reasons to believe that they often do not. One reason is that there are often market failures that allow some people with more power to reap returns that are higher than their marginal productivity—these excess returns are what economists call *economic rents*. Consider Figure P.1, which presents data on cumulative productivity growth since 1948 and average pay growth for non-supervisory workers who are directly involved in production (in other words, hourly workers that are not salaried managers, and who comprise 80 percent of the workforce).

Before 1973, the iron link between productivity and wages held for these workers, just as assumed in Classical economic models. But since the mid-1700s—roughly when our modern era of growing inequality began—productivity has grown at *eight times* the rate of a typical worker's pay. And since 2000, productivity has been growing at *ten times* the rate of a typical worker's pay. In other words, the benefits of higher productivity are not going to the vast majority of workers, but elsewhere in the form of economic rents.

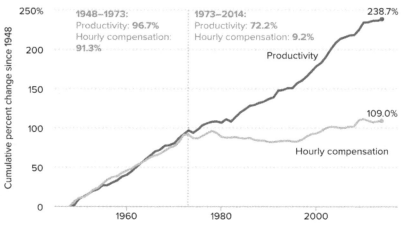

Source: Bivens and Mishel (2015), used with permission.

*Figure P.1   Growth of productivity and pay of production/
            non-supervisory workers, 1948–2014*

Another reason why wages may not reflect actual productivity is because most
wages are determined within the context of where you work: your wage is a function of your level within a company, your years of service, the evaluations of peers
and supervisors, the industry your company operates in, where your job is located,
and the profitability of the company in addition to measures of productivity. In
other words, wages reflect social norms, aggregate productivity, and complicated
professional networks as much or more than individual productivity. If this wasn't
true, then why is it that an average immigrant from Mexico can increase their
wages by 250 percent simply by migrating to the US, or a Haitian by 1,000 percent,
or a Nigerian by 1,500 percent? In this context, when we talk about why wages
have become more unequal, we are not only talking about why some individuals
are paid more than other individuals, but why some groups of people are paid more
for doing similar activities than other groups of people. These are complicated
questions for which Classical economic wage theory gives us few satisfactory
answers. Thinking carefully about these questions—and others like them—gets us
much closer to the big questions we want to address in this book about what causes
inequality, its impact on society, and how we deal with it.

    This book has eight chapters, each organized around a question. Chapter 1,
'How Do We Measure Unequal? The Who, Where, What, When, and How of
Inequality', focuses on how we define and measure economic inequality. Many
of our debates about inequality boil down to the fact that there are many different

definitions and types of inequality, and many different data sources with which to measure it. Here we introduce the most common sources of inequality data and frame some of the important questions for discussion throughout the rest of the book.

Chapter 2, 'How Unequal Are We? Six Major Facts', summarizes the empirical data on wealth and income inequality across the globe in six major facts, highlighting how inequality in income and wealth within countries is growing, but inequality in income across the globe (ignoring nationality) is falling.

Chapter 3 is entitled 'Why Might Inequality be Necessary? Incentives, Freedom, and Efficiency'. Before I discuss the reasons to be worried about inequality, it is important to understand why some scholars have argued that we shouldn't worry about inequality, or should even be happy about it. This "let the market decide" approach to inequality has a long history, not only in economics but also in philosophy. In this chapter we will examine the arguments that inequality simply reflects efficient differences in productivity that should be rewarded, that inequality incentivizes higher productivity, that providing equality of opportunity should be our focus rather than promoting equality of outcomes, and that economic policy should concentrate on dealing with poverty and not inequality.

Chapter 4, 'Why Does Unequal Matter? The Economic Externalities of Inequality', gets to the heart of the matter: Why exactly should we be worried about economic inequality? Here, we examine why there may not be a tradeoff between equity and efficiency but in fact a virtuous/vicious circle between the two. This chapter will focus on the social nature of productivity and wage determination; the role that inequality plays in degrading social capital, polarizing our political systems, reducing public health, and reducing social mobility; how inequality can lead to financial fragility and macroeconomic instability; and recent research on the ways that our perceptions of fairness and our relative positions in social hierarchies impact productivity.

Chapter 5, 'Why has Domestic Inequality Risen, and Fallen, and Risen?', examines why inequality within countries is rising today in most countries. Over the very long run, inequality has risen and fallen across the globe in long waves. In this chapter, we will examine why there have been these ebbs and flows in inequality, paying particular attention to why domestic inequality fell in the mid-1900s in most countries but has risen dramatically since 1980. Many hypotheses have been offered to explain rising inequality today, such as: globalization, skills-based technological change, rising returns to capital (particularly intangible capital), changes in fiscal policy, rising market power and economic rents, and changes in family structure. We will investigate each of these potential factors.

Chapter 6, 'Why are the Three Most Important Factors in Global Inequality Location, Location, and Location?', changes our viewpoint and examines inequality not from a country-specific perspective, but from a global perspective. Here, the focus is on differences in income and wealth between countries and across the entire world population. The biggest fact in global economic inequality is that the vast majority of inequality across people can be explained by one simple word: where. In other words, *where* is much more important than *who*, which indicates that the social determinants of productivity and the networks we work within are much more important than individual productivity. The focus in this chapter is to understand why location is so important to everyone's potential income, and, in the process, understand why inequality, poverty, and wealth are so persistent across place and time. We will also investigate why global inequality has been falling, but why there remain tremendous incentives for people to migrate from poor countries to rich countries.

Chapter 7, 'Is Inequality a Problem We Can Solve?', examines the efficacy of public policies that could moderate inequality, weighed against their potential costs. This includes examining structural reform policies that change the workings of markets (such as changes in labor laws, creating more market competition, and improving education) and fiscal policies that transfer resources from the richer to the poorer citizens (such as increasing the progressiveness of taxation and providing everyone guaranteed incomes). The goal here is to broadly consider the policy menu that governments have to choose from when they set a goal to reduce inequality.

Finally, Chapter 8 is entitled 'What is the Future of Economic Inequality?' There is always value in looking forward, even when forecasting in economics is murky enough to make any prediction about the future very likely to be wrong. I conclude this book with a discussion of the most likely continuing trends in economic inequality and what factors will be most likely to drive the distribution of income and wealth in the future. Despite the fact that this book is about the seemingly dour topic of economic inequality, I hope to leave you with a sense of optimism by convincing you that rising economic inequality does not have to be the inevitable outcome of capitalism. In fact, we can have a world that is both more productive and more fair, and that there are tools at our disposal that can gain us entry to this world if we can first educate ourselves about the full causes and consequences of economic inequality, and then choose to take appropriate action.

NOTES

1. Pinker (2018).
2. Lucas (2004), p. 20.
3. Solow (2003).
4. Mencken (1916), p. 209.

1. How do we measure unequal? The who, where, what, when, and how of inequality

Before we get into the big "why" issues, we first have to agree about exactly what we are talking about when we talk about inequality. How can we quantify inequality? Talking about data is never the sexiest topic in economics, but the fact of the matter is that obtaining reliable, accurate, and well-defined data is one of the biggest challenges in understanding economic inequality. There are many different types of inequality that we could talk about, and many different sources of data that could be used to measure inequality. A great deal of the public debate surrounding inequality is often at cross-purposes because different people have different ideas about what constitutes inequality and how they choose to measure it. Many people believe in equality as a *principle*, but there is often little agreement about *what* should be made equal.

You can think of this opening chapter as a deep breath before we dive in and immerse ourselves in the big and challenging questions related to the causes and consequences of economic inequality. In this chapter, we examine the many ways that economic inequality can be defined and how we can bring data—or sometimes fail to bring data—to each of these definitions.

In general, confusion about how we measure inequality generally centers around five eternal questions that shape any empirical debate in the social sciences: Who are we talking about? Where are we talking about? What are talking about? When are we talking about? And how are we going to talk about it?

WHO ARE WE TALKING ABOUT?

The most basic "who" question relates to whether we are trying to measure inequality across individuals or households. There is often no clear answer as to whether equality should be measured across individuals or households if we want a clear answer to the question "how unequal are we?"

There are different ways to measure inequality across individuals. Measuring inequality across individual workers tells us a lot about wage and salary inequality that relates directly to our jobs. It can also tell us how much inequality can be attributed to worker productivity, to differences in earnings, and to individual professions. On the other hand, measuring inequality across all individuals, regardless of whether they work or not, gives us a clearer picture of welfare, or the resources available to each person whether they work or not.

However, most measures of inequality take place across households. Measuring inequality across households tells us more about welfare and standards of living because people's standards of living are not just a function of how much money they earn, but also who else is earning money in the family and how many people need to share each paycheck. Of course, measuring household income creates a number of complications. First, households differ in size. In my house, when my family and I go out to eat I have to multiply menu prices by 6. For other households, that might be 2 or 4 or 8. As a result, economists usually standardize household income to account for the number of family members (called *equivalency scaling*). However, it is important to remember that differences in household size are not simply due to differences in the number of children. There has been a significant increase in single-parent households; in the US, only 6 percent of children were raised in single-parent households in the 1960s, but by 2016 this had risen to 27 percent of children.[1] This has had a dramatic impact on household inequality for obvious reasons— such as fewer households with two parents working—and less obvious reasons related to child-rearing and education that we will discuss later. As a result of these differences in household composition, two households might share the same equivalency-scaled income levels but have very different standards of living.

The second complication is that whatever income a household has, the power to spend this income is not distributed equally. In many households, men dominate spending decisions. As a result, it would be incorrect to assume that every male-led household will have the same standards of living as a female-led household. For example, there is empirical evidence that when women have greater power over resources, more money gets spent on children and less on luxuries.[2]

A third complication is that changes in labor force participation can make it hard to compare household income across time. In the US, only 22 percent of women worked in 1947; today that number is 59 percent. More women working leads to higher household income, but it also leads to more inequality between those households in which women work and those in which they don't. We will also see in a later discussion that the increased number of women entering the labor force has also magnified inequality between households because working, educated women are more likely today to marry working, educated men.

One final complication is that households leave out a lot of people who are not part of a household: people in the military, nursing homes, and those who are homeless or who are refugees. As a result, these often-forgotten people are also forgotten in our household income data.

In spite of all of these complications, please keep in mind this general rule: When I talk about inequality in income or wealth in this book, unless otherwise stated, I am talking about inequality among households, not individuals. This is because, as we will see shortly, our most reliable data on incomes comes from sources in which only households report, not individuals.

A second aspect of the "who" question relates to categorical differences related to race and gender. Race is determined by ancestry: it is primarily socially and culturally determined, not genetically determined. While it is only a social construct, race remains one of the most important and enduring factors in creating economic inequality. To pick just a couple of data points from the US, in 1963, the average white family earned $43,000 more than the average African American family (in constant dollars); by 2013 this difference has risen to $123,000.[3] In 2009, the typical black household holds wealth of $5,667—barely one-twentieth of the wealth of a typical white household. Hispanic households only hold about one-eighteenth of the wealth of a typical white household.[4] Home ownership, employment rates, and life-expectancy are lower at every level of education for blacks and Hispanics than for whites.

Gender inequality is also very real. Women tend to work more hours (formal and informal) than men and are paid less for it. In the US, women earn only about 78 percent of what men earn. While some of this difference can be explained by things such as the risk of the job (men tend to work in more risky jobs), a number of jobs have been "feminized" through social norms that lead to implicit or explicit wage discrimination against women. However, the wage gap between men and women has shrunk in most countries since 1960, and almost all of this improvement can be explained by an increase in female educational attainment; today women outnumber men in college within 29 of 32 developed countries.[5] However, gender inequality exists, even at the top of the income distribution. Only 13 percent of the highest earners in the US are women, and only 3 percent of the world's billionaire wealth is held by self-made billionaire women.[6] In fact, in the US there are more male CEOs named John than there are women CEOs (and the same holds for David as well).[7]

One final "who" question that must be answered relates to membership: Who are we including and who are we excluding? When we talk about inequality on a national level, we need to be clear who gets counted. Are we including only citizens? Are we including recognized refugees or those with legal residence without citizenship? Or are we including all residents? These are difficult questions to answer because not everyone who has legal residence or even citizenship in one country has the same rights as other citizens in other countries. For example, the *Houku* system in China severely restricts the ability of those born in rural areas to migrate and enjoy public services in many urban areas. Likewise, many external immigrants can live in many developed countries but with severely restricted economic and civil rights. In these cases where people are purposefully treated differently, it is not clear that we should treat everybody the same in our inequality statistics. In other words, a country with a great deal of *income inequality* but that has severe *rights inequality* may not necessarily be more equal in terms of quality of life. However, these differences are simply not captured in most of our economic inequality data, as most of our data is collected from all citizens without regard for others who live in the country but under a different legal status.

When we talk about differences across race, gender, or citizenship status, we cannot avoid the topic of discrimination—that people are purposefully treated differently because of their categorical status, and that belonging to a category conveys privileges and costs, either consciously or implicitly. As we will discuss later in the book, there is a strong presumption in economics that discrimination is inefficient, and as a result that it should not persist in a market economy because firms that discriminate will be forced out of competitive markets. However, it is hard to reconcile efficiency and perfectly competitive markets with a growing body of research that finds that persistent discrimination is a fact of life. In fact, we will see that discrimination may be inefficient but still persists because of psychological biases and the fact that markets are not perfectly competitive. To highlight just one study of discrimination in the job market, white male job applicants with a criminal record are more likely to be called back for a job interview than black men without a criminal record.[8]

So be warned: In the interest of conciseness, our inequality data will often aggregate across people and households and talk about inequality in the US, or inequality in Britain, or even global inequality. But these summary statistics about inequality will themselves hide a great deal of inequality across groups of individuals. I will keep this in mind as this book proceeds, and I hope that you will as well.

WHERE ARE WE TALKING ABOUT?

One of the most underreported facts in inequality is that geography plays the primary role in who has what. For reasons that I will elucidate throughout this book, the three most important factors in inequality are the same as the three most important factors in the real estate business: location, location, and location. In talking about inequality, *where* we are talking about is more important than *who* we are talking about.

Where matters in many different ways. When I refer to *domestic*, or *within-country inequality*, I am talking about national inequality within the US, within the UK, or within China, for example. When talking about within-country inequality, it is domestic households led by citizens (not just simply residents in most data) that are the category of interest. On a day-to-day basis, when we see that our neighbor's house is bigger than ours or we hear that Kanye West and Kim Kardashian bought a gold toilet seat (I wish I made this up), it is within-country inequality that is foremost in our minds, because this is where we live our lives.[9]

However, levels of domestic inequality within countries, as I will explain in the next chapter, are dwarfed by *between-country inequality*, or the inequality across different countries. For example, per capita income in the US is more than 180 times larger than it is in the Republic of the Congo.

Finally, we will also examine *global inequality*, which ignores nationality and compares households (to the extent that the data allows) across the globe. As a result, global inequality essentially combines within-country inequality and between-country inequality.

Thinking hard about the differences in within, between, and global inequality gives us a more nuanced view of what is happening to inequality across the world. We will see that between-country inequality appears to be getting worse if we just look at the incomes of the richest countries compared to the incomes of the poorest countries. But if we take into the account the population size and rapid growth of China and India, then between-country inequality is actually declining. As a result, even with within-country inequality rising in most countries today global inequality is still falling. This seeming contradiction—that inequality is rising inside of most countries but declining across the world's population—lies at the heart of what makes this such a confusing economic era.

One more important statistical issue related to location must be addressed: Whenever we talk about where, we have to not only consider the fact that incomes are different across the globe, but currencies and prices are also different. We not only need to adjust for exchange rates—which is relatively easy given that there is market data for this—but we also need to adjust for the fact that poorer countries generally have lower prices and, as a result, households get more purchasing power for a given level of income. For example, five US dollars will buy you more food in Nigeria than in Japan. Thankfully, economists have put together the International Price Comparison Project (ICP), which is the largest empirical study in the history of economics.[10] The ICP collects price data at regular intervals in all countries in order to construct what are called *purchasing power parity (PPP) exchange rates*. PPP exchange rates are the exchange rates at which, in theory, a person could buy the same amount of goods across countries with the same amount of income. Market exchange rates can be very different than PPP exchange rates because the prices of similar goods and services can be very different across countries. To pick one example, in 2011 the market exchange rate averaged 46 Indian rupees for every US dollar. However, the PPP exchange rate as measured using ICP data was only 15 rupees per US dollar. In other words, you get three times the purchasing power in reality than the market exchange rate for rupees would suggest; or, to say this in another way, Indians actually have three times the standard of living they would appear to have if you used unadjusted market exchange rates. This is a big deal, which is why using PPP exchange rates is absolutely essential to having any sort of accurate measure of between-country or global inequality.[11]

Of course, there are problems with the PPP exchange rate data that we use. First, the ICP compares the prices of similar bundles of goods across countries. On one hand, assuming that consumption baskets are the same across countries makes it easy to compare prices. But on the other hand, the goods that are typically consumed in countries can be very different. If Americans, Japanese, and South Africans buy very different things, how are we to compare their relative costs of living? Likewise, even people within the same country don't pay the same prices and purchase the same things. In some countries, the differences between prices in urban and rural areas are at least as great as they are across borders; Shanghai's prices are closer to those of New York than they are to a rural village in the far west of China. The ICP makes some technical adjustments for these problems, but they are fraught with ambiguity. The point here is not to say that PPP exchange rates are biased or uninformative, but instead to emphasize that they must be used with cautious skepticism. Every piece of data related to economic inequality is imperfect; however, this is not the same thing as saying that the data is uninformative.

The urban versus rural divide is not just important in regards to differences in prices, it is also real in regards to differences in income levels. In China, urban incomes are three times those of rural incomes in 2015, up from only twice as large in 1983; these regional differences are the largest factor in the overall rise in inequality in China.[12] In the US, a significant portion of the rise in income inequality in the late 1990s was driven by rising incomes in only five counties: Manhattan (New York), King County (Seattle), and the three counties that comprise Silicon Valley (California).[13] Likewise, regional inequality has also been driven by high concentrations of firms in specific industries that are either doing well, or not so well. In the US, when the finance and IT sectors boomed, Manhattan and Silicon Valley boomed as well, while the downturn in the automobile and heavy manufacturing industries led to busts in Detroit and other Midwestern rustbelt cities. It is rising regional inequality in developed countries like the US and the UK that has driven the big divide in region voting patterns seen in these two countries during the 2016 US presidential election and the UK Brexit vote.

WHAT ARE WE TALKING ABOUT?

When we talk about what is unequal, the most commonly used data used to measure economic inequality are *pay (earnings) data, income data, wealth data,* and *consumption data.* Let's talk about each of these and how they differ.

Pay, or *earnings,* refers to compensation for work. Pay data incorporates wages and salaries, but excludes capital income from savings and corporate profits. It is data that is associated with a job, not necessarily a particular person. So we can talk about the earnings of elementary teachers, software engineers, and CEOs. Pay data is the easiest data to collect in rich countries because employers (particularly large ones) are easier to track over time, there are fewer firms than households, and they often have administrative obligations for reporting such data. The value of pay data is in its reliability and comparability across jobs, despite the fact that there can be differences in how firms define hours worked or enforce labor regulations. Most importantly, pay data allows us to measure one important cause of increasing economic inequality: Earnings have grown more unequal between different jobs, and even among people doing the same job at different firms. This is something that we will examine as we talk about the causes of increasing inequality today.

Unfortunately, pay data also has two significant limitations. First, it ignores capital income from savings and investments, or other sources of income that households may be able to collect, making it much too narrow a measure of overall economic inequality. Capital gains, dividends, stock options, interest, and rental income are all ignored in pay. A second problem is that pay data is quite limited in many poorer countries where many workers work on an informal basis (40 to 60 percent of all workers in many less-developed countries), meaning that most employees are missed in any pay data collected only from registered firms.

Income is a flow variable, meaning it is measured over a period of time, typically a year. Income is broader than pay because it includes income from work and income from capital (stocks, bonds, trusts, rents). To give you an idea about how important capital income is in determining overall income inequality, consider data from the US on capital gains, which is income received from the appreciation of an asset such as the sale of a stock, bond, or real estate. If capital gains were excluded from income, the top 1 percent would go from receiving 22.5 percent of all income to 19.3 percent of all income.[14]

The best way to collect income data would be from income tax records. Income tax data is more reliable—because there are potential penalties for falsifying it—and it gives us the best data on those with the highest incomes. It would be nearly impossible to get accurate income estimates of the richest people in the world without income tax data. The problem is that while income tax data is available for the US, many other countries, particularly poorer countries, don't have income taxes (they pay consumption taxes) or income taxes only apply to a small portion of the population. Complete income tax data only exists for 29 countries, and comparing data across these countries and even within the same country over time is very difficult because of different and changing tax laws. There is also the problem that people, but particularly the rich, hide income. They do this in legal ways, through deductions, loopholes, exclusions, offshoring, or by changing their behavior to allow them to avoid taxes. They also do this in illegal ways as well, through tax evasions such as underreporting or manipulating stated income.

Survey data of households is popular when good income tax data is not available—it is probably our best source of income data in most countries. The most common of these are International Household Income surveys. These surveys are conducted across countries and ask the heads of households to specify the range that their income falls into—for example, $10,000–$20,000, $20,000–$30,000, etc., all the way up to a truncated top income of $999,999. However, this survey income data still has flaws. The definitions of what counts as income is not standardized across countries. Also, it is clear that people may not fill these surveys out accurately or truthfully—this is likely to be a particularly big problem among the richest households, who have more complicated financial pictures and are often reluctant to report income they might have hidden away (or offshored) from tax authorities. However, surveys also miss poorer households (who might be homeless, for example) and miss important sources of income in poorer households, particularly "in-kind", or barter income. As a result, these surveys underreport the very rich and the very poor, meaning that they understate actual income inequality by as much as 10 percent.[15] The final problem with income survey data is that sample sizes are limited, and participation is biased. In 2013, 200,000 surveys were distributed in the US, 100,000 in India, but only 10,000 in most countries. Many surveys are not returned, and participation rates have been falling across the globe.[16] In the US, the nonresponse rate was 15 percent in 2017. Based on areas where nonresponse rates are the highest—which was in the richest and poorest neighborhoods—nonparticipation in the survey may lead to 10 percent underestimation of actual income inequality.[17]

Because of rising interest in the topic of inequality, there is more survey data being collected today than ever before. For example, the Luxembourg Income Study is a standardized survey with lots of microeconomic data on individual households, but is only collected in 50 rich countries. The United Nations, World Bank, and many regional organizations and national central banks have been collecting their own income survey data as well. Much of this data is becoming more standardized over time, but the fact is that perfect comparability across countries will never be possible because of differences in how different countries tax income, pay for healthcare and education, or enforce accounting standards.

There is one more important factor in measuring income: How do we deal with government? The government taxes most households, transfers income to some people (in particular the poor and elderly), and provides public goods such as education and healthcare to everyone. How do we account for all of these government programs when measuring income?

In fact, there are three different kinds of income that we can use to measure inequality. *Market income* is income from market activities: wages, salaries, and capital income. There is no adjustment for government taxes and transfers and, as a result, market income tends to be the most unequal across households.

Gross income is market income plus government transfers, such as public pensions, medical and educational payments, and unemployment insurance. Gross income really looks at the total resources available to a household, but is also somewhat unrepresentative of actual welfare because it ignores the fact that people have to pay for these government benefits.

Finally, there is *disposable income*, which subtracts income tax collections from gross income. Disposable income does not count consumption or sales taxes that people have to pay, and it is important to keep this in mind given that poorer households tend to spend a bigger share of their income on consumption. Disposable income is the best measure of what a household actually has to spend, and generally is the best measure of the actual quality of life of individual households. Disposable income is generally less variable than market or gross income because the tax systems in most countries are more or less progressive, meaning those with higher income pay higher tax rates. However, in poorer countries where government is less effective and more income is earned informally, there are often smaller differences between market, gross, and disposable income. Also, in countries that rely more heavily on consumption taxes, gross income will be closer to disposable income.

Wealth is a stock variable, meaning it is measured at one point of time. Instead of looking at income that is measured over a fixed period of time, wealth looks at the accumulated assets from savings, the returns on investment, and any inheritance or transfers received by households. To calculate wealth, you must assess the value of a household's financial assets (stocks, bonds, real estate, cash), their nonfinancial assets (houses, real estate, art, jewelry, cars), and subtract any liabilities (debt or other borrowings) that they have. Unfortunately, traditional measures of wealth focus on tangible assets and ignore many intangible assets such as the value of education, networks, and other social connections. These intangible assets are increasingly important in explaining inequality, as we will talk about later.

The big advantage of wealth data is that we can measure what is going on with the very rich because most survey data on incomes is truncated at

$1 million, while wealth data is not truncated in the same way. Wealth data primarily comes from three different data sources, and economists have tried to put these sources together as best as they can. First, wealth data can be obtained from countries that have a wealth tax, such as Sweden. However, wealth taxes do not exist in most countries and tend to be paid by only a small number of people when they do exist. Second, wealth can also be also imputed from the capital income that people report to tax authorities or on income surveys. These imputations involve complicated estimation methodologies that are fraught with missing data, modeling assumptions, tax avoidance, and changing tax laws among other problems.[18] Finally, probably the best source of wealth data is from personal wealth surveys. The US Federal Reserve and European Central Bank conduct wealth surveys regularly, although they tend to have high nonresponse rates from the richest people, and it is always unclear how truthful people are willing to be about how much they are really worth. Other common surveys of wealth are found in *Forbes* magazine's "500 Richest People in the World" and *The Sunday Times'* "Rich List". While these look at only a small number of rich people, there is actually good reason to think that the participants in these lists are more truthful, or might even overstate wealth because of the status associated with making these lists.

Wealth is dramatically more unequal than income. Some people are extremely wealthy, while roughly one-third of those living in developed countries such as the US have zero or negative wealth, meaning that their debts are greater than their assets. In fact, half of the world's population owns 100 percent of the wealth, meaning that wealth is not anything close to a global norm. Wealth data alone cannot give us the full picture of inequality because so many people's wealth cannot be accurately measured. But without talking about wealth, it is impossible to get the full picture of economic inequality.

Consumption, in a very real sense, is what matters. We work and save to consume, not just to earn an income. Consumption is the primary determinant of our current welfare and standards of living.

Because people tend to smooth their consumption over time, inequality in consumption tends to be lower than inequality in income, which is much more variable. For example, the children of rich parents have the backstop of their parents' wealth which makes them better able to smooth their income over the course of their life even if they are not earning any income—a backstop that the children of poor people do not have. In this sense, inequality in consumption tracks true inequality better than income inequality.

All of this said, there are problems with using consumption data to measure inequality. First, we collect data on consumption expenditure, not actual consumption. As a result, consumption data (like income data) misses a lot of informal consumption (e.g. growing your own food, barter, trade in household services). There are also difficulties in adjusting for different costs of living in different regions and among different people that makes getting an accurate picture of consumption across households difficult. But there are also more fundamental problems associated with using consumption as a measure of inequality. Income gives you more than just the power to consume. Having income gives you the power to control resources, and people with income are empowered in ways that the poor can never be, regardless of their consumption choices. In the words of Amartya Sen, income gives people "capabilities" and options in life to make their own decisions and choose how they would like to participate in society.[19] Two people might have the same consumption levels, but there are decidedly more options for the person who has a high income and chooses to limit their consumption than there is for the person who has little income and has their consumption dictated to them. As a result, income is a better measure of the true constraints created by inequality.

Another reason why income matters more than consumption is that income also reduces risk, and reducing the risks associated with life is just as valuable as maintaining high current levels of consumption. You will not have to be convinced of this if you have ever missed a meal from lack of money, or have not known how you will pay your next school fee, or have ever seen someone you love refused medical treatment because they cannot pay for it. Someone who lives frugally but is still rich will never really know these stresses and how they impact the quality of life.

The good news is that we don't really have to choose between income and consumption to understand trends in inequality. Consumption inequality closely tracks income inequality, although the growth in consumption inequality has not been as rapid.[20]

WHEN ARE WE TALKING ABOUT?

Time has to be an element of consideration when examining inequality for a couple of reasons. First, prices and the cost of living rise over time, so we must use *real data* (i.e. adjusted for inflation and changes in the price level) when comparing data over time. Of course, calculating price levels and the cost of living is difficult to do, for the reasons we talked about when we talked about PPP. But even if our estimates of the cost of living are imperfect, they are better than ignoring the problem. In this book, I will always be using real statistics when comparing data from different points in time.

Time also has to be considered because our inequality data are always associated with a specific moment in time—they are photographs, not films. As a result, if we plotted everyone's incomes from the poorest to the richest, this graph could look exactly the same year after year, but specific people would have moved to different spots on the curve. This often has to do with people's ages: Many people start out at low levels of income, see their incomes grow until they near retirement age, then typically see their incomes fall. In other words, individual income tends to be hump-shaped over a lifetime, and demographics such as the average age of the population can play a role in shaping overall income inequality at any one point in time. For example, the baby boom of the 1950s and today's declining birth rates have led to aging populations in most developed countries. If older people are wealthier than younger people (which tends to happen in countries that are growing), then older populations should also have more wealth inequality.

Age is not the only factor that determines where an individual ranks relative to their peers. One of the things we will examine later in this book is how much "churning" is actually occurring across income rankings. When ranking incomes, are people moving up and down the income ladder a great deal over time and over their lives? Or are the people that are born at the bottom and at the top of the income ladder staying at the bottom and the top? In other words, are there high or low levels of *income mobility*? When there is little income mobility, people's stations in life are largely predetermined and their incomes are not necessarily a function of their own hard work and abilities, but of the income class that they were born into. More churning and greater income mobility might be more consistent with a meritocratic society in which people's income class reflects their contributions to society (although "merit" is always a loaded word, for reasons I will discuss later).

Finally, time plays a big role in measuring inequality because the quality of our data has improved over time. As a general rule, the further back in time you go, the weaker is the evidence. Today we have sophisticated income and wealth surveys. In the 1900s, we had to primarily rely on income tax records. In the 1800s and before, most inequality data that exists comes from social tables collected in some countries, regions, and cities that recorded demographic, income, and wealth records by hand. From these incomplete social tables, contemporary scholars can infer broader measures of inequality. Going even further back in time, the best evidence of inequality can be found in anthropological data patterns, such as land ownership in Roman Egypt, variation in house sizes in Aztec Mexico, and inheritance shares in Babylonia.

HOW ARE WE TALKING ABOUT IT?

Collecting data points on income or wealth is fine, but they are just data points. How do we organize this data and summarize it in ways that allow us to understand what this data is actually telling us about economic inequality?

Let's begin by clarifying what we mean by a *distribution*. The easiest way to visualize a distribution is to create a graph that plots the *amount of a resource* (wealth, income) from the lowest to highest levels on the horizontal axis and the *number that possess this level of the resource* on the vertical axis (either households or individuals). This graph will likely be hump-shaped, meaning that there will be more people in the middle than are very rich or very poor. It will be truncated on the left, because few people will have zero and nobody can have negative amounts of the resource. On the right end, this distribution is likely to have a long tail that stretches far to the right because there will be a small number of very rich people. We would consider a distribution to be more equal if it looked more like a normal distribution, with a large number of people in the middle and few at the poor and the rich ends—in other words, more hump-shaped and symmetrical. A distribution will be more unequal the more that the distribution flattens out, is pushed to the left, and stretches further to the right. Figure 1.1 presents three hypothetical distributions of income across households. Distribution A would be the most equal—there are more households in the middle, and fewer at the extremes. Distribution C would be most unequal, as there are more poor and rich and fewer middle-class households.

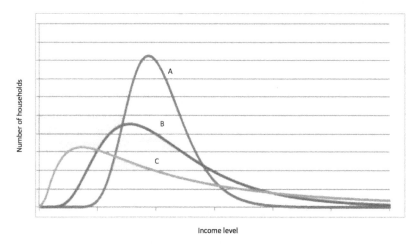

Figure 1.1   Hypothetical income distributions

The distributions in Figure 1.1 are hypothetical. In fact, if we were to make this graph using real data from a country like the US, it requires some manipulation of the data to visualize the entire distribution on one graph because those at the highest end of the distribution earn so much more than those at the bottom and the middle of the distribution that a simple plot will place most households at what looks like zero with a long line stretching out along the horizontal axis.

Measures of inequality, then, are really ways to describe the shape of distributions without resorting to a simple, and less informative, plot of the number of households living at various levels. Our measures of inequality are ways to quantify disparity within groups that are more concrete than using an "eyeball test".

So, how exactly are we going to characterize the inequality of different distributions? The first—and most important—issue is to clarify whether we are going to measure absolute inequality or relative inequality. *Absolute inequality* is the absolute differences in levels between individuals. For example, if one household makes $50,000 and another $20,000, their absolute level of income inequality is $30,000. For an entire population, a measure of absolute inequality could be the *range* of the data (the highest value minus the lowest value) or a *decile ratio* (the level of the household that just qualified for the top 10 percent minus the level of the richest household in the lowest 10 percent of the distribution). Absolute measures of inequality are intuitive, but they have a number of problems. First, measures of absolute inequality will always rise if an economy is growing and average incomes are rising. For example, in 2008 (in 2005 dollars), the richest 1 percent of the world earned at least $71,000 per year, but median income across the globe was only $1,400, and the poorest 10 percent earned less than $450.[21] Thus, a 1 percent increase in income for the top 1 percent would be the same size as a 58 percent increase in the income of the bottom 10 percent. If we focus only on measures of absolute inequality, we will always conclude that inequality is getting worse, even if the incomes of the poor are growing much faster than the rich over time.

Relative inequality is a better way to measure reality because, in economists' minds, we think that everything is relative. People instinctively weigh gains relative to where they started, not from where they have never been. If a poor and rich person both find $100 on the street, who should be happier for it? The poor person, obviously, because it changes their financial situation by more—in other words, it will be a larger percentage change in their income. Relative measures of inequality recognize that a $1 income gain to the poor should be weighted more heavily than a $1 income gain to the rich if the goal is to accurately measure the impact of inequality. If a country doubles the income of their poorest while the incomes of the richest only slightly improve, we should recognize that inequality has fallen in relative terms and that overall well-being has improved, even if measures of absolute inequality have risen.

There are three different measures of relative inequality that we will use throughout this book. The first is the *Gini coefficient*, named after the Italian statistician Corrado Gini. The Gini coefficient summarizes the entire distribution of income, from the very top income to the very lowest income, in a single number between zero and one that measures the extent to which the distribution of any resource across individuals differs from perfect equality and perfect inequality. A Gini of one means one person owns everything, a Gini of zero means that everyone owns the exact same amount. As a result, a higher level of the Gini coefficient means higher inequality. A Gini coefficient reduces the entire distribution to a single number, so obviously a lot of information is obscured by a Gini coefficient. But the conciseness and simplicity of interpreting a Gini makes it a useful tool in describing inequality.[22] To get an idea about what the Gini coefficient looks like in the US, Figure 1.2 presents the Gini coefficients for market, gross, and disposable income since 1979.

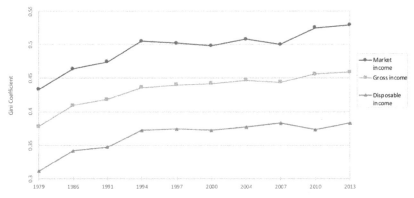

Source: Luxembourg Income Study Database (2019).

Figure 1.2　　*Gini coefficients for market, gross, and disposable income in the US*

Here we can see that as measured by the Gini coefficient, income inequality in the US has been rising steadily since 1979. For example, market inequality rise from .43 in 1979 to .53 in 2013. The disposable income Gini rose from .31 to .38, which is also a proportionally substantial increase. We also see that market inequality is greater than gross income inequality, which is greater than disposable income inequality, as we would expect.

There are some important things to keep in mind about Gini coefficients so that we use them appropriately and don't misinterpret, or over-interpret, what they can tell us. The Gini does not depend on the size of the population, or whether we are using absolute or relative data, or what currency units the data is measured in. In other words, Ginis are easy to calculate and easy to compare across countries.

A Gini coefficient will stay the same when percentage changes across the distribution are equal, but this means that the dollar-amount changes in income will be unequal, and the difference between the highest and lowest incomes will increase. In other words, it is a measure of relative inequality, not of absolute inequality. As a result, Gini coefficients do tend to paint a more conservative picture of inequality and minimize the huge differences in levels between the very rich and the very poor. For example, in the US, the 1 percent richest Americans earn at least 158 times the Americans in the bottom 10 percent. Or, to put it in another way, the top 1 percent can earn in a little more than two days what it takes the bottom 10 percent almost a year to earn. These staggering differences in income are somewhat hidden by Gini coefficients, which essentially report an "average" level of inequality among a population. Likewise, the extent of poverty, or people who have absolute income levels that fall below minimum standards of living, are ignored by Gini coefficients. The bottom 10 percent of the world's population is living on about $1.90 day (in 2011 dollars).[23] Thinking about the real difficulties of living on so little brings the reality of global poverty home in a way that a Gini coefficient cannot.

One less obvious problem with using Gini coefficients is that having a Gini coefficient value of one is actually not possible in the real world because everybody but one very lucky person would starve. This raises the question of the maximum feasible Gini—what should we consider a "high" level of the Gini if a value of one is impossible? One approach would be to estimate the minimum level of subsistence needed to feed the population, then subtract this amount from total income and then estimate the distribution of this "surplus" resource. For example, if total income was four times the minimum subsistence level of income to keep everyone alive, then the maximum Gini would be .75—in which case, everyone lives at subsistence except for one person, who owns everything else. If total income was twice the minimum subsistence level, the maximum Gini would be .5. This illustrates an important problem with comparing Ginis across countries: Rich countries will tend to have higher maximum Gini coefficients because they will have more surplus income (i.e. more income above subsistence levels). According to estimates, if the minimum subsistence level of income is $300 per person (in 1990 dollars), a country with a per capita GDP of $1000 has a maximum Gini of .76, while for the US the maximum Gini is close to one. However, it is probably more appropriate to consider the "socially acceptable minimum income" when making these calculations instead of just what income is needed to keep people alive. In this case, the maximum Gini for rich countries can be much lower—in the US, as low as .6.[24] This puts the current Gini coefficient of disposable income in the US of .38 in a much clearer context: it is two-thirds of maximum possible inequality, and rising.

The second measure of relative inequality that we will use in this book is *income shares*. Income shares capture the percentage of the total income owned by a particular group within the overall distribution. Examples would be the income earned by the top 1 percent, or the income shares broken into groups of 10 percent of the population (deciles), or the income shares broken into groups of 20 percent of the population (quintiles). When using income shares, we are trying to better describe the overall shape of the distribution.

Income shares are more complicated to report than Gini coefficients, but have the potential to convey more detailed information on inequality across the entire distribution.

By expressing data in terms of income shares, we are expressing data in terms of percentiles and not levels, meaning that they are not dependent upon the units of currency we are using, so they can be easily compared across countries.

Of course, income shares aggregate data and obscure some important information; data broken into deciles will convey more information than data broken into quintiles (but also are messier to report and comprehend). However, the biggest thing to keep in mind when looking at income shares is that the same people will not necessarily be in the same percentiles across time. Once again, there is churning within the distribution as people move up and down the relative distribution over their lifetime. We will discuss how much churning there is, and why this is important, when we talk about income mobility. For now, it is important to recognize that income share data imposes the condition that for one person to rise to a higher percentile ranking, another person must fall in the percentile rankings. Or, to say this another way, even if everyone in the lowest income share were to see their absolute incomes improve, they could still fall further behind those in higher percentiles in terms of relative income, and we would observe higher overall measured relative inequality.

There is one final measure of inequality that we will use in the book when talking about global inequality, or inequality across the entire world population, which is known as *Theil's statistic*, named after the University of Chicago statistician Henri Theil. Theil's statistic is very complicated to calculate, but relatively easy to understand. It is useful because it can serve as a measure of overall inequality which can also be separated into a measure of how groups within the overall population differ.[25] Theil's statistic is a relative measure of inequality, like the Gini coefficient, but is not limited to being between zero and one. In fact, the absolute level of a Thiel's T statistic is meaningless by itself unless it can be tracked over time, in which case it can be used as a measure of how inequality is changing.

Here is where Theil's statistic becomes particularly useful. Let's say you have two groups of people in a population; for example, men and women. When using Theil's statistic to measure inequality, it is true that the inequality of the entire population will be equal to the weighted-average of the differences in income among men and the differences in income among women (within-group inequality), and the difference in average incomes between men and women (between-group inequality). As a result, Theil's statistic can be deconstructed into a measure of within-group inequality and between-group inequality that gives us a much fuller picture of what is going on with the overall distribution.

Theil's statistic is also useful if we think about the groups as countries—in other words, defining different groups by geography. Using Theil's statistic to measure inequality, we can break global inequality into the proportion of inequality that occurs within countries (i.e. differences in income between US citizens, Chinese citizens, etc.) and inequality that occurs because average income differs between countries (i.e. per capita income is higher in the US than in China). As we will see, this allows us to think about how much of global inequality is attributable to inequality that exists because of unequal economic and social conditions across individuals within countries, and how much global inequality is associated with unequal economic and social conditions in different countries.

IN CONCLUSION

So this is probably the most tedious chapter in the book—sorry to lead off with it—but unless we can understand what kinds of inequality we are talking about and how we measure them, we will never be able to understand the more interesting questions related to current trends in inequality and its impact on our lives.

After reading this chapter, you might come to the conclusion that inequality can't be measured—there are too many different ways to define inequality, too many data problems, and no simple measure that can capture its complexity. But I think that this is the wrong conclusion to draw. There are good reasons to be skeptical about economic data, but not to be cynical. As we are going to see in the next chapter, it is true that different data give us different pictures about the *level* of inequality, but the *changes* in inequality are much more apparent. Whether we are talking about equality as measured by market income, disposable income, wealth, pay, consumption, individuals, households, ethnicity, gender, country, survey data, tax data, citizenship, urban, rural, social mobility, Gini coefficients, or income shares, our confidence intervals regarding the data are shrinking over time, the data is becoming more correlated, and the *trends* in inequality have become pretty clear. Describing these trends in economic inequality is the subject of the next (and much more interesting) chapter.

NOTES

1. US Bureau of the Census (2016).
2. Doepke and Tertilt (2016).
3. Pew Research Center (2014b).
4. Pew Research Center (2011).
5. Hsieh et al. (2018).
6. See Edlund and Kopczuk (2009) and Freund and Oliver (2014).
7. Wolfers (2015).

8. Pager (2003).
9. Watkins (2013).
10. ICP data can be found at: http://siteresources.worldbank.org/ICPEXT/Resources/ICP-2011-report.pdf. For a more detailed description of how PPP exchange rates are used to adjust income surveys across countries, see Lakner and Milanovic (2013).
11. You might ask why don't market exchange rates always reflect actual differences in purchasing power? There are three principal reasons. First, market exchange rates are quite volatile and are subject to large swings—20 percent or more in short periods of time—even though the actual domestic purchasing power of the currency has changed very little. The second reason why there is often a difference between market and PPP exchange rates is that many governments manipulate exchange rates and keep them above or below levels to which they would gravitate in the free market. For example, until recently, China's central bank kept the RMB exchange rate undervalued against the dollar in order to facilitate its export markets, meaning that the market exchange rate for the RMB was below its PPP exchange rate. Third, exchange rates over time tend to adjust to reflect the fact that internationally traded goods should sell at roughly the same price across countries. The more goods within a country that are not internationally traded—local foods, real estate, services, etc.—the more likely that a market exchange rate that only equilibrates the prices of internationally traded goods can be consistent with persistently large differences in the price of local goods across countries.
12. Naughton (2017).
13. Galbraith (2012).
14. Atkinson (2015).
15. Hlasny and Verme (2019).
16. *The Economist* (2018a).
17. Korinek et al. (2006).
18. Kopczuk (2015).
19. Sen (1985).
20. Attanasio and Pistaferri (2015).
21. Milanovic (2016).
22. How exactly is a Gini coefficient calculated? Imagine a graph that plots the cumulative population—up to 100 percent of the population—on the vertical axis and cumulative amount of a resource—up to 100 percent—on the horizontal axis. If we plotted what percentage of the population got what percentage of the resource in a world of perfect equality, the distribution would be a 45-degree line and the area under the line would be a triangle. In a world of perfect inequality, there would be no line and no area, only a single point where one person got 100 percent of the resource. The Gini coefficient, then, is a geometric measure of how far away the actual distribution of the resource is from this "ideal" triangle. A higher Gini means that the actual distribution of resources is farther away from perfect equality. See also Peltzman (2009) if you don't like my description of calculating a Gini and would like to read someone else's.
23. World Bank (2018).
24. See Scheidel (2017) for a more detailed description of how these calculations are made.
25. For a brief tutorial on calculating Theil's T statistic, see the University of Texas Inequality Project (2018) at http://utip.lbj.utexas.edu/tutorials.html.

2. How unequal are we? Six major facts

Inequality is rising as an issue of primary importance in our civic debates, but this is despite—not because of—most people's understanding of how economic inequality is changing. Surveys have shown that people across the world are shockingly ignorant about economic inequality and underestimate the extent to which inequality exists despite the voluminous research on inequality that has taken place over the last two decades. According to one 2010 survey, less than half of all Americans believed that inequality in the US had increased, despite ample evidence that it has.[1] Americans also think CEOs are paid about 30 times the average worker; in reality, that number is 350 (at an average annual salary of $12.5 million). And it is not just Americans who are uninformed. In each of 40 countries surveyed, people underestimated the amount of income inequality in their country, and only slim majorities of the population in places where inequality has increased at the fastest rates—such as the UK, Australia, and China—recognized that inequality had actually increased.[2]

There are likely a few reasons for this. First, as we saw in the previous chapter, there are a lot of different ways to measure inequality and it is easy to be confused, discouraged, or misled by the data. Also, inequality data is always interpreted through our subjective notions of what is "fair", and what is considered fair differs greatly between people and countries. For example, a majority of both Americans and Dutch think that the income distributions in their countries are "fair", even though measured inequality is much higher in the US than in the Netherlands. On the other hand, 75 percent of the French think their current distribution of income is unfair, despite having much lower measured inequality than the US.[3] It is clear that our perceptions of inequality are biased by our desire to see what we want to be true, which in turn is shaped by a complex set of social norms.

I think that another factor in explaining people's misperceptions of inequality comes from the fact that people are influenced by the national myths that we tell ourselves. In America, the "land of opportunity" and "everyone is middle-class" mindsets are a powerful narrative that shapes how we view economic reality. More Americans think that they are middle-class (44 percent) than lower-middle-class (28 percent) or upper-middle-class (13 percent). Very few people think of themselves as lower-class (12 percent) and upper-class (1–2 percent).[4] As we will see in this chapter, however, where Americans see themselves on the income ladder and what they think their chances are of moving up it has little relation to the reality of inequality in the US.

Keeping these challenges in mind, the purpose of this chapter is to take a closer look at the inequality data across the globe. The goal is to present the most balanced and clear summary of the complexity of the inequality data that is available, while also trying to be as concise as possible in order to avoid swamping you with data. The most crucial statistics are summarized in six important facts about inequality across the globe.

Fact #1: Income Gini coefficients have risen significantly since 1980 within most countries of the world.

The Gini coefficient on income—described in the previous chapter—is a statistic that summarizes inequality into one number between zero (perfect equality) and one (perfect inequality). While there are important differences in the *level* of Gini coefficients across countries, the trend in Gini coefficients worldwide is upward. Inequality is increasing in every part of the world except the very poorest regions and countries—the Middle East, sub-Saharan Africa, and Brazil—where it has stabilized at very high preexisting levels.

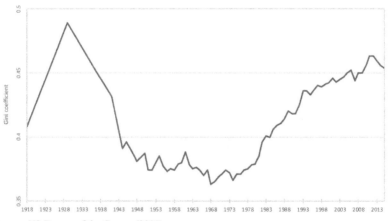

Source: US Bureau of the Census (2015).

Figure 2.1   Gini coefficient for gross income in the US

Let's begin by looking at the US, which is an example of the general trends in inequality across rich countries. Figure 2.1 presents the Gini coefficient for gross income in the US since 1918. What jumps out of Figure 2.1 is that a century ago the trend was towards falling inequality, not rising inequality.

The US experienced a sustained drop in its Gini coefficient from 1929, when it nearly equaled .5, until roughly the mid-1970s, when it had fallen to .36. We will refer to this period as "The Great Compression". The Great Compression took place across developed countries and was the result of a number of factors, most importantly the financial crises and wars of the 1930s and 1940s (which significantly reduced the wealth and the incomes of the rich), and the adoption of more progressive fiscal policy that transferred more income from the rich to the middle-class and the poor. The current trend of rising inequality in the US began in the mid-1970s and continues to today, where it is approaching 1920s levels of inequality with a gross income Gini coefficient of .45. This estimated Gini almost certainly underestimates true inequality given the trouble that income surveys have in measuring the incomes of the top 1 percent (see previous chapter).

Table 2.1 presents Gini coefficients on disposable income (which should be lower than market or gross income) for a selected group of countries. Let's begin by looking at Panel A, which presents these countries ranked according to the level of their Gini coefficients in 2015 (or the most recent year for which data is available). There is obviously a lot of variability here, but there are some general conclusions that can be drawn from this data. First, it is generally true that rich countries have lower levels of inequality and poor countries have higher levels of inequality. Given that we are looking at disposable income, this is in large part because rich countries have stronger governments and more progressive social safety net programs. There are also some clear regional differences. Inequality is highest in the Middle East, sub-Saharan Africa, and particularly in China and India. Among rich countries, inequality is highest among the Anglo-Saxon countries (US, UK, Canada, and Australia), lower in continental Europe, and at the lowest levels in the Nordic countries.

When we turn to Panel B of Table 2.1, we see these same countries ranked not in terms of their current Gini coefficients, but by changes in their Gini coefficients since 1980. Once again, there are no universal truths here, but we can make some general observations. First, most rich countries have seen a rise in inequality. Second, increases in inequality have been the largest for the fastest-growing countries. Third, those countries that have seen slower growth in their Ginis, or who have actually seen a decline in their Ginis, are typically slower growing countries that already had high levels of inequality at the beginning of the period. As a result, there does appear to be some convergence in Ginis across the globe—those countries with high Ginis in 1980 have typically seen the smallest increases or declines in inequality, while those with the lowest Ginis have seen the biggest increases in inequality. Finally, inequality has risen in a few countries that have not been growing fast, such as Russia and Egypt, suggesting that the political changes that have taken place in these countries have played an important role in changing inequality.

Panel A: Ranked by level of most recent Gini

Country	1980 Gini	2015 Gini	Change in Gini
South Africa	0.561	0.577	0.016
China	0.317	0.510	0.193
Hong Kong	0.374	0.499	0.125
Chile	0.483	0.499	0.016
India	0.415	0.499	0.084
Egypt	0.405	0.470	0.066
Mexico	0.473	0.459	-0.015
Indonesia	0.393	0.457	0.063
Brazil	0.513	0.449	-0.064
Russia	0.302	0.439	0.137
Malaysia	0.483	0.428	-0.055
Kenya	0.484	0.416	-0.068
Turkey	0.452	0.398	-0.053
Nigeria	0.372	0.390	0.018
Iran	0.508	0.388	-0.120
Singapore	0.369	0.388	0.019
Argentina	0.379	0.386	0.007
United States	0.316	0.378	0.062
Uganda	0.375	0.376	0.001
Israel	0.306	0.369	0.063
Pakistan	0.356	0.362	0.006
Morocco	0.356	0.357	0.001
Spain	0.319	0.343	0.024
Italy	0.327	0.333	0.006
Australia	0.279	0.332	0.053
United Kingdom	0.276	0.329	0.053
Canada	0.280	0.312	0.031
S. Korea	0.289	0.307	0.018
Japan	0.243	0.299	0.056
France	0.323	0.293	-0.025
Switzerland	0.314	0.293	-0.021
Germany	0.259	0.290	0.030
Ukraine	0.276	0.263	-0.013
Sweden	0.206	0.257	0.051
Finland	0.211	0.256	0.044
Norway	0.232	0.249	0.017

Panel B: Ranked by change in Gini

Country	1980 Gini	2015 Gini	Change in Gini
China	0.317	0.510	0.193
Russia	0.302	0.439	0.137
Hong Kong	0.374	0.499	0.125
India	0.415	0.499	0.084
Egypt	0.405	0.470	0.066
Indonesia	0.393	0.457	0.063
Israel	0.306	0.369	0.063
United States	0.316	0.378	0.062
Japan	0.243	0.299	0.056
United Kingdom	0.276	0.329	0.053
Australia	0.279	0.332	0.053
Sweden	0.206	0.257	0.051
Finland	0.211	0.256	0.044
Canada	0.280	0.312	0.031
Germany	0.259	0.290	0.030
Spain	0.319	0.343	0.024
Singapore	0.369	0.388	0.019
Nigeria	0.372	0.390	0.018
S. Korea	0.289	0.307	0.018
Norway	0.232	0.249	0.017
Chile	0.483	0.499	0.016
South Africa	0.561	0.577	0.016
Argentina	0.379	0.386	0.007
Pakistan	0.356	0.362	0.006
Italy	0.327	0.333	0.006
Uganda	0.375	0.376	0.001
Morocco	0.356	0.357	0.001
Ukraine	0.276	0.263	-0.013
Mexico	0.473	0.459	-0.015
Switzerland	0.314	0.293	-0.021
France	0.323	0.293	-0.025
Turkey	0.452	0.398	-0.053
Malaysia	0.483	0.428	-0.055
Brazil	0.513	0.449	-0.064
Kenya	0.484	0.416	-0.068
Iran	0.508	0.388	-0.120

Table 2.1   *Gini coefficients on disposable income across countries*

Note: Gini coefficients are for disposable income, where 1980 and 2015 data are used (or the oldest or most recent data available).

Source: Solt (2016) and SWIID database, accessed at http://fsolt.org/swiid/.

To summarize, there does appear to be a clear trend towards more domestic inequality—most countries are seeing their Ginis rise, and there are relatively few countries that have seen their Ginis fall. Countries that have seen the fastest increases in inequality are fast growing (China and India), Anglo-Saxon (US, UK, Canada, and Australia), or have become more authoritarian (Russia, Egypt).

The fact that there are some general trends, but no hard and fast rules, when describing changes in Gini coefficients across countries suggests that there is no predetermined level of inequality that every country inevitably gravitates towards. In general, what we see here is that when similar countries share similar policies, similar income levels, and similar growth rates, they also share similar levels of inequality. But these levels of inequality can change over time. Those countries that have seen the biggest changes in their social, political, and economic systems—such as China, Russia, and Iran—are also the countries that have experienced the biggest increases or decreases in overall inequality as measured by Gini coefficients.

Fact #2: The top 10%, top 5%, top 1%, top 0.1%, and top 0.01% income shares within countries are rising particularly fast.

Across the world since 1980:

- The top 1 percent has earned twice as much income as the bottom 50 percent.[5]
- The top 1 percent earns 27 percent of all income, the bottom 50 percent earns only 12 percent of all income.[6]
- The share of income going to the top 1 percent and top 5 percent has increased within every country for which there is reliable data.[7]
- The share of total income going to the top 10 percent has increased in every region of the world. The top 10 percent earn 61 percent of all income in the Middle East, 55 percent in India, 54 percent in sub-Saharan Africa, 47 percent in the US and Canada, 37 percent in Europe, and 41 percent in China. The rise of the top 10 percent has been fastest in India, the US, Canada, and China.[8]

In other words, it is at the top of the income distribution that we have seen the largest changes in inequality. The rich are pulling away on a relative basis across the globe. The super-rich more so. And the super-duper rich (a technical term) the most.

Figure 2.2 reports the percentage of gross income going to the top 1 percent across a selection of countries. The data in this figure excludes capital gains, and as a result it understates both the level and the changes in the share of

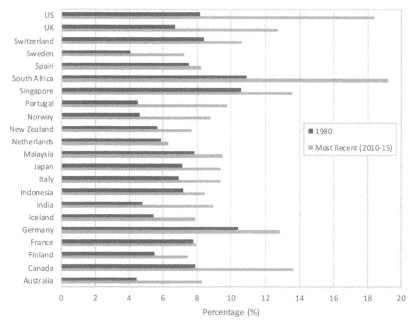

Note: Income shares include gross income across individuals, excluding capital gains.

Source: Atkinson (2015).

Figure 2.2   Percentage of gross income going to top 1%

income going to the top 1 percent. These conservative estimates still show that the share of income going to the top 1 percent has increased in every single one of these countries, with the largest increases in India, China, South Africa, and, in particular, the Anglo-Saxon countries (Australia, the UK, Canada, and the US).

The US is the most extreme example of what is happening at the far top-end of the income distribution in many countries. In the US between 1979 and 2007, 60 percent of all the gains in market income went to the top 1 percent, while only 9 percent went to the bottom 90 percent.[9] The top 10 percent today (households that earn more than $120,000 a year and have a group average of $310,000 in yearly income) earns 50 percent of all income, and the top 1 percent (households that earn at least $470,000 in income and have a group average of $1,340,000 in yearly income) earns 20 percent of all income, putting both at pre-depression level highs.[10] Of this top 1 percent, it is the top 0.1 percent (who have income of at least $2 million and average $6.1 million in income) and top 0.01 percent (who have income of at least $9.8 million and average $28.7 million in income) who have done the best: The top 0.1 percent raised its share of total income by four times what it was in 1970, and the top 0.01 percent raised its share of total income by six times. The pulling away of the very rich was interrupted by the Great Recession of 2007–9. However, in the first three years of the recovery between 2009 and 2012, the top 1 percent more than returned to form and captured 95 percent of the total gains in income in the US.[11] To put it another way: almost all income earned over the last decade in America has gone to only about 2.3 million households making half a million dollars a year or more.

Looking at the households that are part of these top income shares, we can also see other sources of inequality. One of the starkest is that only 6 percent of households in the top 20 percent are black. While the number of rich who are minorities is growing, it still lags behind the overall pace of demographic change in the US population.[12]

Fact #3: Global wealth inequality is growing even faster, and the number of billionaires is booming.

Income inequality is extreme. Wealth inequality is staggeringly extreme. Consider these facts about global wealth:

- In 2010, the wealth of the world's wealthiest 388 people was needed to equal the bottom half of the world's population, or 3.5 billion people. In 2017, it only took the richest 62 people in the world to have total wealth that is equal to the wealth of the bottom half. In 2018, it now only takes the 28 richest.[13]
- The 20 wealthiest on the Forbes 400 list own more than the bottom half of the US population. All together, the Forbes 400 members have as much wealth as all African Americans plus one-third of the American Latino population combined.[14]
- There were 2,043 billionaires across the globe in 2017, up by 233 since 2016, holding more than $7.7 trillion in wealth. Only 227 of these billionaires are women. Only ten are black. Only three are black women.[15]
- The US is the most unequal industrialized country in terms of wealth, and getting more so. In the US, the share of wealth going to the wealthiest 1 percent has doubled between the mid-1970s and today.[16]
- Global average wealth is $56,540 per household. However, median household wealth is only $3,582.[17]

As we talked about in Chapter 1, wealth is difficult to measure for many reasons, particularly the fact that wealth is not taxed in most countries (only income from that wealth) and that the richest people find ways to protect or hide their wealth from tax authorities when it is. As a result, most of what we know about wealth comes from survey data. However, in the countries for which we do have reasonable data, wealth inequality is growing dramatically, whether measured by a Gini coefficient on wealth or by the wealth share going to the top 10 percent or top 1 percent. The share of wealth going to the top 1 percent has risen in all countries since the mid-1980s, and has roughly doubled in the US, China, and Russia, while rising less slowly in the UK and France.[18] In other words, while the levels of inequality in wealth are proportionally much higher than the levels of inequality in income, the trends in wealth inequality are similar to the trends in income inequality across countries.

Once again, the US is an extreme example of these global trends in wealth inequality. The income cutoff for the top 1 percent in the US is about $470,000. In contrast, the wealth cutoff for the top 1 percent is an astonishing $4.4 million! Note that both groups include about 1.6 million households. This leads to a very high Gini coefficient on wealth in the US of .85, compared to the Gini coefficient on gross income in the US of .45.[19]

Those in the top 1 percent of wealth in the US (who have at least $4.4 million in wealth, and who average $15.5 million in wealth) own nearly 44 percent of all the wealth in the US. This is up from 22 percent of all wealth in the US in the mid-1980s. However, almost all of this increase in the share of wealth going to the top 1 percent (and the top 10 percent as well) has gone to those in the top 0.1 percent of wealthiest Americans (those who have at least $23.1 million in wealth and average $81.7 million in wealth).[20] In fact, now the 20 wealthiest Americans own as much wealth as the bottom 50 percent of US households.[21]

Of course, rising wealth inequality also contributes to rising income inequality. In the US, the income from capital gains going to the top 1 percent rose from one-third to two-thirds of all capital gains—once again, most of this going to the top 0.01 percent. This is in large part because the extremely rich have much more financial wealth (as opposed to wealth in housing) that allows for returns to compound over time. The richest 10 percent own 90 percent of stocks, bonds, trusts, business equity, and investment real estate. In addition, there is also evidence that the returns on capital have risen relative to wage income, further increasing the disparity between the incomes of the rich and the incomes of the poor.[22]

Finally, it is worth reiterating that these aggregate figures obscure lots of inequality between different groups of people. For example, American white families hold about 20 times the amount of wealth of black families, and the gap in wealth between the average black and white families increased by $151,000 between 1984 and 2009.[23] Disparities in wealth are about three times larger between black and white households than disparities in income, and this holds across all income levels, rich families and poor.[24] Wealth also differs significantly across education levels. Those with a college education have ten times the wealth as those with less than four years of high school.[25]

Fact #4: The middle-class in rich democracies is shrinking and economic mobility is stagnant.

The middle-class can be defined in many ways, but let's start by defining it as households with per capita incomes between 25 percent above and 25 percent below median income in a country. As you can see in Figure 2.3, the percentage of the population in the middle-class has been falling in every major developed democracy since 1980, with the largest declines in those countries that have the highest levels of inequality: the US, UK, and Canada.

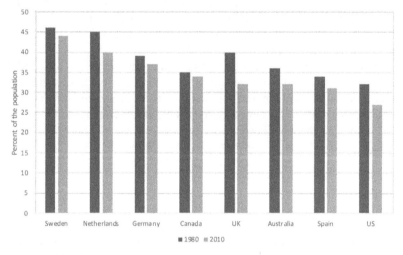

Note: The middle-class is defined as those who have per capita incomes that are 25 percent above and 25 percent below median national income.

Source: Luxembourg Income Study Database (2019).

Figure 2.3   *Percentage of the population in the middle-class in rich democracies*

If you define the middle-class more broadly, you find similar results. The US Census Bureau and the Federal Reserve define the middle-class as those with between two-thirds and twice the level of median income (between $42,000 and $126,000 for a family of three, a very wide spread).[26] Using this definition, the middle-class in the US has fallen to slightly less than half of the population for the first time in its history, down from 61 percent in 1971.

It is the rise of the top 10 percent, and particularly the top 1 percent, across the world that is leaving less relative income for everyone else, including the middle-class, however you choose to measure it. Figure 2.4 clearly shows how the dramatic rise in the income share of the top 1 percent directly correlates with the steep decline of the income shares going to the poorest 50 percent, many of whom qualify for the middle-class. While the top 1 percent now earns more than 20 percent of total income, the bottom 50 percent has seen its share fall from 21 percent to only 13 percent of total income. I'll state this again because it is so remarkable: The bottom 50 percent earns only about two-thirds of what the top 1 percent earns in the US.

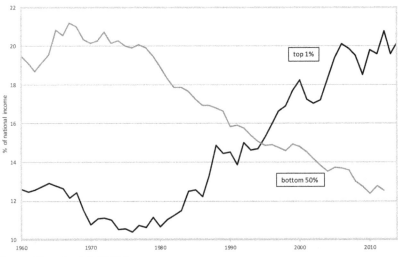

Source: Alvaredo et al. (2018a).

Figure 2.4   *Gross income shares of the top 1% and bottom 50% in the US*

The middle-class not only feel vulnerable because their income is stagnant, but also because they have so little wealth to serve as a safety net. About three-fifths of middle-class wealth is invested in housing, and the average debt-to-income ratio of a middle-class household is 125 percent. Compare this to the rich who have only 9 percent of their wealth in their houses and a debt-to-income ratio of only 38 percent. In fact, many middle-class families live in "asset poverty". In 2013, the average working family in the US had enough reserves to sustain its normal spending for less than a week![27]

A shrinking middle-class is not the only thing contributing to socioeconomic angst within richer countries. There has historically been a feeling in many countries that while you might be poor today, there is a good chance that you could be richer tomorrow. There was a feeling that hard work and ingenuity—coupled with the support of capitalism and democracy—would give enough people the boost they need to move up the income distribution over time—or at least that their children would advance beyond where their parents started. However, new longitudinal data that has surveyed the linkages between parental income and the income of their children suggests that many rich democracies are not the land of opportunity that we once mythologized them to be. Specifically, *intergenerational earnings elasticity* data has been created that calculates the correlation between paternal earnings and a son's adult earnings using children born during the early to mid-1960s and measuring adult outcomes into the mid-to-late 1990s.[28] The lower the intergenerational elasticity, the less likely a child's earnings will be highly correlated with paternal earnings, meaning that lower intergenerational elasticity implies greater income mobility in a country. This data suggests that there are big differences in intergenerational income mobility between countries: the US has half of the intergenerational income mobility as Canada, and the country with the highest mobility, Denmark, has more than four times the mobility as the country with the lowest, Peru. To put these numbers in some context, the intergenerational earnings elasticity of .47 in the US is similar to the correlation between a parent's height and the height of their children.[29] In the words of the economist Alan Krueger:

> The chance of a person who was born to a family in the bottom 10 percent of the income distribution rising to the top 10 percent as an adult is about the same as the chance that a dad who is 5' 6" having a son who grows up to be over 6' 1" tall. It happens, but not often.[30]

Figure 2.5 plots these intergenerational earnings elasticity data across countries along with Gini coefficients in each country—this graph is often referred to as "The Great Gatsby Curve". What we see here is that countries that have low intergenerational elasticities (i.e. less highly correlated incomes between parents and sons) also tend to have low income inequality, and vice versa. Although we cannot say that one causes the other—likely, there is some dual causation here for reasons that we will discuss later in the book—we do know that the pain caused by one magnifies the unhappiness caused by the other.

By almost any other measure, income mobility across time is stagnant or falling across developed countries.[31] Given that education is a key factor in

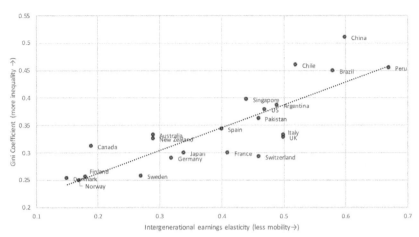

Source: Data on intergenerational earnings elasticity comes from Corak (2016). Data on Gini coefficients is from disposable income Ginis from Solt (2016).

Figure 2.5   Intergenerational mobility and income inequality

future income mobility, the lack of progress in many measures of educational achievement in the US and elsewhere is a harbinger of worsening inequality in the future. There is a stronger link between income and educational achievement in the US than any other developed country.[32] For example, poor students with high test scores are about as likely to graduate from college as richer students with low test scores.[33] Only 21 percent of high school sophomores from the bottom 20 percent earned a bachelor's degree over the ten years following their high school graduation, while 74 percent of those in the top 20 percent earn a degree.[34]

In the US, a lack of education and stagnant income mobility are most strongly correlated with two factors: race and having unmarried parents. In regards to race, black children have less upward mobility and more downward mobility. Black children born into the bottom 20 percent are twice as likely to be stuck there than are white children, while black children born in the middle 20 percent are twice as likely to fall to lower quintiles as white children are.[35] With regards to marriage, 80 percent of children raised in the bottom 20 percent will rise out of this quintile if their parents are married. For those children whose parents are not married, less than half of them escape.[36]

Fact #5: The global middle-class and poor are gaining ground (relatively).

Time for some good news. While it is true that the middle-class and poor have suffered relative losses within rich countries, if we consider the world as a whole, there has never been a better time to be alive. Growth in emerging market economies—particularly within China and India because of their fast growth and enormous populations—has pushed a remarkable number of people out of poverty and into the global middle-class. In many ways, this is the most important global event—not just economic event, but *any* event—of the last 40 years. The remarkable improvements in standards of living, life-expectancy, and quality of life that have been achieved in much of the poorer world has been unmatched by any other period in human history.

The global Gini coefficient on market income, which treats the entire global population as one, has fallen from .69 in 1988 to .65 in 2013, at the same time that global per capita income growth has been greater than 3.5 percent a year. Most of this growth has been in emerging market countries. In 2000, rich countries accounted for 60 percent of world GDP; today, they account for less than half, and by 2030 will account for less than 40 percent of world GDP.[37] However, while there has been an important reduction in global inequality as measured by the Gini, it is important to note that the global Gini is still higher than the Gini coefficient within even the most unequal of individual countries.[38]

Global poverty has plummeted. As measured by the current standard of extreme poverty being anyone who lives on less than $1.90 a day (at purchasing power parity), the number of extreme poor has plummeted from 42 percent of the world's population in 1981 to 9 percent today![39] While the world's population has increased by 4 billion people, somehow the number of people living in extreme poverty actually fell by 1 billion people. The immense impact of these changes on human welfare is staggering to think about.

As I mentioned above, China and India have a lot to do with these improvements—they are quickly becoming home to the global middle-class. China has reduced the number of people living in extreme poverty by roughly 600 million people since the late 1970s—a population nearly twice the size of the US! (It is hard to avoid using exclamation marks when you talk about the remarkable reductions in global poverty over the last four decades.) India has reduced the number in extreme poverty by more than 100 million. Unfortunately, poverty has not plummeted everywhere. Today, half of the global poor live in sub-Saharan Africa. While the percentage of people living in extreme poverty has fallen from 54 to 41 percent of the population of sub-Saharan Africa, the actual number of people living in extreme poverty has increased from 225 million to 400 million due to high population growth rates in the region.[40]

If you put fact #4—the declining middle-class in the rich world—together with fact #5—the rising global middle-class—you get a decidedly mixed

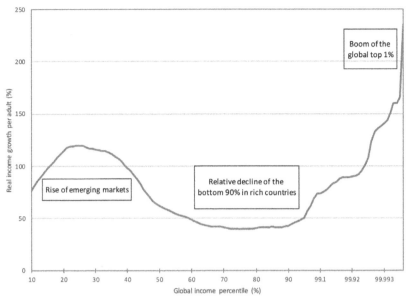

Source: Alvaredo et al. (2018a).

Figure 2.6   Total income growth across the globe, 1980–2016

picture of what is happening to overall global inequality. The best way to visualize this is to look at what is referred to as the "elephant curve", first depicted by the economist Branko Milanovic. Figure 2.6 presents the elephant curve, which graphs the relationship between income gains on the vertical axis against global income percentiles in order to illustrate which income shares have experienced the largest income gains since 1980. From this graph we see winners at either end of the curve. Emerging market economies have experienced large gains, particularly in China where incomes have increased by roughly 400 percent over this period, resulting in the sizeable growth of the Chinese middle-class. But the global top 1 percent (which would include most people in the top 10 percent of the US or other developed countries, and translates to earning about $50,000 a year per capita, or $200,000 for a household of four people) has experienced even larger gains—they are the trunk of the elephant. When looking at the elephant curve, note the non-standardized percentiles at the bottom, which flatten growth gains at the very top—if the entire top 10 percent was lumped together, the elephant would be mostly trunk. The fact is that the bottom 50 percent captured 12 percent of all global growth during this period, while the top 1 percent received more than twice that amount, or 27 percent of all global income growth.

The elephant curve also illustrates the relative losers over this period: the middle-class of the rich world in the US, Europe, Australia, Japan, and New Zealand. Their income gains have been smaller than elsewhere, and smaller than they have become accustomed to in previous generations. For the first time, many middle-class children in these countries are not doing significantly better than their parents, and coupled with the economic dislocation that accompanies globalization and technological change, they are not feeling happy about it. To give you some idea of the catch-up that is occurring between growing emerging markets and the developed world, in 1988 the richest person in the bottom 20 percent in the US had an income six times larger than the poorest person in the top 20 percent in China. Today, those people have the same levels of income. Once again, this is because incomes outside of the top 10 percent have been stagnant in the US, but growing strongly in China.[41]

Fact #6: Where, not who, is still the biggest story in global inequality.

As we discussed in Chapter 1, when measured using Theil's statistic, global inequality can be decomposed into two separate sources: *within-country inequality* (who you are within a country) and *between-country inequality* (which country in the world you live in). The fact of the matter is that three-fourths of global inequality can be explained by between-country inequality and only one-fourth by within-country inequality.[42] In other words, where you are matters much more than who you are. Place matters three times as much as person. The accident of where you are born is the most important factor that determines your lifetime income potential.

The implications of this fact are staggering. One implication is that there is a huge *citizenship premium* associated with being able to live and work in a rich country. Branko Milanovic expresses the citizenship premium this way: consider a citizen of the Congo, the poorest country in the world. If this Congolese person migrated to the US, they would see their income rise by a factor of 92; migrating to Sweden increases income by a factor of 71, to Brazil by a factor of 13, but to Yemen by only a factor of 3.[43] These incredible returns to migration illustrate two important points. First, the citizenship premium captures the huge economic incentives that the poor have to migrate to rich countries. Second, we cannot explain the citizenship premium—and most of the world's inequality—until we first understand why place matters more than who you are, your education levels, or how hard you work. Why does where matter so much?

To connect fact #6 to fact #5, it is true that place matters less than it used to. This is, once again, driven by the convergence of income in China, India, and other emerging market economies with the developed world. But in the midst of this convergence, there is also divergence between those at the very top and the very bottom. Rich countries are still growing faster, and pulling away, from the least developed and slowest-growing countries that are primarily in sub-Saharan Africa, the Middle East, Latin America, and Eastern Europe. The ratio of per capita income in the 15 richest to the 15 poorest countries in the world has risen from roughly 40 in 1990 to approximately 60 today (all 15 of the poorest countries in the world today are in sub-Saharan Africa).

It is important to note that place matters within countries as well as between countries. In other words, a great deal of national inequality is also associated with where you live. For example, urban incomes across the world are higher than rural incomes. In China, incomes in urban areas are nearly three times what they are in rural areas.[44] In the US, the differences in urban and rural incomes are much smaller, but other important differences remain. Children born in the poorest 20 percent in Detroit have half the likelihood of making it into the top 20 percent as a kid born in the poorest 20 percent in San Francisco.[45] Increasingly, as we will discuss in more detail later, Americans live in rich areas surrounded by other rich people, or poor areas surrounded by other poor people. The number of people living in poor neighborhoods (less than two-thirds of metropolitan median income) and rich neighborhoods (with more than 150 percent of metropolitan median income) has doubled in the US since 2000, and residential segregation has increased more rapidly for black and Hispanic families than for white families.[46] There are good reasons to think that this geographic separation between the rich and the poor is not just the result of higher economic inequality, but is driving inequality higher as well.

IN CONCLUSION

"It was the best of times, it was the worst of times … it was the spring of hope, it was the winter of despair …". I put this quote from Charles Dickens at the beginning of this book because it perfectly captures today's age.

For those at the bottom and the top of the global income distribution, it has been the best of times. The global poor are moving towards the global middle-class and extreme poverty is plunging. It has also been very good times for the top 10 percent, great times for top 1 percent, and extraordinarily great times for those even higher up the global income distribution. In regards to wealth, most of the world's wealth is now concentrated in the hands of a small number of people in a way that is hard to put into any historical context; the possible exception is the fourteenth-century Malian king Mansa Musa, who made a fortune in salt and gold—so much so that he collapsed world gold prices when he gave away a small part of his fortune.

For those in the middle of the global income distribution—the bottom 90 percent in most developed countries—it may not have been the worst of times, but it has not been good. Inequality levels across countries vary, but trends towards growing inequality are clear. Across countries, Gini coefficients are rising, while the top 10 percent and particularly the top 1 percent are lapping the bottom 90 percent. This is particularly true in the Anglo-Saxon developed countries. For the middle-class in rich democracies, this era has seen diminished expectations and rising anger and cynicism.

Obviously, we want to talk about why this is all occurring. Can we provide explanations for the six important facts that we have identified in this chapter? But before I provide any explanations, I want to take a step back. Should we care about economic inequality? Are there reasons to think that higher inequality threatens social stability or economic progress? In the next chapter, we first examine the arguments that inequality doesn't matter in and of itself, and that egalitarian angst is all for naught.

NOTES

1. Institut Français d'Opinion Publique (2010).
2. Kiatpongsan and Norton (2014).
3. Ibid.
4. Pew Research Center (2014a).
5. Alvaredo et al. (2018a).
6. Ibid.
7. Milanovic (2016).
8. Alvaredo et al. (2018a).
9. Scheidel (2017).
10. Piketty et al. (2018).
11. Saez (2013).
12. Reeves and Matthew (2016).
13. Oxfam (2018).
14. Collins and Hoxie (2017).
15. Dolan (2017).
16. Wolff (2017).
17. Credit Suisse Research Institute (2017).
18. Alvaredo et al. (2018a).
19. Bourguignon (2015).
20. Saez and Zucman (2016).
21. Jones (2015).
22. Wolff (2017).
23. Shapiro et al. (2014).
24. McKernan et al. (2013).
25. Wolff (2017).
26. US Bureau of the Census (2015) and Pew Research Center (2015).
27. Wolff (2017).
28. Corak (2013).

29. Huggett et al. (2011).
30. Krueger (2012).
31. Evidence suggests intergenerational mobility was stable in the US for those born between 1950 and 1970. See Chetty et al. (2014a).
32. Pew Economic Mobility Project (2011).
33. Hoxby and Avery (2013).
34. Kena et al. (2015).
35. Reeves and Matthew (2016).
36. Reeves (2014).
37. OECD (2010).
38. Hellebrandt and Mauro (2015).
39. World Bank (2016).
40. Ibid.
41. Milanovic (2016).
42. Lakner (2017).
43. Milanovic (2016).
44. Wanli (2015).
45. *The Economist* (2017a).
46. Reardon and Bischoff (2011).

3. Why might inequality be necessary? Incentives, freedom, and efficiency

The working premise of this book is that rising economic inequality is bad for society and poses a threat to our economic well-being and social cohesiveness. But in any honest debate—and that is what this book is trying to provide—all premises must be critically examined. The fact of the matter is that some of the best and brightest minds in economics, philosophy, sociology, and history do not believe that inequality is necessarily something to worry about. In the words of one such economist, Harvard's Martin Feldstein, "income inequality is not a problem in need of a remedy".[1] Those who share this belief include Nobel Prize winning economists such as Milton Friedman and Robert Lucas, who contend that a society in which equality is imposed on it by government is worse in every important aspect than one in which people's rewards rise and fall based on the value of their contributions to society. Lucas argues that: "Of the tendencies that are harmful to sound economics, the most seductive, and in my opinion the most poisonous, is to focus on the questions of distribution."[2]

Before we examine the reasons to be concerned about rising inequality, we first need to clearly understand the rationales of some of our most important thinkers on why we should not be worried about inequality, or should even be happy about it when compared to the alternatives. We can summarize these "What, me worry?" arguments into four different perspectives on inequality—not mutually exclusive and closely related to each other in important ways—that each contend that economic inequality is a necessary evil that should be accepted, not corrected.

CLASSICAL INEQUALITY AND AUSTRIAN ECONOMICS: THE "JUST DESERTS" PERSPECTIVE ON INEQUALITY

The Classical view of inequality dates back to Adam Smith and essentially applies the principles of supply and demand in perfectly competitive markets to understanding the causes of inequality. In the Classical view, inequality simply reflects differences in productivity that should be rewarded if resources are to be used in their most productive ways in order to maximize overall efficiency. In other words, inequality is just a measure of incentives. Higher wages and greater inequality signal where resources are needed most; this creates economic incentives to move talent and capital to where it is most valuable. When resources are used in their most productive ways, the economy is operating in the most efficient manner possible and our standards of living are maximized. With perfect equality, there would also be zero economic incentive to work hard, get an education, save money, start a business, take a risk, or create a new technology that ultimately drives the economic growth that benefits us all.

The critical Classical assumption that provides the foundation for justifiable inequality is that labor markets are perfectly competitive. As a result, every firm must compete for the best workers, driving wages to the point where workers are paid their marginal product. By marginal product, economists mean the value of the output produced when a unit of labor is added to production. In the Classical model, the competition for labor ensures that every worker is paid their marginal product, and wages only rise as workers' productivity rises. It is in this sense that inequality is justified—richer workers are the most productive workers. The richest landlords are those with the most productive land. The richest entrepreneurs are those with the best business ideas. These inequalities are "natural" in the sense that there is no judgment about what makes some workers more productive than others or why some landlords own the best land. These endowments are just the way things are, and market efficiency demands that they be paid their marginal product or else these endowments will be used less profitably elsewhere.

Economists would characterize this result—where everyone's labor is paid their marginal products—as the *Pareto efficient* outcome for society. A Pareto efficient outcome is one in which there is no way to make one person better off without making someone else worse off. If society imposed a tax on the richest and most productive workers and allocated that revenue to the poorest and least productive workers, this outcome would not be Pareto efficient because the most productive workers would lose because of it. However, according to Classical thinking, the costs of redistributing income are really felt by all. When the most productive workers are taxed, they might choose to work less and deprive other workers of the value of their contributions. In addition, by giving some workers incomes that are greater than their productivity, redistributing income has reduced their incentives to work harder or to improve themselves, significantly reducing their contributions to society as well.

To put this another way, the problem with taxing LeBron James is not only that he might play basketball less and we would lose the enjoyment of watching him, but that by making basketball less lucrative, taxes reduce the incentives for other people to play basketball and develop their own skills. If everyone benefits when LeBron plays basketball, why should we discourage it with a distortionary tax?

Classical economists do not believe that *all* inequality is good, just natural inequality. Inequality that is created by government interference in the economy or by imperfectly competitive markets is bad inequality, because it creates inequality while also being inefficient. Monopolies, labor unions, government regulations, and taxation can create market failures and economic rents that lead to unnatural inequality. Classical economists recognize that there is a need for limited taxation to pay for public goods that will be inadequately provided by the market alone. These taxes could even be progressive and paid primarily by the rich if the well-off are the primary beneficiaries of services from these public goods, such as law enforcement, national defense, and public education. However, the appropriate role of government intervention is always limited to two goals: (1) making markets more competitive and (2) moving wages closer to the true marginal products of workers. The role of government is not to reduce inequality *per se*.

Taken together, the economist Gregory Mankiw calls this the "just deserts" perspective of Classical inequality. In Mankiw's words:

> According to this view, people should receive compensation congruent with their contributions. If the economy were described by a classical competitive equilibrium without any externalities or public goods, then every individual would earn the value of his or her own marginal product, and there would be no need for government to alter the resulting income distribution. The role of government arises as the economy departs from this classical benchmark. (Distortionary) taxes and subsidies are necessary to correct externalities, and progressive income taxes can be justified to finance public goods based on the benefits principle.[3]

One important implication of Classical inequality is that wage growth should reflect productivity growth. In other words, as we become more productive, wages should rise in equal proportion. Is this true? Refer back to the Preface and Figure P.1, where you can see that before 1970, the iron link between productivity and wages held for US workers, just as assumed in Classical economic models. But in our modern era of growing inequality, productivity has grown at *eight times* the rate of a typical worker's pay since 1970 and at *ten times* the rate of a typical worker's pay since 2000. In other words, the benefits of higher productivity have not been going to workers. This is strong evidence of uncorrected-for market failure and growing economic rents that create inefficient inequality.

Another school of economics noted not only for its acceptance but also its celebration of inequality is the Austrian schools of economics, named after its two intellectual leaders, the Austrians Friedrich Hayek and Joseph Schumpeter. Austrian economics places its primary emphasis on technological development and the role that entrepreneurs play in driving productive—but also costly—evolutionary change in economic systems.

Hayek's *The Road to Serfdom* is one of the most influential conservative books of the last century.[4] In this book, Hayek lauds the efficiencies of the free-market system and warns of the dangers of government central planning aimed at promoting equality, specifically the extreme form of egalitarianism adopted in communist countries such as the Soviet Union. Hayek's critique of government planning focuses on the role of information. Information is always limited: as Adam Smith noted, no single individual knows enough to make a pencil because nobody could possibly learn each and every step needed to produce each and every input necessary to build a pencil. But prices and markets—Smith's "invisible hand"—are able to make pencils because prices create incentives for people with specialized knowledge to make what is needed, while markets are a means of bringing these individuals together. Likewise, no group of people, no matter how large or intelligent, knows how to feed a city, but somehow people get fed through the actions of millions of people coordinated through billions of transactions with the only goal of acting in their own self-interest.

In markets, vast quantities of information are conveyed through prices and wages. Prices and wages reflect the cumulative knowledge of large groups of people and send signals about where resources can be used most productively. As a result, market outcomes are always preferable to government-directed outcomes because a small number of government bureaucrats can never know enough by themselves to efficiently plan an economy. Centrally planned economies will always be guilty of "malinvestment" by failing to allocate resources to their best possible uses because bureaucrats are not omnipotent. Even government manipulations of markets that are not as invasive as central planning can still be harmful. Whenever governments interfere in markets so that prices do not reflect the full benefits and costs of a transaction, they also distort information and incentives, which leads to less efficient investment decisions. As a result, according to Hayek and in agreement with Classical economists, the best governments follow laissez-faire policies and intervene in markets only to provide public goods under the narrowest of definitions, or to prevent monopolistic or collusive behavior. In fact, Hayek argued quite explicitly that wealth and inequality are necessary prerequisites for innovation and cultural progress.[5]

Joseph Schumpeter, in his book *Capitalism, Socialism, and Democracy*, focuses on the role of dynamic entrepreneurs in improving standards of living over time. According to Schumpeter, "The fundamental impulse that sets and keeps the capitalist engine in motion comes from the new consumers, goods, the new methods of production or transportation, the new markets, the new forms of industrial organization that capitalist enterprise creates."[6] Like biological evolution, technological development generated by this competition does not take place at a constant rate. Instead, innovation is the result of big ideas that are developed sporadically (mutated, to use a biological term) within different industries. Initially, these new technologies are not unambiguously good for economic growth because new technologies replace old technologies, leading to obsolescence and requiring resources to be reallocated, retrained, and replaced. This is the basis of Schumpeter's theory of creative destruction, where new technologies eventually lead to growth, but are initially chaotic and require costly retrenchment. For every Google there is a print newspaper, and for every MP3 player there is a cassette player. Technology builds on itself, but it also relegates some of what has been built before it to the trash bins of history. This enriches successful entrepreneurs in extraordinary ways, it raises standards of living for society as a whole, but it also creates losers.

However, for this process to work efficiently, firms must be allowed to fail. The deaths of firms and industries are essentially the way that the "dead brush" of capitalism is cleared to allow new growth to occur. Without failure, resources will continue to be allocated to less productive businesses, leaving fewer resources available for the entrepreneurs that will potentially drive the next great wave of technological innovation. Without failure, capitalism cannot thrive. For this reason, Schumpeter worried about the dangers of socialism in democratic nations. Whenever people have jobs and wages that are protected in the interest of equality and fairness—whether it is a bailout of a failing firm, a labor regulation making it costly to fire workers, or a protectionist trade policy—there is the potential to block new technologies. Schumpeter also believed that the social safety net provided by the modern welfare state discourages risk-taking and fails to incentivize the entrepreneurial spirit that is at the root of capitalist success.[7]

There may have been no better proponent of Austrian economics—even though he lived in the era before Hayek and Schumpeter—than President Theodore Roosevelt, who clearly viewed himself as a version of Schumpeter's superman entrepreneur:

> It is not true that as the rich have grown richer the poor have grown poorer. Successful enterprise, of the type which benefits all mankind, can only exist if the conditions are such as to offer great prizes as the rewards of success. The captains of industry who have driven the railway systems across this continent, who have built up our commerce, who have developed our manufacturers, have on the whole done great good to our people. Without them the material development of which we are so justly proud could never have taken place.[8]

Roosevelt and Schumpeter would see nothing wrong and very many things right with the booming income and wealth of the top 1 percent we talked about in the last chapter. They would be encouraged by the fact that 70 percent of all of the business owners in Forbes 400 started their own companies and did not just inherit them, up from only 40 percent of business owners on the list in

1980. They would also be happy to see that the number of people on the Forbes 400 list that grew up with family members on the Forbes 400 list fell by more than half (from 60 percent to 30 percent of the list) since 1980. Most of the 4th, 5th, and 6th generations of family wealth have disappeared from the Forbes 400 list over time (although many of these families are still very wealthy, just not Forbes 400 wealthy), just as Schumpeter would have hoped to see in an entrepreneurial economy.[9]

It seems strange to say, but the first Austrian economist may have been the Greek philosopher Plato, who lived 2,300 years before Hayek and Schumpeter. In *The Republic*, Plato talks about people's desire for *thymos*, which can be translated as self-respect, admiration, and ambition for these things. But *thymos* in some people becomes *megalothmia*, the need to be recognized as superior to others.[10] In its extreme, *megalothmia* becomes a tyrannical desire for achievement. Plato argued that productive societies must find a way to channel the ambitions of the most ambitious people towards productive outlets—i.e. entrepreneurship—and away from theft and manipulating political systems. In Plato's view, Mark Zuckerberg and Genghis Khan are not as different as they must first seem. Ensuring that our economic system channels ambition towards productive outlets becomes crucial to maintaining social stability and a high quality of life. However, the cost of stability is inequality.[11]

Let me conclude this discussion of Classical and Austrian economics by saying that a few economists from the Classical period in economics (the 1800s and early 1900s) were worried about inequality, but they largely failed to accept that there were economic solutions to inequality. Thomas Malthus feared population growth and the "iron law of wages". According to Malthus, a slowly growing capital stock could never keep pace with an exponentially growing population, which would lead to a continual decline in the productivity of labor. Eventually, falling productivity would mean that wages would be driven below subsistence levels until population growth corrected itself—in other words, until famine occurred. Likewise, David Ricardo worried about the "scarcity principle": that a growing population would make a fixed supply of land relatively more and more valuable, driving up land rents to such levels that extreme inequality between very wealthy landholders and subsistence-income farmers would be the norm. Karl Marx shared similar worries as Malthus and Ricardo, but without the belief in perfectly competitive markets. In Marxist theory, the owners of capital exploited the fact that there was a surplus of unemployed workers so that wages would never rise to the marginal product of labor. Competition among entrepreneurs assured that only the firms that exploited workers the most would survive. As a result, all income growth would accrue to the owners of capital, while most of the labor force would be trapped in subsistence levels of poverty.

Ricardo came to the conclusion that property taxes might be a necessary evil to prevent mass poverty and ensure social stability. On the other hand, Malthus, an English cleric, believed that the only solution to the iron law of wages was sexual abstinence. Marx, of course, believed that the entire capitalist system was unsustainable and needed to be overthrown and replaced with a communist system that would foremost emphasize equality, not Classical economics.

THE TRADEOFF BETWEEN EQUITY AND EFFICIENCY: THE "BIGGER PIE" PERSPECTIVE ON INEQUALITY

The incredible economic growth experienced across the world since the industrial revolution has improved almost everyone's quality of life, regardless of how you measure quality of life. Our economic pie has gotten bigger thanks to economic growth made possible by higher levels of productivity and increased efficiency. Steven Pinker points out that if the world's output in 1700 was baked in a standard 9 inch pie pan, the world's output today would be a pie more than 10 feet in diameter.[12]

Many economists accept as a truism that there is a strict tradeoff between equity and efficiency—that any attempt to redistribute income or wealth (changing how we slice the pie) will change economic incentives and move resources away from their most productive uses and limit economic growth (and change how big the pie is). When this happens, it can hurt everyone, rich and poor alike. Much of this belief originates with an appeal to the concept of Pareto efficiency, which we just discussed. When an economy is operating at a Pareto efficient point, then it must be true that for someone to have more, at least one person has to have less. While Pareto efficiency says nothing about what the optimal outcome for society as a whole actually is, it does imply that if we are at a Pareto efficient point, there is an inescapable tradeoff at work: policies that aim to make one group of people better off will also make another group of people worse off. As a result, if we are at a Pareto efficient outcome (and that is a big *if*), redistribution policy is inherently about picking winners and losers. Because of this, many economists, such as Robert Lucas in the introduction of this chapter, argue that society should not distract itself from the big issue of growth by thinking too much about redistribution. Instead, policymakers should keep their sole focus on increasing overall efficiency and identifying ways that society can make more, not on designing policies to take from Peter to give to Pauline, or vice versa.

Many conservative economists argue that redistribution does more than just distract us from focusing on efficiency—it directly reduces efficiency in ways never fully appreciated by Classical economists. Supply-side economists argue that taxes do not simply redistribute resources in inefficient ways, but they also radically reduce people's incentives to work, save, and invest in capital. In fact, taxes are so distortionary that redistributing income from the poor to the rich inevitably makes both groups worse off. Supply-siders believe that taxing the rich is extremely costly for a number of reasons. First, the richest are the most productive members of society (according to Classical thinking), so taxing them will impact productivity the most. Second, the richest have most elastic labor supply—they can more easily leave the labor force than those in the poor and middle-class. Third, rich people save more and create more capital. Finally, globalization allows the rich to move their wealth around the world and shelter it more easily in tax havens, meaning that taxing the rich is particularly harmful to national capital accumulation. For all of these reasons, it is counterproductive to penalize the rich when they do so much for the economy.

Taxes on the poor and middle-class are also costly according to supply-siders, although less so than taxes on the rich. Taxes on the poor and middle-class create significant disincentives to invest in an education by reducing future income benefits. Because education is the most important avenue for generating income mobility over time, supply-siders believe that low tax rates for everyone are the most effective means of generating more social mobility and greater income equality in the long run.

Entrepreneurship is another important avenue for income mobility, and, like Austrian economists, supply-siders worry about the long-term impact of taxes and the welfare state on entrepreneurship for a number of reasons. First, the welfare state reduces entrepreneurship by making people more dependent on handouts, less likely to work or to innovate, and less productive—i.e. to suffer from "learned helplessness".[13] In other words, social safety nets lead to cultural deterioration and future economic stagnation. Second, supply-siders also worry that redistributive taxation will channel entrepreneurship into profitable but potentially more destructive activities such as political rent-seeking and crony capitalism. Many conservatives fear that welfare states are inherently vulnerable to becoming captured by elites and becoming "predator states", where both efficiency and equity are sacrificed for the self-enrichment of the powerful. As a result, supply-siders worry that the growth of the welfare state will lead to more inequality, not less.

This idea that taxing the rich can hurt everyone is most vividly captured by what is referred to as the Laffer curve, which can be seen in Figure 3.1. The Laffer curve is not the least bit amusing to conservatives, and captures the idea that the disincentives of higher tax rates are so great that governments will actually collect less tax revenue once tax rates exceed a certain level. This is because as tax rates rise, workers will stop working, the rich will stop investing, and entrepreneurs will stop innovating. Many supply-side economists believe

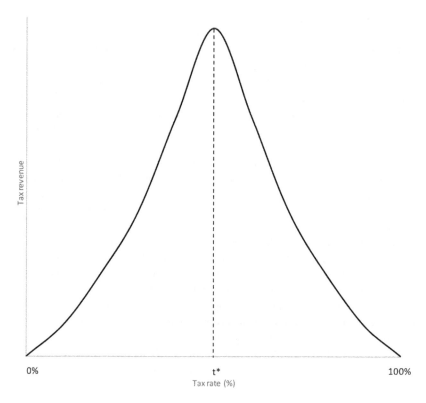

Figure 3.1   The Laffer curve

that this tax revenue maximizing rate—t* in the graph—is between a 20 and 35 percent tax rate.[14] This tax rate will allow the government to collect enough tax revenue to fund only the most essential government services. Raising tax rates above this level in order to finance aggressive income redistribution will actually lead to the collection of less tax revenue, reducing the government's ability to fund a minimal welfare state. As a result, taxes should be kept low in order to increase efficiency and maximize economic growth, allowing the overall benefits of higher growth to "trickle down" to those at the bottom of the income distribution. In supply-side thinking, low taxes and limited government are the best ways to foster a more egalitarian society.

The basic insight of the Laffer curve is intuitively persuasive, and there is evidence that exceptionally high tax rates can reduce the incentives to work, get an education, become an entrepreneur, invest, or honestly report your income.[15] However, the real debate between most economists is related to the more important empirical questions: At what tax rates do taxes become so distortionary that tax revenue begins to fall? 20 percent? 50 percent? 90 percent? What is the shape of the Laffer curve? Is it a half-circle or a parabola, meaning are the disincentive effects of taxes constant or do they change quickly past certain thresholds? And is the Laffer curve symmetrical, or are there different impacts of changing tax rates below t* than changing tax rates above t*?

These are all interesting questions for economists to debate. However, to the extent that this debate can be summarized succinctly, the best evidence suggests that the left side of the Laffer curve is steeply sloped (higher tax rates have a strong positive impact on tax revenues) and that t* is much higher than 35 percent—possibly as high as 70 percent.[16] This is because the impact of higher tax rates on labor supply is very small. Studies have generally found that a 10 percent increase in the tax rate only reduces labor supply by between 0 and 3 percent.[17]

Supply-siders and many conservative economists see additional avenues through which income redistribution directly reduces productivity. Some have argued that inequality is a prerequisite for efficiency. This idea is best captured in the nineteenth-century steel magnate Andrew Carnegie's "Gospel of Wealth" philosophy.[18] Carnegie believed that the price of material progress is wealth inequality because of the importance of economies of scale in production. In most manufacturing industries, the best way to increase efficiency and reduce costs is to operate at the biggest scale possible. However, operating at scale also means that most of society's productive resources must be held in the hands of a small number of business owners. As a result, efficiency requires the concentration of wealth and inequality, and there is no way around this. Carnegie argued that wealth should be encouraged to accumulate because it promotes efficiency, even if that means that many industries become monopolized. However, Carnegie also argued that those few elites who come out on top have a moral responsibility to give their wealth away during their lifetimes—voluntarily, not compelled to do so by the government. In his opinion, accumulated wealth should be treated as a trust fund for society and given away when tycoons die, not passed down through inheritance because children will never give inherited wealth away. "The man who dies rich, dies disgraced."

While Carnegie's arguments seem self-serving, the idea that scale, efficiency, and inequality are intrinsically linked is not just a tenet of conservatives and supply-side economists, but of economists across the political spectrum, including Karl Marx and John Maynard Keynes. Marx believed, as we discussed before, that the concentration of wealth is necessary for enhanced efficiency because efficiency requires the exploitation of workers, and those capitalists who are the most despotic are sure to earn the highest profits. Keynes believed that accumulated wealth is crucial to accumulating capital at a scale that can put new technology into production. In fact, picking up on this insight of Keynes, many economic historians argue that the industrial revolution was not really a technological revolution as much as a financial revolution.[19] In Keynes' words:

> it was precisely the *inequality* of the distribution of wealth which made possible those vast accumulations of fixed wealth and of capital improvements which distinguished that age from all others. Herein lay, in fact, the main justification of the Capitalist System. If the rich had spent their new wealth on the own enjoyments, the world would long ago have found such a regime intolerable. But like bees they saved and accumulated, not less to the advantage of the whole community because they themselves held narrower ends in prospect.[20]

EQUALITY OF OPPORTUNITY IS MORE IMPORTANT THAN EQUALITY OF OUTCOME: FREEDOM, FAIR RACES, AND "FRUITS OF LABOR" PERSPECTIVES ON INEQUALITY

Philosophical libertarians agree with Classical, Austrian, and supply-side economists about the dangers of income redistribution, but the fundamental source of their fears is quite different. Taxes and the welfare state may reduce efficiency and create distortions, but libertarians primarily fear larger and more intrusive governments because they believe that government redistribution reduces freedom of choice. According to the libertarian view, the welfare of society is maximized when people are free to do as they choose as long as it doesn't hurt anyone else. Libertarians such as the economist/philosopher John Stuart Mill argue that maximizing liberty also maximizes societal welfare over the long run by allowing people to follow their own distinct desires, giving everyone the greatest chance to fully develop as a human being and achieve happiness. Libertarians believe that liberty is the fundamental goal around which society must be organized, not equality or efficiency.

Libertarians see inequality as the result of free choice, and in that sense, it is a reflection of a healthy society. When someone decides to be a poorly paid artist, or to drop out of school early because they dislike it, or to choose leisure over consumption, they are simply following their own path towards maximizing their own happiness. Redistributing income from the rich to the poor without the rich's consent is a fundamental impingement of freedom. A welfare state backed by the power of the government to coerce its citizens is fundamentally unjust because it restricts the freedom of some individuals to do what they want. By heavily taxing the rich, the government is essentially forcing them to work for the state, violating the most basic individual freedom: ownership of the self. Redistributive governments might think of themselves as Robin Hoods, but libertarians view them as simply thieves because they do not respect the liberty of the rich or the poor: they take with coercion and give in a paternalistic way.

The philosopher Robert Nozick states the libertarian case in a somewhat different way. He rightly asserts that there is no such thing as an ideal income distribution and no such thing as an optimal level of inequality that perfectly balances society's desire for both equity and efficiency. As a result, whenever governments redistribute income, they are imposing an arbitrary pattern of income distribution through coercion that directly interferes with individual liberty and people's ability to keep the "fruits of their own labor". Such coercion can only be justified when the goals are clear and incontrovertible— something that will never happen when it comes to the divisive idea of what constitutes a fair and equitable society. As a result, Nozick argues that governments have no right to redistribute income. The rich are free to give away their own income if they choose to, but there is no justification for the state to forcibly take from one person and give to someone else, even if the majority of the population supports such action. In Nozick's words: "only a minimal state, limited to enforcing contracts and protecting people against force, theft, and fraud, is justified. Any more extensive state violates personal rights not to be forced to do certain things, and is unjustified."[21]

What makes for a fair and equitable society in the minds of libertarians? According to Nozick, a society is fair if its rules are fair. As long as everyone has to abide by the same laws that are universally enforced, society is fair. Everything after that is up to the individual, not society. As long as inequality is the result of each individual's own decisions and actions, then the right to freedom comes with the responsibility to enjoy or suffer the consequences of your actions. As a result, the government's role is to not guarantee outcomes, but to protect individual choice and to make sure that limited rules are fairly enforced.

This idea that governments should only promote the equality of opportunity, not the equality of outcomes, is an important one in libertarian thinking. The philosopher John Rawls, from whom we will hear more in the next chapter, defines equality of opportunity in the following way: "those who are at the same level of talent and ability, and have the same willingness to use them, should have the same prospects of success regardless of their initial place in the social system."[22] In other words, as long as inequality can be tied to merit, then it is acceptable. Former Federal Reserve chair Ben Bernanke states the libertarian view of merit in this way: "A bedrock American Principle is that idea that all individuals should have the opportunity to succeed on the basis of their won effort, skill, and ingenuity … Although we Americans strive to provide equality of economic opportunity, we do not guarantee equality of economic outcomes, nor should we."[23]

What does equality of opportunity mean? To many libertarians, it simply means non-discrimination. In other words, the government should not play favorites in any way and provide the same privileges and protections to everyone. But the problem with this view of equality is that it ignores the problem of endowments, or intrinsic differences between us. If someone who is fit races against someone with one leg, is it a fair race? Libertarians would say yes as long as they start at the same point at the same time and run the same course. The Nobel Prize winning economist Milton Friedman explains why in this way:

> Life is not fair. It is tempting to believe that government can rectify what nature has spawned. But it is also important to recognize how much we benefit from the very unfairness we deplore. There's nothing fair ... about Muhammad Ali's having been born with the skill that made him a great fighter ... But wouldn't it have been even more unfair to the people who enjoyed watching him if, in the pursuit of some abstract ideal of equality, Muhammad Ali had not been permitted to earn more for one night's fight ... than the lowest man on the totem pole could get for a day's unskilled work on the docks?[24]

In other words, it is the unfairness of life that makes it worth living, and to prevent unfairness would be neither practical nor desirable. The closest to fairness that we can get is to provide everyone equal opportunity for freedom to pursue our desires based on our own abilities.

The idea that most of the endowment differences between people are natural—meaning that people are born with these differences and there is nothing constructive to be done about them—is a prevalent idea among libertarians. In fact, there is a great deal of empirical evidence that economic outcomes in life are heavily influenced by natural endowments such as genetics. Because genetic differences cannot be corrected for without extreme restrictions on freedom, libertarians believe that they should simply be accepted. For example, a review of studies of identical twins separated at birth—which are commonly used to separate differences in heritability from environment—finds that economic outcomes are as inheritable as personality and many medical conditions.[25] In fact, this study concluded that 33 percent of the variation in household income can be explained by genetics, while only 11 percent can be explained by differences in environment.

However, critics of Libertarianism argue that many endowments are not natural but unnatural—they reflect differences in family environment, unequal access to education and government services, and explicit or implicit forms of discrimination in society. In other words, there are few abilities that are truly "natural", but instead are tied to social and economic privilege. In Rawls' definition of equality of opportunity, he emphasizes the point that people of the same talent, ability, and willingness to use them should have similar outcomes. But the problem is that talent, ability, and willingness are inherently shaped by the people we interact with and the legal and economic institutions that governments put in place to support us. There is no possibility of having a truly non-discriminatory society as long as there exists unequal access to certain privileges. As a result, it might actually be easier to achieve equality of outcome than equality of opportunity, because it is easier to redistribute income through government policy than it is to provide true equality of opportunity by guaranteeing equal access to every social or governmental institution.

To say this in a somewhat different way, the idea of a meritocracy-driven society where everyone has the same equality of opportunity is a myth, because success itself contributes to more success. When merit is rewarded, it leads to unequal conditions, which then improves access to the institutions that create future success (such as education, political influence, social connections, etc.) that undermines mobility. As we will talk about more in the next chapter, education is the means most widely promoted by libertarians as the key to rewarding merit and ensuring social mobility. However, education is also one of the factors that are most responsible for perpetuating inequality of opportunity and outcomes in modern society. As we will see, it is a plain fact that the educational access of children is closely correlated to the income levels of their parents. As a result, only rewarding merit also discourages income mobility at the same time.

Another limitation of the libertarian argument is that the distinction between heritability and environment—between natural and unnatural endowments—is not quite as clear as it initially appears. One interesting study examined twins that had been misidentified and raised as identical, when in fact they were not genetically identical, and vice versa. The findings suggest that whether parents *thought* the twins were identical was a greater predictor of the similarity of the twins across a variety of economic and social factors than whether they *actually were* genetically identical.[26] In other words, socialization plays a big role in outcomes—even within the same families with the same parents—and it is often difficult to clearly separate the impact of environmental variability from the impact of genetic variability.

One final challenge to the libertarian viewpoint is that protecting freedom often requires coercion. Is anarchy really freedom? Even libertarians don't think so. Libertarians argue that governments do have the right to use their power to restrict certain behaviors; for example, to protect people from theft or bodily harm. Inequality is predicated on property rights, which are a form of coercion because they restrict one person's liberty from using someone else's property. So just as Nozick argues that there is no socially optimal distribution of income, there is also no perfectly free society in which people have absolute liberty. Whether we are talking about egalitarianism or liberty, no sustainable utopia is possible. Societies must find reasonable balances between freedom and equality, not preference one at the complete disregard of the other. Critics of Libertarianism assert that coercion to promote equality of outcomes is less objectionable when it is broadly, fairly, and legitimately applied. If the political system is fair, then the redistribution of resources imposed by that system can also be fair, even if some people are disadvantaged by it.

ABSOLUTE MATTERS MORE THAN RELATIVE: THE "SIZE OF THE SMALLEST PIECE" PERSPECTIVE ON INEQUALITY

What makes for a just society? Libertarians have one idea. Plato had a very different idea. He argued that a just society is simply one in which everyone is doing the work they have been assigned to do as a part of the class they were born into, and not interfering with the work of members of other classes. In his mind, the greatest good is achieved when everyone is working towards their *telos*: their natural goal, or innate purpose for living, which is defined for them at birth. Modern liberal societies have very different ideas from Plato, obviously. But one thing that philosophers can agree upon is that there is no valid and general principle that specifies the optimal distribution of income and wealth. Philosophers—and economists as well—tend to argue about the direction in which the government should influence the distribution of income, but not about what the optimal goal for this distribution should be.

As a result, some economists and philosophers argue that focusing on relative income, relative indicators of justice, and relative measures of well-being is guaranteed to frustrate and encourage envy. Wherever you are on the distribution (unless you are the richest, which at the time of this writing is Jeff Bezos), there is always someone doing better than you. The problem with focusing too much on relative inequality is captured in an old Soviet joke about two poor friends: the only difference between them is that one has an undernourished goat and the other doesn't. When asked what he wants most in life, the peasant without a goat says "for my friend's goat to die".

Instead, an approach that fosters more societal happiness is to ignore relative inequality and concentrate on absolute measures of well-being, specifically poverty. As opposed to redistributing income across the entire population, the focus should be on helping to raise up those living in poverty and limiting the tax penalties on everyone else.

The philosopher Harry Frankfurt has argued against focusing on relative inequality and instead focusing on a "doctrine of sufficiency". In his words: "From the point of view of morality, it is not important that everyone should have the same. What is morally important is that each should have enough."[27] Doing worse than others does not mean that you are doing badly. When the sole focus is only on relative position, you are giving others the power over you to define your ambitions. Frankfurt believes that governments should not foster relative envy. Instead, the primary aim of government should be to make sure that everyone has their basic needs met, and leave it at that.

The alleviation of poverty has generally found more acceptance among economists than the broader goal of minimizing inequality. Adam Smith noted that the mark of a dysfunctional society is one where some people are so much poorer than others that they have to live and dress in such a way that they cannot go out into public without shame. Other economists such as Lester Thurow have argued that the alleviation of poverty is a public good—it confers benefits on all of society, such as the elimination of crime, improved civil society, and better public health. As a result, eliminating poverty creates positive externalities that the government should promote by redistributing income to the poor (but not necessarily to those above the poverty level).[28]

Maybe the most persuasive argument for focusing on poverty and not equality comes from the Nobel Prize winning economist Amartya Sen[29], who accepts the libertarian argument that the best measure of a just society is how free it is. In Sen's view, societies make a mistake when they sacrifice personal freedoms in an attempt to spur economic growth and reduce poverty through brute force. However, it is also true that increasing the incomes of the poorest facilitates freedom by giving them a broader range of choices that they could potentially make; income increases people's "capabilities" in Sen's terminology. Higher incomes mean greater freedom to choose the job you want, not just a job that you need to survive. Higher incomes are also needed to pay for an education, which allows people to make more informed choices and which improves their quality of life in many different ways. Higher incomes also increase access to healthcare, increasing health and life-expectancy. As a result, limiting poverty is one of the most effective ways of increasing freedom.

Focusing on poverty means moving away from focusing on improving the relative position of the middle-class. This could be justified by recognizing that the middle-class has made huge gains on an absolute level over time. Ask yourself: Who would you rather be, John Rockefeller in 1900 or you today? Rockefeller might have had servants and mansions, but he did not have a cell phone, a washing machine, vaccinations, and airplanes. It is quite true that the average American lives a life that would have been impossible for kings to enjoy just a few decades ago. In fact, it can be argued that the middle-class today enjoys lifestyles closer to those of the top 1 percent than it has done at any time in the past. The middle-class spends a lower fraction of its income on necessities than it ever has before and has access to the same information technology, public health advances, and transportation improvements (without the first-class seating) that the super-rich enjoy.[30] In many ways, technology and globalization have transformed what it means to be poor, at least in developed countries.

Are we doing a better job at eliminating poverty than we are at reducing inequality? On a global level, yes. As discussed in the previous chapter, there are fewer people living in absolute poverty across the globe than at any time in history. But within specific countries such as the US, the answer is less clear. In the US, the poverty line is measured at constant purchasing power, not at a constant standard of living. Basically, the US poverty line is calculated by taking the cheapest meal plan that can feed a family and multiplying it by three based on the assumption that a family spends one-third of their money on food. However, this assumption that families spend one-third of their income on food is something that has not been true since the 1960s. Today, Americans only spend only about 13 percent of their income on food, thanks in part to rising costs for housing, education, childcare, and healthcare. In other words, the way the US measures poverty has little do with the actual standards of living that can be maintained at this income.

Given this hard-to-defend definition of poverty in the US—which in 2017 is roughly $22,500 for a family of four—the number of people living in poverty in the US has declined from 33 percent of the population in 1948 to 12 percent of the population in 1969, but has remained relatively constant since then. In 2016, the official poverty rate was 12.7 percent, meaning that 43.1 million Americans were living in poverty. While many of the people that are poor today will not stay poor over their entire life, more than half of all Americans will live at least one year below the poverty line at some point between the ages of 20 and 65.[31] The most disturbing fact is that 25 percent of all children in the US live in poverty—something that plays directly into the low rates of income mobility in the US.

It can also be argued that relative poverty in the US is worse than the official statistics indicate for at least two reasons. First, the poverty line does not measure actual purchasing power. Many goods that are essential to the poor—particularly housing, education, and healthcare—have seen their prices rise faster than the overall rate of inflation, reducing the real goods and services that the poor can afford. Second, the poor also have very little wealth, meaning that they have no financial cushion and are exposed to a great deal of risk. One-quarter of all Americans say they could not come up with $2,000 if given a month to do so, and an additional one-fifth could only do so through pawnshops or taking payday loans.[32] Because of these realities, it appears that to a very real extent, focusing on reducing poverty as opposed to focusing on reducing inequality is more of an academic discussion than one with tangible consequences. The simple fact is that in the US and other countries, neither is happening.

However, the most persuasive argument that relative poverty matters more than absolute poverty is that it is always relative that matters. Let's return to thinking about John Rockefeller in 1900. No one would think that John

Rockefeller was poor because he didn't have a car or a phone. In many ways, the poor today have more access to a wider and more valuable range of goods and services than Rockefeller had. But that doesn't stop them from being poor. Poverty is as much about status as it is about consumption. It is not based on how little some people do have, but also what they see other people have but they do not.

IN CONCLUSION

In this chapter we have talked about bigger pies, fruits of labor, just deserts, and the freedom to choose. Is this making you hungry? We might need a fair race to burn off the calories.

The stated purpose of this chapter was to examine why inequality might be a necessary evil in a capitalist, democratic country that values personal liberty and the highest standards of living possible. But the real purpose of this chapter was to begin to think a little more clearly about this question: What is fair? Classical economists, Austrian economists, supply-siders, and libertarian philosophers have somewhat different ideas as to what is fair, but generally agree that the closest we will get to fair is to allow for the freest markets and the widest expanse for individual choice that is possible.

The philosopher Michael Sandel says that there are three theories of justice: (1) to maximize welfare, (2) to provide freedom, and (3) to promote virtue.[33] The theorists in this chapter believe that free markets and free choice achieve each of these three forms of justice. First, allowing markets to work optimizes efficiency and welfare by maximizing the size of the pie. Second, allowing free choice ensures freedom. And third, competition and a focus on meritocracy and "just deserts" promotes the virtues of hard work, saving, personal responsibility, and entrepreneurship. In other words, inequality is not only efficient, it is also just. Focusing on attaining some abstract notion of "equality" will not only lead to a less efficient economy, it will also lead to a less fair society.

To this, many others respond that the conservative thinkers in this chapter conceptualize the world as they would like it to be, not the world as it actually is. In fact, there are many reasons to think that an unequal society cannot be just, and it also cannot be either efficient or free. In other words, inequality is not a necessary evil of a just, efficient, and free society; it is a fundamental barrier to a just, efficient, and free society. Critics of these conservative thinkers think that efficiency and liberty are not put at risk by equality, but that equality is a prerequisite for efficiency and liberty. It is to the critics of these conservatives, and to the proponents of a more active egalitarianism, that we turn to next.

NOTES

1. Feldstein (1998).
2. Lucas (2004, p. 20).
3. Mankiw (2013), p. 32.
4. Hayek (1944).
5. Robin (2013).
6. Schumpeter (1942, p. 83).
7. The links between Social Darwinist thinking and Austrian economics are clear. From the Austrian viewpoint, the rich are naturally selected by competition within markets.
8. Roosevelt (1901).
9. Kaplan and Rauh (2013).
10. Fukuyama (1992).
11. These views are also shared, in somewhat different form, by Aristotle and Friedrich Nietzsche.
12. Pinker (2018).
13. Lindbeck (1995).
14. Klein (2010).
15. There is evidence that across OECD countries, high top marginal tax rates on personal income (greater than 70 percent) reduce productivity growth and reduce entrepreneurial activity. See Arnold (2008).
16. Diamond and Saez (2011).
17. Saez et al. (2012) and McClelland and Mok (2012).
18. Carnegie (1889).
19. Ferguson (2009).
20. Keynes (1920, p. 19).
21. Nozick (1974, p. ix).
22. Rawls (1971, p. 73).
23. Bernanke (2007).
24. Friedman (1980, p. 137).
25. Benjamin et al. (2012).
26. Conley et al. (2012).
27. Frankfurt (2015, p. 7).
28. Thurow (1971).
29. Sen (1985).
30. Bourdreaux and Perry (2013).
31. Rank (2004).
32. Lusardi et al. (2011).
33. Sandel (2009).

4. Why does unequal matter? The economic externalities of inequality

Inequality has long been a concern in almost every society and across every class. But why, exactly, does what other people have impact how we feel about what we have? In the fractured debate over the consequences of economic inequality, many ideas and theories have been posed as to why inequality matters. In this chapter, I want to discuss some of these ideas and connect them under the following unifying theme: those who argue that inequality matters are really arguing that it is not just market interactions that are important, but the relationships between people both inside and outside of markets that matter. In other words, there are social consequences for every individual interaction that cannot be ignored (although they often are ignored in economics). The social consequences of inequality not only impact our individual welfare, but they also impact our efficiency in a variety of ways, meaning that an unequal society will also be an inefficient one.

In this chapter I will talk about ten—yes, ten—ways that our individual behavior is shaped by inequality, how these behaviors impact society, and how these societal changes then, in turn, impact individuals in complex ways. As a result, changes in inequality within countries produce positive and negative externalities that can create poverty traps and virtuous circles that fundamentally shape the nature of our friends, our families, our societies, and our economies.

UTILITARIANISM

One of the oldest—and probably least persuasive—arguments that inequality is harmful can be attributed to the philosophical school of Utilitarianism, which has historically played an important role in the way that economists think about societal welfare. Utilitarianism refers to the ideas first posed by the philosopher Jeremy Bentham, who argued that the focus of public policy should be on maximizing the sum of individual utilities—i.e. aggregate utility. In Bentham's words: "the greatest happiness for the greatest number is the measure of right and wrong".[1] In other words, governments should attempt to maximize pleasure and minimize pain for the largest number of people. Utilitarian thinking is embedded in most economic policy analysis models on the assumption that a calculus can be made about whether an action causes pain (reduces utility) or pleasure (increases utility). Most economic models then measure aggregate welfare by adding up everyone's individual utilities in order to ascertain whether society as a whole benefits or loses as a result of this policy.

While utilitarians argue that the focus of policy should not be on the inter-personal distribution of utility but on aggregate utility alone, they still believe that income redistribution is justified. This is because everyone experiences diminishing marginal utility, meaning that the first goods consumed by an individual give more utility than the last goods consumed. The implicit idea here is that because we become satiated, someone who consumes a lot benefits less from additional consumption than someone who consumes a little. This is the reason why utilitarians believe that an income distribution in which everyone is equal maximizes aggregate welfare: If everyone has the same utility function, then taking $1 million from a rich person and giving $10,000 to 1,000 poor people would increase aggregate welfare. Thus, by extension, perfect egalitarianism maximizes social welfare.

There are some serious flaws with utilitarian logic, however. First, many things are impossible to assign a utility value to. How much utility is a year of life worth relative to an additional ham sandwich? How much are we to value restrictions on individual freedom, or even human rights violations, against the "greater good" of maximizing aggregate utility? Many of the things that make life worth living are not mere objects that can be quantified, although utilitar-ians and economists often assume that they can. Second, some people have differences in preferences, meaning that inequality might actually maximize social welfare if those who value consumption the most have higher incomes. On the other hand, those who get more utility from leisure should be happy to work and earn less. Third, what if the rich get pleasure out of their superiority to the poor? Should that be weighted in aggregate utility? And finally, what about the possible efficiency losses associated with redistributing income that might lead to a reduction in aggregate utility?

In regard to this last question, the economists Peter Diamond and Emmanuel Saez developed a model in which diminishing marginal utility holds, but that also incorporates distortionary taxes that reduce productivity and economic growth. Under reasonable assumptions, they find that the optimal tax rate for society is 73 percent—much higher than current top tax rates in the US and most other countries. This is indicative of just how important diminishing mar-ginal utility can be to social welfare, and creates a strong *prima facie* argument for some amount of income redistribution.[2]

Despite its limitations, there are two important insights from Utilitarianism that will inform our discussions going forward. The first is that we should evaluate policies as utilitarians suggest: based on their *consequences*, not on ideology or strict morality. And second, Utilitarianism asks us to think about well-being more broadly than simply maximizing growth or enhancing efficiency, which is the narrow definition of welfare adopted by many of those who fail to accept the dangers of inequality.

INDIVIDUAL PRODUCTIVITY IS A FUNCTION OF LEAKS AND MATCHES

There is no such thing as individual productivity, unless you are Robinson Crusoe. Living on his isolated island, Robinson Crusoe was completely dependent upon himself to make everything, so his productivity was easy to ascertain. But for the rest of us, we work in groups and teams—our productivity is intrinsically intertwined with the work of others, with the capital that we share, and with the ideas and technology that we use. In the modern workplace, my own productivity cannot be separated from my co-worker's productivity.

The primary driving force behind increases in productivity and efficiency is the development of new technology. In other words, it is the creation of *ideas*, or new thinking, that propels most of our increases in productivity and rising wages. When it comes to creating new ideas, however, it is fundamentally important to understand that ideas are different from other goods created in markets. Most goods are *rival*: when I am eating a piece of pizza, someone else cannot be eating that same piece of pizza. But because ideas are not tangible, they are non-rival and can be shared and used in ways that labor, physical capital, or a pizza cannot. Thomas Jefferson, writing to a petitioner regarding a patent dispute, beautifully expressed this insight when he said:

> He who receives an idea from me, receives instruction himself without lessening mine; as he who lights his taper at mine, receives light without darkening me. That ideas should freely spread from one to another over the globe, for the moral and mutual instruction of man, and improvement of his condition, seems to have been peculiarly and benevolently designed by nature ... and like the air in which we breathe, move, and have our physical being, incapable of confinement or exclusive appropriation.[3]

Because ideas are non-rival and intangible, ideas also "leak" and ideas "match". As Thomas Jefferson noted, ideas leak across people and across the globe. We can share ideas so that everyone can benefit from them at the same time. However, this does not mean that the same idea is equally productive everywhere. In many cases, you need to have an existing stock of knowledge and complementary technology and capital to be able to maximize the benefits of an idea. This might be a group of people with the appropriate educational background, an already existing technology that the new idea relies upon, a certain skill set, a particular machine, or specific experiences. In order to leak, ideas also require institutional structures, such as a legal system and a free society, in order to spread. Where all of these things exist, more ideas and better technology will also exist.

Ideas also match because when two ideas come together, they often add up to something much greater than just two separate ideas alone. Good ideas augment and amplify one another. In economics-speak, we say that ideas have positive externalities: they convey benefits on those who had nothing to do with creating the idea in the first place. We all stand on the shoulders of giants—the ideas and networks of those that came before us. Their ideas remain with us today, and are the foundation for future innovations. For example, consider the development of the internet, which required the simultaneous development of computers, communications, software, and protocol technologies, all built upon technologies that had been accumulating piecemeal for generations. According to the technology writer Steven Johnson:

> Like many of the bedrock technologies that have come to define the digital age, the internet was created by—and continues to be shaped by—decentralized groups of scientists and programmers and hobbyists (and more than a few entrepreneurs) freely sharing the fruits of their intellectual labor with the entire world.[4]

In the public's conception of invention, ideas are usually created by lone geniuses grinding away in their laboratories. In popular culture, we glorify the individual technology guru, such as Thomas Edison, Bill Gates, and Steve Jobs. But in reality, the modern history of technology is not the story of the lone genius. It is the story of networking, leaks, and matches. The vast majority of the great ideas and inventions of the twentieth century—germ theory, penicillin, radar, the personal computer, the internet—were not the result of a single individual, but of groups of people working together, one idea feeding off another idea in unexpected ways, with existing ideas being subtly improved upon iteration after iteration, creating linkages towards the development of new technologies that no single mind could have developed in isolation. Even the prototypical genius inventor Thomas Edison didn't build his light bulb by himself, but as part of an extensive team of people with diverse skills and backgrounds, and in an environment that encouraged experimentation and idea sharing.

Understanding the ways that ideas leak and match—and the ways that our individual productivity is really a function of the networks we belong to and the people we work with—goes a long way in explaining why there are no true "just deserts" for our work. Steve Jobs was lucky to be born in the US and live in Silicon Valley during a period of intense creativity in which many other brilliant people helped amplify and implement his ideas. If he were born instead in a small West African village, Jobs' ability to put his talents to use would have been significantly reduced. Saying this does not diminish Jobs' achievements, but simply recognizes the fact that our individual productivities are linked in ways that are impossible to fully unravel. There is something profoundly unknowable about how much of our income any of us can legitimately claim to have "earned".

The leaking and matching of our ideas and talents has important implications for understanding the nature of inequality. First, it provides a powerful argument that eliminating inequality and barriers to inclusion actually benefits everyone, not just the person who directly gains. Each of us is only as productive as the networks that we inhabit. By being more inclusive and incorporating more and more diverse people in our networks, we create more leaking and matching of ideas. This allows each of us to become more productive and enjoy greater prosperity.

This leads to the second big implication of leaks and matches: there is a tradeoff between equality and efficiency, but it is the opposite of that envisioned in the Classical model. Instead of inequality enhancing efficiency, inequality actually reduces efficiency by limiting the ability of people to gain access to the education and social connections needed to join networks and contribute to the productivity of those around them. Every person that fails to maximize their own potential also reduces the ability of many others to reach their full potential. It is in our own self-interest to make sure everyone has the best chance to become the most productive member of society that they can become.

Finally, leaks and matches lead to poverty traps and virtuous circles. Each one of us is only as productive as the people we work around and network with. When someone lives around other less-educated people with fewer ideas, their own capability to create ideas and their incentive to invest in an education are reduced. This is the essence of a poverty trap. Virtuous cycles exist when new ideas make everyone more productive, increasing everyone's capability to create new ideas and also creating incentives to invest in more education.

An important implication of poverty traps and virtuous cycles is that self-segregation perpetuates income inequality. Americans increasingly live in rich areas surrounded by other rich people, or poor areas surrounded by other poor people. As a result, not only are cities the most unequal places in most countries, but in the US metro-level inequality has increased dramatically over the last 30 years.[5] The number of those living in poor neighborhoods (less than two-thirds of metropolitan median income) and rich neighborhoods (with more than 150 percent of metropolitan median income) has doubled in the US since 2000.[6] This income segregation also has a racial component: residential segregation into poor/rich neighborhoods has increased more rapidly for black and Hispanic families than for whites.[7]

Wealth and poverty are geographically concentrated because more ideas and wealth will be created where people are highly educated, have more existing ideas, are already wealthy, and can most easily network with each other. Think back to the "citizenship premium" discussed in Chapter 2—where you are born explains three-fourths of all of the variation in income across the globe. Who you are—the "just deserts"—explains relatively little of the income variability across the globe. The largest benefit of migration is that all workers, both high and low skilled, are more productive in rich countries where they can take advantage of idea networks and better institutions. We will talk a great deal more about leaks and matches when we talk about global inequality later in Chapter 6.

Geography plays a huge role in inequality within countries as well. This is most evident in the urban/rural income divide. Today, roughly half of the world's population lives in an urban area, and by 2050 this number will be nearly 70 percent. Increasingly, people are not just moving to cities, but to megacities of more than 10 million people. While there were five of these megacities in 1970, in 2015 there were 23. People are pulled to cities and particularly megacities because of the higher wages that jobs in urban areas provide. And why are wages higher? Because people are more productive in cities where they have better access to more people, more technology, and the increased possibility of leaks and matches associated with it. In the US, 63 percent of patents are developed by the populations of just 20 cities.[8] Innovation in any city increases exponentially with its size. A city that is ten times larger than another city is seventeen times more innovative—a city 50 times bigger is 130 times more innovative.[9] These astonishing findings stem from the fact that cities are filled with networks where the individual skills of each person complement other people's skills within complex formal and informal networks. Some of these networks are created by firms, but others are created in the coffee houses, reading groups, neighborhood parks, restaurants, etc. that comprise thriving, growing cities. A city is not just a place; it is thousands of connected networks.

Some cities are richer today than others, but also some cities are able to create more leaks, matches, and upward mobility over time for their residents. In one fascinating study, a group of economists led by Raj Chetty at Stanford used income tax records to estimate how income mobility differs across "commuting zones" in the US (basically, urban areas) for children born between 1971 and 1982.[10] They measure the intergenerational elasticity of income between parents and children, where a *higher* level of elasticity means *less* income mobility (i.e. higher elasticity means that a child's income is more closely correlated with their parent's income). They find that not all cities are created equal in terms of income mobility. For example, the probability that a child reaches the top quintile of the national income distribution starting from a family in the bottom quintile is only 4.4 percent in Charlotte, North Carolina but 12.9 percent in San Jose, California. Figure 4.1 presents a "heat map" for mobility across regions of the US, where the darker areas represent less mobility, the lighter areas the most mobility. Overall, relative mobility is lowest for children who grew up in the Southeast—places like Alabama and Mississippi in particular. It is highest in the Mountain West and the rural Midwest, in places like Iowa and Colorado, and in the largest metropolitan areas. According to the authors, some commuting zones in the US have mobility that is comparable to the highest mobility countries in the world—places such as Canada and Denmark—while others have some of the lowest estimated mobility across countries for which data is available. They find that mobility across regions is lowest where: (1) the level of segregation by race and income is highest, (2) the level of income inequality is highest, (3) the quality of schools is lowest, (4) the numbers of social networks people are involved in are low, and (5) the child was most likely to be raised by a single parent.

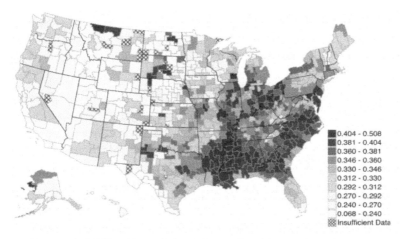

Source: Chetty et al. (2014b), with permission of the Equality of Opportunity Project.

Figure 4.1   Intergenerational income mobility across commuting zones in the US

This is strong evidence of the importance of leaks and matches, which are maximized where families and social networks are strong, barriers to inclusion are low, educational achievement is high, and income and social equality exists. It is strong evidence in support of the argument that inequality has large costs that cannot be captured in simple Classical models of perfect competition where externalities are the exception, not the rule. Instead, externalities are *the* fundamental aspect of efficiency. Until we begin to see productivity as a social phenomenon, not an individual one, we cannot understand why inequality is so costly to efficiency and to our society.

FAIRNESS INTRINSICALLY MATTERS

In economics, it is all relative (just like most of the rest of life). Measures of absolute income are an abstraction—they are just numbers. It is only when we express income in terms of purchasing power, and particularly when we compare our purchasing power to others' purchasing power, that we begin to more completely comprehend the reality that they represent.

In large part this is because we are inherently social animals and instinctively think of ourselves in relation to others. We have an inborn need to attach ourselves to other people, and we are compelled to interact and share ideas. As social animals, social status matters to us: the desire to attain status is as strong as the need for sex or social interaction. Social status, as much as some of us would like to claim otherwise, instinctively defines our own self-worth. We suffer from status anxiety when we suffer relative status deprivation. A wide range of psychological studies show that if you think about people who are superior to you in some respect, it makes you feel worse about yourself. If you think about someone inferior to you in some respect, it makes you feel better about yourself.[11] In fact, psychologists find that we make judgments on each other's social status immediately upon meeting—it is our first priority.[12] In the words of Ralph Waldo Emerson, "'Tis very certain that each man caries in his eye the exact indication of his rank in the immense scale of men, and we are always learning to read it."[13]

Social rank is so important to us that we don't care as much about doing well as we care about doing better. A mass survey of 5,000 British households found that, surprisingly, the richest 20 percent were actually slightly less satisfied with their lives than the poorest 20 percent. What really mattered was each individual's relative pay compared to people in their same occupational category, adjusted for age and educational levels. Those who were better paid than their professional peers were the happiest.[14] Similar results have been found in many other countries and professions across the world. Neuroscience studies have used brain imaging to show that people are primarily concerned with winning more money than their competitors and less about the actual amounts of money won. In fact, doing better than others creates the same responses in the brain as sex and drugs.[15] However, our primary peer groups are the people closest to us in social status. In the words of Bertrand Russell: "Beggars do not envy millionaires, though of course they will envy other beggars who are more successful."[16]

Because social rank matters so much to us, fairness and equality also matter a lot to us. As we discussed in the previous chapter, Plato believed that a fundamental human desire is *thymos*: our desire for self-esteem, respect, and recognition by others "as a human being" that deserves worth and dignity. According to Plato, *thymos* is the reason we are capable of self-sacrifice and willing to risk our lives in the struggle for the social good. *Thymos* is also closely tied to our innate sense of justice. According to Plato, too much inequality violates this sense of self-esteem and, as a result, is inherently unjust. Too much inequality leads people to feel that the value of their work, and of themselves as human beings, is not being recognized by their boss or by society. In essence, extreme inequality is a violation of our human rights and impairs our ability to be free people. As a result, in Plato's utopia, no one would be more than four times richer than anyone else in society (women and slaves excluded). Plato would not be surprised at all to read modern studies that suggest that nations with higher inequality have lower professed levels of happiness, and that happiness is not linked to rises and falls in income, but only to rises and falls in income inequality.[17] Plato would have also agreed with H. L. Mencken, who once defined wealth as "Any income that is at least $100 more a year than the income of one's wife's sister's husband."[18]

One interesting way to test how much fairness matters to people is to observe how people play what is called "the ultimatum game". The ultimatum game involves two players. The first player is given some money and instructed to share it with the second player. If the second player accepts the offer, they divide the money accordingly and both get to keep their share; if the second player rejects the offer, then neither player gets anything. The strictly rational way to play this game is for the first player to offer the second player only a very small amount of the total. The second player should still accept this seemingly bad deal because getting something is better than getting nothing. However, when this game is actually played by real people, most second players will reject any offer that is less than 50 percent of the total, punishing the first player (as well as themselves) for failing to make a "fair" offer.

So why do people punish others when they also hurt themselves in the process? Because we all rely upon reciprocity, and if we do not punish those who violate our innate sense of fairness, then we are inviting uncooperative outcomes that degrade our self-esteem. In other words, it violates our innate sense of *thymos*. Fairness is a social norm developed to support our self-esteem, and is learned through punishing those who do not play fair.[19]

Before we examine the economic ramifications of our desire for fairness, let's take one additional philosophical detour and ask ourselves this: What constitutes a fair society? Without going into an encyclopedic review, let's focus on how the philosopher John Rawls answered this question. Rawls argued that a fair society is an egalitarian (but not equal) society. Here's his thinking, which is often referred to as the "veil of ignorance" principle.[20] Suppose that we gathered together to agree on a social contract. If you didn't know what your position was going to be in the income distribution of your society, what kind of distribution of income would you choose? Rawls argues that each of us would choose an egalitarian distribution where inequality was only justified to the extent that it could be used to benefit the poorest and most vulnerable. In other words, only inequality that enhances aggregate productivity is acceptable. For example, paying doctors more than dishwashers is justifiable inequality because it incentivizes people to invest in an education that helps us all. But paying doctors hundreds of times more than dishwashers excessively compensates them for their investments, and is not justifiable and not fair.

In addition, inequality that is the consequence of luck or the "natural lottery" is not fair. This includes inequality that results from those privileged by their family, education, health, or even innate ability.[21] These factors are arbitrary from a moral perspective—they are not earned and do not necessarily enhance everyone's well-being, and so they cannot be justified. Rawls argued that instead society should enhance equality by following the "maximum principle": society should only be unfair to the extent that it maximizes the conditions of the least well-off. In other words, whenever the rules and institutions of societies favor one group of people over another, they should always favor the poor over the rich. In Rawls' words:

> Those who have been favored by nature, whoever they are, may gain from their good fortune only on terms that improve the situation of those who have lost out. The naturally advantaged are not to gain merely because they are more gifted, but only to cover the costs of training and education and for using their endowments in ways that help the less fortunate as well. No one deserves his greater natural capacity nor merits a more favorable starting place in society. But it does not follow that one should eliminate these distinctions. There is another way to deal with them. The basic structure of society can be arranged so that these contingencies work for the good of the least fortunate.[22]

While this is a beautiful idea in principle, in practice there are many challenges to Rawls' maximum principle. The economist Gregory Mankiw has asked whether the maximum principle should apply not just to income but to kidneys as well.[23] Should people be forced to give up a kidney to those in need? In addition, the maximum principle gives us no clear idea as to how much inequality is acceptable to help the poor. Is Plato's idea of the richest earning four times as much as the poorest too much inequality or too little? Is Mark Zuckerberg's wealth justifiable because the poor benefit from using Facebook?

As we discussed in the previous chapter, one thing that liberals such as Rawls agree upon is that even if a society could provide complete equality of opportunity, it still would not necessarily be fair. A just society demands more than just reducing income inequality, lowering discrimination, and creating legal equality. It demands addressing "natural endowments" that impact inequality in more indirect ways, such as genetics, social class, parental input, culture, socioeconomic networks, and educational opportunities. Fairness requires more than simple open competition, namely an equal chance to prepare and develop merit. In other words, there has to be truly equal access to things such as education, and our social policies should favor those who are not favored with natural endowments that help them gain better access to these things. To return to our overused footrace analogy, Rawls would ask how much better does a disabled person have to be to win a race with someone that is not disabled? That is a measure of the true cost of inequality, and that is the inequality that our societal institutions should serve to minimize.

Because fairness matters to people, it impacts the economic decisions that people make, which in turn has fundamental implications for economic efficiency in a number of ways. First, there is a great deal of evidence that firms don't simply set wages according to supply, demand, and marginal products as assumed in Classical theory. Instead, wages are often the result of a bargaining process between two human beings in the context of social norms of acceptable behavior. There is often no "aggregate wage" that firms and workers can use as a reference, so they use the relative wages of the people around them and then negotiate based on these wages in a way that might be referred to as "relational wage setting". As a result, firms worry a great deal about relative wages and perceptions of fairness, even across workers who do different jobs in the company. Both horizontal (same level) and vertical (above and below) equity matters to firms because they know that it matters to their workers. Very interestingly, 80 percent of the increase in earnings variability for all workers from 1997–2007 came from differences in wages across firms, not differences within firms.[24] In other words, it matters as much *who* you work for as *what* you do. Within specific companies, wages tend to be relatively equal, presumably because of fairness concerns. Across different companies, fairness matters less and inequality is more extreme.[25]

One way that relative wages matter to productivity is through what is called *efficiency wages*.[26] Efficiency wages refer to the fact that higher wages increase a worker's productivity. An innate understanding of efficiency wages was captured in the old Soviet saying: "They pretend to pay us and we pretend to work." Workers that are paid a higher relative wage work harder because it boosts their morale and fosters a harmonious work environment. On the other hand, when workers feel their work is undervalued, they get their job effort in line with their lower wages by not working as hard. Workers who are paid higher efficiency wages also work harder because they have more to lose if they are fired from their job. Finally, workers that are paid more are likely to remain in their jobs, reducing the training costs that firms incur when there is worker turnover. For example, a study of employees in the University of California system found that workers in jobs with higher levels of pay inequality had the highest rates of worker turnover.[27]

There is also evidence that perceptions of unfairness reduce worker effort, in part by making them feel like their work is not valued and meaningful.[28] In one interesting experiment, economists paid two groups of workers the same amount. When one group suffered a wage cut, their performance declined by twice as much as when both groups of workers suffered the same wage cut at the same time.[29] In a similar experiment, higher wages had a positive impact on the productivity of workers who believed they were not being treated fairly before the wage increase, while those who thought they were already being paid fairly did not experience any increase in productivity when their wages rose.[30] Likewise, using data on firm-level pay disparities, research suggests that firms with the largest pay disparities—particularly firms where the CEO is overpaid and workers underpaid relative to the market—have the worst firm performance.[31]

Fairness can also impact efficiency in ways other than through wages and worker effort. It can also change our patterns of spending, causing us to allocate resources in unproductive ways. In the late 1800s, Thorstein Veblen examined the purchasing habits of the rich with an anthropological eye and the spirit of an evolutionary biologist.[32] Veblen came to the conclusion that much of what the rich spend their money on was "conspicuous consumption": consumption that signaled social dominance by being gaudy and purposefully unproductive. What better way to show people how superior you are than to show others how much money you can waste on useless things?

The economist Robert Frank has modernized the views of Veblen by highlighting the increasing importance of "context sensitive goods".[33] These are goods in which their value is related to their relative position among other goods. A good example of a positional good is housing. Because the biggest houses in the best neighborhoods within the best school districts are most desirable and are fixed in supply, they are essentially "winner-takes-all" goods. The competition for these goods becomes extreme, pushing up their prices beyond any narrowly defined measure of economic value. An analogy would be to an arms race, where there are winners and losers in a zero-sum contest, and the winners only win by investing more and more resources into winning.

These context sensitive goods encourage overspending and misallocations of resources by everyone in society. For example, in real estate markets they foster housing bubbles, excessive debt, and financial crises. But the key is that economic inequality worsens the problem of context sensitive goods. Everyone has to compete with the rich, and, as a result, the poor and middle-class are forced to spend an increasing proportion of their income (and accumulate debt) on context sensitive goods such as housing in the neighborhoods with the best schools, all to the detriment of the overall welfare and the stability of society. In the words of Joseph Stiglitz, "Trickle-down economics may be a chimera, but trickle-down behaviorism is very real."[34]

INEQUALITY NEGATIVELY IMPACTS EDUCATION AND HEALTH

There is a growing body of evidence that inequality, not just poverty, reduces overall economic efficiency by reducing education and public health outcomes.

Let's begin by talking about education, which in today's society is more closely related to class and social status than even income, wealth, or birth. If human capital in the form of formal education was distributed through perfectly competitive markets, then income inequality would make little difference to economic outcomes. The most talented and hard-working would be able to borrow as much as they needed to pay for their education and always get into the best schools because resources always flow to their most productive uses in perfectly competitive markets. But in reality, this is not even close to the way the world works. Ability is hard to evaluate, and assessing an individual's return from getting an education is even harder. As a result, there is absolutely no guarantee that the students that would benefit the most from an education will also be the students who are born to afford it. Many students are regularly credit rationed, meaning that they cannot borrow as much as would be optimal to fund their desired levels of education. Children from richer families can rely upon their parents' income and assets. But many families of poorer students often can't afford the incredible investments needed for higher education, let alone the costs associated with a "free" public secondary education.

As a result, there can be a vicious cycle between education and income, where income inequality leads to human capital inequality, which in turn worsens income inequality. Those parents who can afford private schools and cello lessons are likely to raise children that can afford these things for their children as well, while those parents who can't will likely have children who can't, regardless of their innate ability and effort.

Figure 4.2 looks at data from a group of children born in the US between 1984 and 1987 and examines the correlation between these children's college attendance rates and what income percentile their family falls into. As you can see, the correlation is amazingly strong: on average, a 10-percentile point increase in parental income increases the probability of college attendance by 6.7 percent.[35]

In addition, the correlation between education and income is most extreme at the most extremes. At the top end of the income distribution, there is "opportunity hoarding", where the most exclusive (and scarce) opportunities

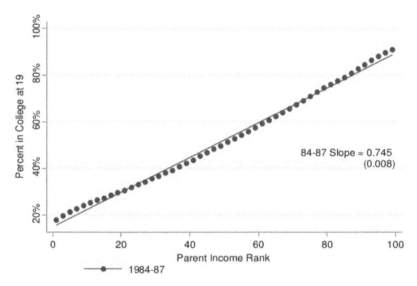

Source: Chetty et al. (2014a), with permission of the Equality of Opportunity Project.

Figure 4.2   *College attendance rates vs. parent income for children born between 1984 and 1987*

are reserved for those elites that can gain access to them.[36] The nepotism here is not explicit but implicit. For example, to gain access to an elite school, you have to maintain perfect grades and test scores as well as participate in a wide variety of extracurricular activities. These goals are more easily achieved when supported by a team of tutors, workshops, lessons, cars, and parents that have the free time to make these things happen. Likewise, things such as exclusionary zoning (restrictions on high density housing, plot size restrictions, property tax financing of schools) in the best public-school districts push up home prices to such an extent that only the richest parents can afford to buy their children into the best "free" public schools. While competition to get into the best schools appears to be meritocratic, it is really more of a birthright.

There is plenty of empirical evidence that the wealth of parents matters more in educational achievement than it ever has before. For example, the gap in math and reading test scores between children from high- and low-income families, regardless of race, is roughly one-third larger among children born in 2001 than among those born 25 years earlier.[37] The same phenomenon holds for college educational outcomes. The correlations between SAT test scores and income have been rising across the income distribution, but particularly at the highest levels of income.[38] Poorer children are less likely to go to college (80 percent versus 29 percent attendance rates in the highest and lowest 25th percentiles). Once they get in college, young people that score in the middle 50th percentile on college entrance tests are five times more likely to finish college if they are rich than poor (51 percent to 8 percent). In fact, high-scoring poor youngsters are less likely to graduate from college than low-scoring rich youngsters (29 percent to 30 percent).[39]

Once again, the more elite the university, the more that income seems to matter. In 2004, children from the top 25 percent of the income distribution were 17 times more likely to get into highly selective colleges than children in the bottom 25 percent.[40] This is in part because children from lower-income families are less likely to apply to selective colleges, and also less likely to be accepted.

Education does not just take place within school, but outside of school as well. The gap in enrichment spending, or money spent outside school on lessons, training, and other extracurricular activities, is growing. Educational enrichment spending is rising for the top 25 percent but flat for the bottom 25 percent.[41] In 2015, the average child in the top 10 percent enjoyed about $6,600 a year in enrichment spending, but in the bottom 10 percent that figure was only about $750.[42] Finally, because they can afford to enjoy more leisure, college-educated parents spend about 45 minutes more time interacting with their children every day than high school-educated parents.[43]

Inequality can also impact educational outcomes through its impact on psychology and esteem. Income inequality and class play a role in creating anxiety amongst poorer students by making them feel inferior, thereby reducing their self-confidence and individual initiative. In just one example of this, a study of students in India found that students of lower castes performed worse on tests that involved solving mazes if they were reminded of their caste right before they took the tests.[44]

Finally, economic inequality can also impact educational outcomes by influencing family structure and parenting strategies. I will have more to say about this in the next chapter when we talk about assortative mating and parenting.

In regards to health, it will surprise no one that individuals with higher incomes have better health outcomes and higher life-expectancy.[45] It will also not surprise anyone that there is a great deal of variability in health across ethnic groups in the US, given that race is closely tied to income. In the ten US counties with the highest life-expectancy, 77 percent of white men live until 70, while only 68 percent of black men live to that age. In these same counties, infant mortality is 5.8 percent among whites but 13.7 percent among blacks.[46]

However, *income inequality* appears to matter independent of *income levels*. Looking across developed countries, of ten major measures of social welfare and public health, such as life-expectancy and infant mortality, only two measures—educational achievement and trust in neighbors—are correlated with the level of income. But all ten are correlated with income inequality. The same holds not just across countries, but within the 50 US states.[47]

One of the more disturbing developments in the US recently has been a decline in life-expectancy of Americans for three years in a row—the first time that this has occurred in more than 50 years. The overall fall in life-expectancy is entirely driven by a decline in the life-expectancy of whites, particularly among males. Among white Americans, deaths from drug over-doses increased by 300 percent between 2010 and 2014. The fact that this comes at a time of rising inequality and a relative decline of the bottom 50 percent in the US suggests that many US white males are dying of underper-forming expectations relative to their history of privilege and success. They are "deaths of despair".[48]

The empirical evidence indicates that higher income inequality worsens public health by lowering life-expectancy, raising infant mortality, lowering height, reducing birth weight, increasing AIDS infection rates, and leading to higher depression and drug use.[49] Unfortunately, the gap between the health of the rich and the poor appears to be growing. The difference in life-expectancy between the top 20 percent and the middle 40 percent is one year for men born in 1920, but for men born in 1950 it is three years.[50] According to the *British Medical Journal*: "The big idea is that what matters in determining mortality and health in a society is less the overall wealth of that society and more how evenly wealth is distributed. The more equally wealth is distributed the better the health of that society."[51]

Why does inequality itself make people less healthy? The public health research suggests that the answer is not because poverty leads to poor health (poverty predicts poor health in the future). It is also not primarily due to the fact that the poor lack access to healthcare, because inequality is linked to worse health outcomes even in countries with universal access to healthcare. Instead, inequality appears to impact health in three primary ways. First, higher inequality is related to fewer public goods devoted to protecting public health, such as clean water, environmental protections, and immunization pro-grams.[52] Second, and more importantly, inequality increases stress, which has a significant impact on health.[53] Countries with higher inequality report that they are less happy and suffer from more depression and anxiety.[54] The health impacts of increased stress from lower social status are particularly severe in children, and affect early cognitive and social development. This eventually influences success in high school, college, and their productivity when they enter the workforce. As Shakespeare's Iago says in *Othello*: "The person who is poor and contented is rich enough. But infinite riches are nothing to someone who's always afraid he'll be poor."

Finally, there is a growing body of psychological evidence that when people are made to feel poorer, they become myopic and focus more on immediate gratification and think less about the future. As a result, they are less likely to save, more likely to gamble and seek quick payoffs, less likely to make investments in their future like education, and generally take what they can get now. In fact, people in less equal countries engage in less exercise and engage in more smoking and drug use.[55] In psychological experiments, the poorest participants who play simple games in more unequal groups were shown to take more risks and preferred high risk/high reward choices that allowed them to potentially close the gap with their richer competitors. However, these increasingly risky behaviors also increased inequality in the group over time, meaning that inequality created more inequality in a vicious circle.[56]

In sum, it appears that the psychological impact of people's relative income is more important than the purchasing power of people's actual income when it comes to health. In fact, people's subjective belief about their status and income is a better predictor of their health than their actual income or education or occupation.[57] Over the last 200 years there has been such sustained progress in health that we have all come to expect that each generation will live longer than the next. Now, it appears that because of higher economic inequality, this might only be true for the richest.

INEQUALITY REDUCES INTERGENERATIONAL MOBILITY

If inequality were a phenomenon that was completely independent of intergenerational mobility, then inequality would not be such a pressing concern for society. By this, I mean that if the inequality that exists today was the result of either random chance or pure merit, it would not only be more acceptable from a moral perspective, but also from an efficiency perspective. If some people did better than others because they earned it, or simply because randomness mandated that someone has to do better than others, it would also be the case that productivity was being maximized, even if fairness was not. And in future years, those that were living at the bottom of the income distribution would have a reasonable expectation that either they or their children would move up the distribution over time, either by merit or by chance.

Of course, the problem is that inequality and intergenerational mobility—inequality today and inequality tomorrow—are inherently linked and feed upon each other. We know that increasing income inequality reduces intergenerational mobility, and lower intergenerational mobility allows wealth to accumulate to a greater extent from generation to generation, worsening wealth and income inequality. We have already talked about two links between inequality and intergenerational mobility: education and health. We just reviewed the empirical evidence that high-income families are able to pass higher quality education and health to their children, making these youngsters more likely to become high earners, and then provide even better education and health for the next generation. There are good reasons to think that education and health are having even larger impacts on social mobility as the importance of education in modern knowledge-based economics increases. In fact, economists have found that countries with higher returns to education have less intergenerational mobility.[58]

In Chapter 2, we discussed a number of facts regarding the data on intergenerational earnings elasticities across countries. Intergenerational earnings elasticities calculate the correlation between paternal earnings and a son's adult earnings using children born during the early-to-mid-1960s and measuring adult outcomes in the mid-to-late-1990s. (This data has a significant lag in it, and is really describing mobility from 20 years ago, not necessarily today.) Remember that the lower the intergenerational elasticity, the less likely a child's earnings will be closely correlated with paternal earnings, meaning that a lower intergenerational elasticity means greater income mobility in a country. Using this data, we know that (1) there are big differences in intergenerational income mobility between countries, (2) countries with higher inequality have lower levels of intergenerational mobility (see the "The Great Gatsby Curve" in Figure 2.5), and (3) income mobility across time is stagnant or falling across developed countries.

Intergenerational earnings elasticities are a measure of relative inequality, meaning how one generation does relative to the next generation in terms of the income percentile they inhabit. But even in terms of absolute intergenerational mobility, there appears to have been a slowdown. In the US, an important part of the "American Dream" is the belief that children will earn more than their parents. And, in fact, the American Dream held for the vast majority of Americans at one time. For those children born in the 1940s, 90 percent of them eventually earned more than their parents. But for those born in the 1980s, only half will be better off than their parents. This is directly attributable to slower aggregate income growth coupled with rising income inequality.[59]

Isn't it the fact that smart parents have smart kids, and this explains the lack of intergenerational mobility? No. Based on estimates of the inheritability of intelligence (measured by IQ), the variability of intelligence, and the correlation between intelligence and income, genetics can only explain, at most, 10 percent of the correlation of income across generations.[60] The other 90 percent is not the luck of genetics, but the result of our social and economic systems.

When it comes to obtaining a deeper understanding of why income inequality reduces intergenerational mobility, it is important to distinguish between the lack of upward mobility and the lack of downward mobility. When we think about the failure to get ahead, we are thinking about the lack of *upward* social mobility. The Nobel Prize winning economist James Heckman, when investigating the reasons for the lack of upward mobility, summarized the empirical results this way: "Early adverse experiences correlate with poor adult health, high medical care costs, increased depression and suicide rates, alcoholism, drug use, poor job performance and social function, disability, and impaired performance of subsequent generations."[61] In other words, we are formed early in life, and being born into poverty perpetuates poverty to future generations. The adverse experiences Heckman is talking about include things that are strongly correlated with family income: physical abuse, divorce, drug use, depression of parent, and imprisonment. These adverse experiences are also related to the neighborhoods that poor children live in: the segregation of the poor leads to the creation of poverty traps where people can't take advantage of the leaks and matches associated with interacting with other privileged people. Instead of leaks and matches, they get cracks and clashes.

Importantly, the math and reading gap between rich and poor students is already large by the time children enter school, and entering school does little to change this gap for most students.[62] In other words, an opportunity gap exists even before a child gets to school—either from their family or from the social groups they are surrounded by—and American schools appear to be unable to close this gap.

However, *downward* social mobility is just as important as upward mobility. The lack of downward mobility is a problem because relative income is a zero-sum game—only 20 percent of the population can be in the top fifth at one time, and when someone enters, someone must leave. The economist Gary Solon, who was one of the first economists to closely examine income mobility, says that: "[Rather than] a poverty trap, there seems instead to be more stickiness at the other end: a 'wealth trap' if you will. There are probably more rags to riches cases than the other way around ... there seems to be better safety nets for the offspring of the wealthy."[63]

The simple fact is that once people reach the upper deciles of the income distribution, there is every chance that they will remain there—unless they are black. The sons from black wealthy families have much more downward mobility than those sons from white families, largely due to much higher incarceration rates. This suggests that discrimination, particularly in the criminal justice system, plays an important role in intergenerational income mobility as well.[64]

What are these safety nets for most of the rich? More income leads to greater education and health, as we have talked about. But the most obvious safety net is wealth itself. As we will examine in the next chapter, there is evidence that the wealthy are able to earn higher returns on their savings and then compound these returns over time, turning their wealth into greater income, then into

greater wealth, etc. To the extent that wealth can be transferred from generation to generation through inheritance, wealth and income sustain itself over
time. In fact, in the US almost half of the wealth inequality can be explained
by inheritance alone.[65] This explains why almost half of those born into the
wealthiest 20 percent in the US stay there over their lifetime.[66]

Inheritance also explains a large part of the wealth gap between black and
white families, as the children of white families are five times more likely to
receive a major gift from their relatives than black children.[67] One-fourth of
the wealth difference between white and black families (the former possessing
10 times the average amount of wealth than the latter) can be explained by
inheritance alone.[68] These greater inheritances of white children contribute to
better health, better education, and less debt—among many other things—and
the benefits of these inheritances get compounded through generations of
white families in ways that both obviously and more subtly reduce income and
wealth mobility.

When fortunes of families do change over generations, they only change
very, very slowly. In a study of elite families with unique surnames in Chile,
China, England, India, Japan, South Korea, Sweden, and the US going back
centuries, the economist Gregory Clark finds that more than half of an individual's income status is determined by their lineage. Family fortunes do rise and
fall, but the process of reversion to the mean is a very long one—on average,
10 to 15 generations (300 to 450 years).[69]

Safety nets for the rich are not only dependent upon their personal wealth,
however. Wealthier and more educated people tend to be around other
wealthier and more educated people. They have richer networks for mentor-
ing, groups, and stronger neighborhood communities.[70] As a result, they are
better able to take advantages of the leaks and matches of knowledge and
ideas. In fact, one of the biggest challenges associated with our increasingly
knowledge-based economy is that those that are the most successful now are
also most likely to be the most successful in the future, because having and
using more ideas allows you to produce and use more ideas. In other words, the
rich often don't have a safety net as much as a safety network.

In an interesting case study of how wealth is as much about privilege as
about money, economic historians have found that during the Civil War in the
US, the richest 1 percent of the Confederate population—almost all of whom
were rich white slaveholders whose primary source of wealth was in human
slaves—lost 76 percent of their wealth between the censuses of 1860 and
1870. But by the next census in 1880, the sons of slaveholders had returned to
the same level of wealth superiority as their fathers had, and by the census of
1900, they had exceeded them.[71] This is a testament to the fact that oftentimes
measured wealth can rise and fall, but the privilege conveyed to elites through

social standing, connections, and discrimination are far more resilient and powerful.

HIGH WAGES AND PROFITS OFTEN REFLECT RENT-SEEKING

When wage inequality reflects differences in individual productivity—however difficult it is to accurately measure individual productivity—then there is an argument to be made that it is efficient. This is the Classical explanation of inequality we talked about in the last chapter. But when wage differences reflect market failures and unequal market power, then it becomes impossible to justify. Economists refer to this as *rent-seeking*: when individuals use their market power to manipulate policy or market conditions in an effort to increase their own personal returns, not the returns to society as a whole. In other words, rent-seeking occurs when returns are linked to gaming the system as opposed to maximizing productivity. Rent-seeking occurs when someone uses a campaign contribution to get a law changed that benefits them personally. Rent-seeking occurs when a monopolist raises their prices in ways that maximize their own profits but create a deadweight loss for society. Rent-seeking occurs when market failures exist that give certain individuals the power to raise their wages above their marginal product, or above what is needed to get them to supply their labor or their capital. When inequality is driven by rent-seeking, then inequality is not only unfair, it is also inefficient.

There is clear evidence that rent-seeking has grown and that the iron link between productivity growth and wage growth—the cornerstone of the Classical model—has broken down. Remember that the Classical model assumes perfect competition, so that productivity growth should directly lead to higher compensation for all workers. But return to Figure P.1 in the Preface, which presented data on cumulative productivity growth since 1948 and average pay growth for non-supervisory workers who are directly involved in production. Before 1970, the iron link between productivity and wages was strong. But since 1973—our modern era of inequality—productivity has grown at *eight times* the rate of a typical worker's pay. And since 2000, productivity has been growing at *ten times* the rate of a typical worker's pay. In other words, the benefits of higher productivity have not been going to workers, but elsewhere in the form of economic rents. In fact, if wages had risen at the rate of productivity during this 1948–2014 period, there would have been no increase in overall income inequality in the US.[72]

Rent-seeking can take many different forms, but let's just focus on a couple of ways that have received the most attention from economists. The first would be skyrocketing CEO pay. In the 1950s, the average CEO in the US was paid 20 times as much as the median employee; today, they are paid 130 times the median employee, and in some firms more than 800 times the median wage.[73] CEOs in the US are paid much more than in other countries, and CEO pay has risen at three to five times the rate of growth in the college wage premium (the difference in wages between college- and high school-educated workers).[74]

There are good reasons to think that rising CEO pay largely reflects the power of CEOs to manipulate their own pay and not their rising productivity and growing value to the firm. One reason to think that the CEO pay boom largely reflects rent-seeking is the fact that CEOs have more influence in setting their own pay than any other employee in a firm. While corporate boards have ultimate control over CEO salaries, CEOs have a unique opportunity to convince their boards of what they are worth—half of CEOs are chair of their own board of directors. Clever CEOs convince board members of their value and stack their own compensation committees with sympathetic ears. In addition, CEOs almost always have much better information than board members, who are generally not involved in the day-to-day operations of the business. As a result, the "Lake Woebegone effect" is common among corporate boards: most boards think that their CEO is well above average. In the words of John Kenneth Galbraith "The salary of the chief executive of the large corporation is not a market reward for achievement. It is frequently in the nature of a warm personal gesture by the individual to himself."[75]

Some studies have found that CEO pay is tied to the overall performance of the company and not directly the result of rent-seeking. For example, studies have found that the CEOs of poorly performing companies are more likely to be fired, and that companies that outperform industry competitors pay their CEOs more.[76] However, the weight of the empirical evidence suggests that a substantial portion of CEO pay is driven by rent-seeking. A number of studies have failed to find a consistent link between CEO pay and specific measures of their individual performance that CEOs more directly control other than the stock price.[77] For example, there is evidence that CEOs often take advantage of overall stock market swings that have nothing to do with their own performance to increase their own pay. A study of CEOs in the oil industry found that these CEOs are paid more when profits rose only because of higher oil prices, which they don't control.[78] There is also evidence that the CEOs of private companies—who have fewer financial reporting requirements and have more power to manipulate their own compensation packages—have seen their pay rise faster than public CEOs.[79]

There is also reason to think that booming pay for other workers—not just CEOs—in certain industries is driven more by rent-seeking than by rising productivity. One obvious sector is the financial industry, traders and executives from which comprise an increasingly large number of the people who make up the top 0.1 percent of the income distribution. Rent-seeking in finance has boomed for a number of reasons. Growing bank concentration has led to monopoly profits and a "too big to fail" mentality that incentiv-izes risk-taking and rent-seeking within the sector (e.g. in the 2008 Global Financial Crisis). Also, deregulation in the financial industry since 1980 has fostered rent-seeking through lobbying for tax and regulatory policies that benefit the financial industry generally, and the executives of financial firms specifically.[80] A decrease in antitrust enforcement has led to more mergers and acquisitions that have generally not benefited shareholders, but have played an increasingly important role in generating huge windfalls for the financiers who arrange these deals.[81] Finally, the increasingly complex nature of finance, which in part has been driven by complex financial innovation and in part driven by the desire to mislead investors, has led to a lack of transparency in finance that allows boards of directors, or any executive determining the compensation of an employee, to be more easily manipulated.

To understand how compensation in the financial sector has boomed, consider the fact that between 2004 and 2012, the 25 highest-paid hedge fund managers earned more than all of the CEOs of the S&P 500 companies combined.[82] This has led to a growing percentage of the extremely rich owing their success to jobs in finance: in the US, finance accounts for 5 percent of all jobs but nearly one-fifth of those in the top 0.1 percent of the income dis-tribution.[83] But even for those not quite at the very top, wages in the financial sector have risen. Until 1990, people in the financial sector earned the same education-adjusted wages as those outside of finance, but by 2006 the finance premium had risen by 50 percent; however, for top finance executives, premi-ums had risen by 250 percent.[84]

Other industries that have experienced skyrocketing pay gaps are the legal and entertainment industries. In some sense, a great deal of what happens in the legal industry is explicit rent-seeking: being a lawyer usually means working or manipulating the rules of the system to the advantage of the lawyer or their client, not necessarily to the betterment of society. But in the legal industry, the skyrocketing incomes of a very small number of lawyers have driven much of the increase in compensation to the industry as a whole. Likewise, pay gaps in the entertainment industry have largely been driven by the extraordinary earnings of a very few individuals. We will return to the pay of these elite earners in the next chapter when we talk about "the economics of superstars".

One final area for increased rent-seeking is in Silicon Valley and the IT industry, where the growth of monopolists such as Facebook, Google, and Amazon has led to skyrocketing profits for these firms and sky-high incomes for many of their employees. Using measures of market share, all three of these firms are monopolies and generating monopolist rents. Google has an 88 percent of share of online search advertising and a 60 percent share of the web browser market. Facebook (and its subsidiaries Instagram, WhatsApp, and Messenger) conducts 77 percent of mobile social traffic.[85] In 2017, Facebook and Google accounted for nearly 80 percent of news publishers' referral traffic and together claimed roughly 80 percent of every new online-ad dollar in the US. Meanwhile, Amazon controls 40 percent of America's online retailing and 77 percent of book sales.[86] Worryingly, the leaders of Silicon Valley see competition as a problem to be overcome, not the engine of economic growth. In the words of the tech oligarch Peter Thiel, "Americans mythologize competition and credit it with saving us from socialist bread lines ... Capitalism and competition are opposites. Capitalism is premised on the accumulation of capital, but under perfect competition, all profits get competed away. The lesson for entrepreneurs is clear ... [c]ompetition is for losers."[87]

DISCRIMINATION

If inequality is the result of discrimination, it is inefficient and unfair. It is inefficient because it prevents the most productive workers from doing the jobs that they are most productive at. Free-market conservatives such as Gary Becker believed that market pressures would eventually make discrimination disappear because of its inefficiency.[88] In Becker's view, firms that discriminate will be less productive and profitable, and will eventually be pushed out of markets by those firms that do not discriminate. Discrimination is also unfair and costly to society because, once again, we are social creatures. It has significant psychological costs because it reduces self-esteem and self-respect, things that matter to people as much as efficiency and income.

From the economic perspective, Gary Becker defines discrimination as a situation in which people who are the same are treated differently. In the labor market, discrimination exists when workers who are equally productive receive different rewards, such as wages, fringe benefits, promotion opportunities, and protection against layoff. Discrimination is something different than prejudice: prejudice is a dislike of, distaste for, or misperception of some person, place, or thing. Discrimination can take place without prejudice, and prejudice does not always guarantee discrimination.[89]

Discrimination is an essential part of the way that we make decisions. As we talked about before, each of us instantly evaluate new people we meet and assign them a social status within an instant of meeting. With this in mind, consider what happens when a decision is being made to hire workers from a pool of applicants for a specific job. Employers cannot perfectly observe the qualifications of the prospective workers, so decisions will be made based on imperfect signals—this is where implicit discrimination comes into play. It is easy for employers to extrapolate from observable information about the prospective worker—gender identity, race, age, etc.—to non-observable information about the worker based on stereotypes, experience, and our inherent tribalism. This is the essence of statistical discrimination. Statistical discrimination occurs when people are judged based on information that is not related to their own merits but to those of their group, providing a justification for employers to treat two applicants differently even when they have the exact same observable qualifications. When statistical discrimination occurs, the employer may have no intention of discriminating and usually believes that they are just making a rational and justifiable business decision.

Maybe the most insidious impact of discrimination is that there is a vicious cycle between observable qualifications and statistical discrimination. When people know that they will be less likely to get a job because of aspects of themselves that they cannot control, they are less likely to make the necessary investments in education or work effort to improve the aspects of themselves that they can control because they know aspects of themselves that they cannot control will always be used against them. In other words, statistical discrimination is in some sense self-fulfilling and easily "validated" by the discriminator. Once again, discrimination not only adds to inequality, but reduces overall productivity and welfare.

Because a great deal of discrimination is implicit, it is inherently hard to measure. However, there are a variety of ways that social scientists have tried to identify its impact. Some of the most interesting studies on racial discrimination involve experiments designed to test for implicit discrimination in hiring. In one study, researchers created fake resumes and submitted them in response to posted job ads. Some of these fake resumes depicted high-skill individuals, others low-skilled. The resumes were then randomly assigned "white" and "African American" names. Not surprisingly, controlling for the reported skill levels, resumes with "white" names got 50 percent more call-backs, even from employers who claim to be equal opportunity employers.[90] In another experiment, trained actors interviewed for real jobs, and white and black actors were paired and given similar fake resumes. The white actors were roughly twice as likely to be offered a job as the black actors.[91]

Other studies have looked for, and found, evidence of implicit bias in our criminal justice system. One study found that the "blacker" a person accused of a crime looks (based on a subjective visual survey by a group of people), the longer the sentence the accused received if convicted. For convicted criminals who were judged to look the "blackest", jail sentences were 7–8 months longer than for those judged to be "whiter".[92] Another study found that black defendants charged with murder were more likely to be sentenced to death than white defendants, but only when the murder victim was white.[93]

Other studies have focused on the impact of gender discrimination. To highlight just one well-known study, women have consistently fared better in blind orchestra auditions as opposed to auditions where the judges could see who was playing.[94]

Discrimination also plays a role in limiting intergenerational mobility and contributing to persistent inequality across groups. In the US, the son of a black millionaire has a 2–3 percent chance of ending up in prison, which is the same probability as the son of a white man who makes less than $35,000. Black boys have less upward income mobility than white boys in 99 percent of American localities.[95]

To make things worse, it also appears that while racial discrimination leads to greater inequality, greater inequality leads to increased racial bias by provoking feelings of entitlement among those at the top of the income ladder, and of inferior social status among those at the bottom.[96] In fact, American states with less inequality, like Oregon, Washington, and Vermont, have less measured implicit racial bias than states like New Jersey, Pennsylvania, and Louisiana, even after accounting for differences in income.[97] This complicated interplay between inequality and discrimination can be most easily seen in our politics. According to one political scientist, the best predictor of a person's attitudes towards welfare benefits aimed at reducing inequality is the extent of that individual's racial prejudice, not how rich that person is.[98] In other words, inequality triggers more racial prejudice, but also predisposes people against policies aimed at reducing inequality.

TRUST AND CONFLICT

In the words of the Nobel Prize winning economist Kenneth Arrow: "It can be plausibly argued that much of economic backwardness in the world can be explained by the lack of mutual confidence."[99] Trust encourages cooperation, it reduces uncertainty by allowing us to have confidence in other people, it reduces the transaction costs associated with trade by limiting the need to verify the honesty of everyone, and trust encourages more specialization that facilitates the use of markets. Trust is also crucial to long-term planning and the provision of finance that encourages savings and investment. "Honesty and trust lubricate the inevitable frictions of social life."[100]

Trust plays a broader role than simply easing interpersonal interactions. Trust is also crucial to having effective governments and productive economic institutions. Having any sort of centralized government requires a transfer of trust from individuals to the state. The same is true for political systems, legal systems, and financial systems. Causation likely goes both ways here: trust facilitates good government, and good government also facilitates trust. Of course, the propensity to trust does not change quickly. Trust takes a long time to build, and accumulated trust can be lost very quickly. For example, measures of trust in the former East Germany remain well below that in the former West Germany 25 years after unification.[101]

Let's reconsider the ultimatum game that we discussed earlier in this chapter—the game in which the first player is given some money and instructed to share it with the second player, who gets to accept the offer or reject it, in which case both players get nothing. As we discussed, the rational way to play this game is for the first player to offer the second player only a very small amount of the total. However, when this game is actually played by real people, most second players will reject any offer that is less than 50 percent of the total, punishing the first player (as well as themselves) for failing to make a "fair" offer. The reason is that we all rely upon reciprocity, and if we do not punish those who violate our innate sense of fairness, then we are inviting outcomes that do not maximize everyone's welfare. In other words, fairness and a sense of trust are social norms that are learned through punishment of those who do not play fair and show themselves untrustworthy. In societies where violations of trust are never punished, trust and fairness never become the norm, to the detriment of society as a whole.

As a result, trust and fairness are linked, as are trust and economic inequality. The first person to worry about a vicious circle between inequality and trust was actually Adam Smith. Despite his caricature as the father of laissez-faire, Smith talked a great deal about the dangers of inequality. Smith worried that people naturally tend to sympathize with the rich: "the rich man glories in his riches, because ... they naturally draw upon him the attention of the world", while "the poor man goes out and comes in unheeded, and when in the midst of a crowd is in the same obscurity as if shut up in his own hovel".[102] This is a problem because, in Smith's mind, the rich are not morally superior to the poor—in fact, they are less likely to be good people because they have earned society's esteem for reasons that are unrelated to their personal morality. As a result, Smith believed that as the rich gain social influence, more people will idolize "vice and folly", "presumption and vanity", "flattery and falsehood", and "proud ambition and ostentatious avidity". In other words, inequality encourages behaviors that make for a less trustworthy and cooperative society, which will inevitably lead to increased conflict.

Can trust be measured? One approach is to use field experiments like the ultimatum game discussed above. Another is to examine survey data, such as the World Values Survey, which asks people across the globe questions related to trust and their perceptions of how honest people are. Another approach is to create experiments in which people directly reveal their sense of trust in a society. In one such experiment, researchers left wallets full of money on public transportation and counted how many wallets were returned.[103] In Norway and Denmark, all wallets were returned; in Italy and Switzerland, less than 40 percent of wallets were returned. There is a great deal of agreement between all of these different measures of trust and studies have found that the greater the levels of measured trust, the higher the rate of economic growth across a broad range of countries.[104] The connections are complicated but are related to the fact that trust is correlated with better schools, better health, better child development, and less tax evasion.[105] This is true across different countries, and even across the different US states.[106]

A great deal of empirical work has investigated the links between inequality and trust. Studies have found that income inequality and trust are negatively correlated and that it is inequality that is influencing levels of trust, not the other way around.[107] In fact, multiple studies have found that inequality is a stronger determinant of trust than unemployment, inflation, absolute levels of income, or economic growth.[108]

Trust is not an abstract concept. It is directly tied to the people, communities, and networks that we interact with every day. Just like ideas have leaks and matches that make people more innovative when they are around other innovative people, being able to live and work in neighborhoods and networks that facilitate trust make us more trustworthy and productive. Those who don't have access to these trust networks will enjoy less of the benefits of trust, be less productive, and be poorer. In fact, there is survey evidence that people living in richer neighborhoods trust their neighbors more than people living in poor neighborhoods.[109] Likewise, being part of a wider variety of clubs and volunteer organizations also appears to facilitate trust by expanding the web of contacts that people have with others outside of their typical social groups. People that identify themselves as active members of a larger number of social groups report higher measures of trust.[110] The fact that inequality is associated with lower group participation and, even more importantly, less diversity in the clubs and groups that they participate in is another negative link between inequality and trust. In the words of the eminent sociologist Robert Putnam:

> Community and equality are mutually reinforcing ... Social capital and economic equality moved in tandem through most of the twentieth century. In terms of the distribution of wealth and income, America in the 1950s and 1960s was more egalitarian than it had been in more than a century....Conversely, the last third of the twentieth century was a time of growing inequality and eroding social capital ... The timing of the two trends is striking.[111]

Inequality not only reduces trust, it can lead to outright conflict in terms of crime and war. A number of studies have found that higher poverty rates increase crime rates.[112] Regarding inequality in particular, there is evidence that higher levels of inequality are correlated with increased crime of all sorts, including higher homicide rates.[113] The links between inequality and crime are similar to the links between inequality and health. First, higher inequality is related to fewer public goods that deter crime, such as education and community policing. The second, and biggest, factor is the psycho-social impact of inequality, which encourages less cooperation, less trust, and more individual-istic and aggressive behavior, including depression and violence.[114]

If you are doubtful about whether inequality is the source of interpersonal conflict, consider a study that focused on one aspect of our life where we directly confront the reality that some people live in a higher class than others: flying on commercial airlines. Data from a vast database of commercial flights shows that air rage incidents are four times more likely to occur when there is a first-class section in the airplane—an increase in violent incidents on planes similar to the effect of a 9.5-hour flight delay. Air rage is also twice as likely if passengers have to board in the front of the plane and walk through the first-class cabin, as opposed to boarding in the middle or the back of the plane. Amazingly, the impact of having a first-class cabin on a flight doesn't just make those flying in coach (economy) more susceptible to anger: first-class passengers were more likely to have an air-rage incident the closer their seats were to the coach section.[115]

There is also evidence that inequality leads to greater internal conflict between different groups of people—sometimes, but not always, associated with discrimination of different racial groups within a country—and even war.[116] Anthropologists have found evidence throughout human history that body height inequality—which is directly related to income inequality—increases the likelihood of war over resources.[117] Interestingly, war itself can either increase or decrease inequality. The less violent and localized the war is, the more likely it is to increase inequality by hurting the poor while benefiting elites through war profiteering and resource acquisition.[118] However, the most all-encompassing and deadly wars tend to reduce inequality through a simple mechanism—they make everyone poor by killing people, destroying capital, ruining markets, worsening institutions, and breaking up networks.[119] This is a topic we will return to in the next chapter when we talk about the evolution of inequality over time within countries across the globe.

INEQUALITY UNDERMINES DEMOCRACY AND PRODUCTIVE CIVIL INSTITUTIONS

There is one thing that many political philosophers have agreed upon: democracy is impossible without a general equality of conditions among citizens. The Greek historian Plutarch said that: "An imbalance between rich and poor is the oldest and most fatal ailment of all republics." Aristotle worried that an unequal society will never support a well-functioning democracy: if the rich rule, it will drift towards plutocracy, and if the poor rule it will quickly deteriorate to a tyranny of the majority, where the poor will simply expropriate the wealth of the rich to the detriment of the entire society. Even in the *Wealth of Nations*, Smith fretted that high inequality leads to a situation where "civil government, so far as it is instituted for the security of property, is in reality, instituted for the defense of the rich against the poor, or of those who have some property against those who have none at all".[120]

Democracy is not a necessary condition for capitalism to work—autocracies from Chile to China have proven this. However, there is strong evidence that democracy fosters higher economic growth by promoting economic freedom and the free exchange of ideas and innovation—leaks and matches, once again.[121] Democracies also do a better job promoting public health and, while the evidence is more mixed, higher educational levels.[122] More importantly, democracy improves welfare by providing citizens self-recognition, social status, and an amount of agency over their own lives. Once again, we return to Plato's idea of *thymos*—democracy inherently recognizes the self-worth of citizens and incorporates them in civic activities. So, if inequality is undermining our democracies, it is also undermining our productivity, our standards of living, and our well-being as individuals and as a society.

Growing inequality undermines democracy in five important, and interconnected, ways. First, concentrated wealth is concentrated political power. In the words of Justice Lewis Brandeis: "The United States could have either democracy or wealth concentrated in a few hands—but not both."[123] The main reason wealth plays such a big role in politics is because, to a real extent, money is the lifeblood of political campaigns and plays a huge role in determining who actually wins elections and sets policy. The US senator Mark Hanna said that, "There are two things that are important in politics. The first is money and I can't remember what the second is."[124] As a result, those with money always have outsized influence over political outcomes and policy. The only question is to what extent the political institutions of a country can limit the influence of money in the political process.

Second, concentrated wealth undermines the existence of a large middle-class within a country. In the eyes of political theorists such as Aristotle and Alexis de Tocqueville, the middle-class is a necessary condition for effective democracy because the middle-class are natural proponents of stability and are not aligned with the extremes of either the rich or the poor. The middle-class has an interest in limiting the power of the rich (by limiting the power of elites to engage in rent-seeking) and counterbalance the poor (who might expropriate property through the tyranny of their majority). According to de Tocqueville, the most important thing about America was its "equality of conditions", not its equality of opportunity:

> When the rich govern alone, the interest of the poor is always in peril; and when the poor make the law, that of the rich run great risks ... The real advantage of democracy is not, as has been said, to favor the prosperity of all, but only to serve the well-being of the greatest number.[125]

A third danger of inequality in a democracy is that it leads to social separatism, tribalism, and conflict. Inequality can feed class warfare that, in turn, feeds political dysfunction, partisanship, a reduction in civil discourse, demagogy, reductions in spending on public goods and the welfare state, discrimination, and politics that appeals to nativism and racial bigotry. According to the legal scholar Ganesh Sitaraman, there are three inherent conflicts in any society: (1) the government can oppress the people, (2) individuals can oppress other individuals through crime, and (3) social groups can oppress other social groups.[126] It is the last two types that are less likely in a more egalitarian society.

Conflict between groups can result in outright hostility or warfare. But it can also lead to other, more insidious, changes in public policy. For example, social separatism can lead to a change in the amount and the types of public goods that are provided by governments within a society. Consider spending on public education. Many rich can afford a private education for their children and may conclude that it is in their interest if education becomes a strictly private good. If they vote that way, and use their resources to convince other people to vote that way, the end result is fewer resources devoted to public education. The same thing happens with private health clubs versus municipal recreation centers, gated communities versus mixed-use zoning, and public transportation versus spending on suburban sprawl. On the other hand, many rich see the most valuable benefits they receive from the government as protecting their safety and property rights. The rich often support more spending on crime and national defense because it is in their own self-interest—maybe more than is justified by real conditions.

Inequality also appears to foster political polarization by changing how people think about government policies and the role of the government itself in society. For instance, evidence suggests that changes in inequality—not in the level of income but its distribution—impacts how people feel about government policies aimed at reducing inequality. Psychology experiments have shown that those who *feel* relatively rich—regardless of their absolute income levels—are less likely to support redistribution.[127] As a result, income inequality can lead to greater political polarization, which, in turn, leads to greater income inequality in a vicious circle. It is little wonder, then, that political polarization in the US is currently at its highest level in recent history and has risen steadily since the mid-1970s. This has occurred at the same time that economic inequality in the US began to rise, and measures of political polarization are closely correlated with changes in the Gini coefficient.[128]

The fourth danger of inequality is that it can gradually turn a democracy into a plutocracy (government run by the rich) or an oligarchy (government run by the few). I will use the term plutocracy here, although I could be referring to either. The fact is that wealth has the power in a democracy to not only influence policies, but also to transform the system so that all of the rules and institutions are directed towards supporting what Marx referred to as the "dictatorship of the propertied class". In other words, the country's political system becomes democratic in form only, not in practice. Democracies are vulnerable to plutocracy because wealth is a claim on future resources. Protecting the future flows of income created by these assets often necessitates controlling the economic and political institutions that shape economic outcomes in a variety of ways. The rich can leverage their money and power using legitimate political tools (and sometimes illegitimate tools) to convince the poor to vote in the rich's economic interest. This creates a feedback loop between inequality today and political systems that sustain inequality in the future, and the rich have huge incentives to change the rules of the game to favor their current hold on wealth. As a result, a plutocracy can appear to be a democracy in which the rule of law and free elections exist, but, in fact, the rules of the system actually favor a small number of elites. In the words of the early American politician John Taylor, "when the 'rich plunder the poor' it is always 'slow and legal'".[129]

The fifth and final danger of growing inequality is a tendency towards populism and nativism in politics. Unfortunately, the growing influence of the rich triggers the opposite reaction among other citizens to punish the rich by appealing to simplistic policies that appear to benefit the majority—the "people" in populism-speak—such as policies that unfairly expropriate the resources of the rich. It encourages zero-sum thinking and disparages the rich as essentially corrupt. In other words, there is the possibility that inequality can trigger a populist overreaction and excessive redistribution that undermines productivity and discourages growth. The post-independence histories of many Latin American and African countries attest to the political attraction of populist politics in extremely unequal societies. Unfortunately, the "us/them" mindset of populism also manifests itself in nativist policies that lead to people blaming immigrants and racial minorities for the ills of society, often triggering discrimination as well as anti-trade and anti-immigration policies that harm economic growth and welfare.

There is an immense amount of empirical evidence that all five of the dangers of inequality are undermining Western democracies, particularly in the US. First, there is an ocean of evidence that money runs politics. In the words of former President George W. Bush at a fundraiser: "This is an impressive crowd—the haves and the have-mores. Some people call you elites; I call you my base."[130] US congressional and presidential election spending increased by more than 50 percent in real terms between 2000 and 2016. The 2016 US presidential election cost $2.4 billion alone. This money is largely coming from the rich: the Forbes 400 wealthiest donate $10,000 to political campaigns for every $1 million increase in their wealth.[131] Fewer than 30,000 people account for a quarter of all political donations in the US and 80 percent of the money raised by political parties.[132]

A great deal of what this money is purchasing are lobbying and campaign donations aimed at capturing politicians' ears and hearts. In 1983, there was $200 million spent on direct lobbying in the US. By 2017, this had risen to $3 billion adjusted for inflation, and three-fourths of this spending was in favor of business.[133] Half of all lobbying groups in Washington, DC represent business and wealthy interests, compared to only 1 percent of lobbying groups who represent blue-collar workers (who comprise 24 percent of the population).[134]

In regards to campaign donations, members and candidates for Congress spend up to 70 percent of their time raising money.[135] This not only leads to less time spent on learning about issues and policymaking, it also means more time spent with rich people and lobbyists, leading to distorted perspectives and like-minded thinking. Sometimes members of Congress simply don't want to learn about the concerns of the poor because, in the words of Upton Sinclair: "it is difficult to get a man to understand something when his salary depends on his not understanding it".[136]

Corporations don't just buy influence through political donations and lobbying. There is evidence that a large portion of corporate philanthropy and corporate giving is aimed not at giving back to society, but at influencing politicians through the non-profit organizations that they are closely tied to. Many politicians establish charitable foundations with the ostensible aim of serving the public good, but in fact give to promote a politician's "pet project", good or bad, in order to buy influence with that politician. Corporate donations (which are usually tax-exempt) that go to targeted non-profit charitable foundations are a hidden way to influence the political process that is not only unregulated and less transparent, but it allows the corporation to appear to be "doing good". Research suggests that corporate donations are five times more likely to go to non-profit charitable foundations which are tied to specific politicians, and even more than that if that politician serves on a legislative committee that impacts the business objectives of that corporation.[137] These corporate donations not only impact legislators' behavior directly, but they also change the behavior of charitable foundations in ways that cause them to be more favorable to corporate interest and more engaged in actively influencing policy in ways that benefit their corporate donors.[138]

All of this lobbying money, campaign donations, and strategic corporate philanthropy buys influence. According to the political scientist Larry Bartels, US senators are five times more likely to respond to the interests of the rich than middle-class citizens. Bartels finds no evidence that the views of poor constituents influence the voting behavior of these senators at all.[139] Other studies find similar results: analyses of voting patterns find that legislators' responsiveness to issues is strongly correlated with the concerns of the top

10 percent and not correlated with the concerns of the poor or middle-class, regardless of party.[140] And what does all of this influence buy? Research suggests that every dollar spent on lobbying leads to a return to firms of between $6 and $20 in tax benefits, in addition to other regulatory benefits that might accrue.[141]

The growing influence of the rich and powerful also appears to be changing the nature of public goods. Areas in the US with more income inequality and greater racial diversity spend less money on public goods like education, but more money on security and safety services.[142] One political science study found that American citizens with net worth of more than $40 million overwhelmingly favor cutting social safety net programs, even in the face of majority support for these programs.[143] In Europe, rising inequality has been found to change political agendas and public spending so that they are more focused on "social order" issues such as crime and immigration.[144]

The increased political power of the rich increases cynicism and creates a growing sense that voting and civic engagement don't matter. In the US, while 80 percent of the top 10 percent vote, only 40 percent of the bottom 10 percent vote. The median voter—so important in many political theories—is richer than the median American because the poor are less likely to vote.[145] Disenfranchisement also is driven by the facts that (1) many felons can't vote (this disenfranchises roughly 2 percent of the US population), (2) most congressional districts have been gerrymandered into safe districts, and (3) the use of the electoral college and not the popular vote for US presidential elections means that the outcome in many states is determined even before the election begins, reducing the value of many votes. These constraints on inclusive and equal voting increase cynicism and the influence of the rich in a vicious circle.

INEQUALITY CAN LEAD TO MACROECONOMIC INSTABILITY

A final threat posed by growing inequality is that increasing inequality can lead to greater macroeconomic instability, feeding recessions, depressions, booms, and busts. There is evidence across countries that greater inequality makes a country more vulnerable to swings in the business cycle.[146] These economic contractions are extremely costly to a society, not just in terms of lost income but in terms of disrupted lives—higher suicide and homicide rates, higher poverty levels, lower birth rates, lower life-expectancy, and higher divorce rates amongst other measures of well-being—that have economic, social, and personal consequences that persist for a very long time. During the 2008 Global Financial Crisis, the most vulnerable groups—minorities, the poor, the less educated—were disproportionately impacted. Long-term unemployment led to a loss of job skills that have permanently reduced the productivity and wages of many people. Whole communities, from suburbs in Florida to downtown Detroit, were devastated.

Why might inequality lead to greater macroeconomic instability? A group of economists known as *underconsumptionists*—important influences on the thinking of John Maynard Keynes—worried that richer households would save a greater proportion of their income than poorer households. According to underconsumptionists, as inequality grows and the rich receive a larger fraction of total income, aggregate savings will rise and the gap between aggregate income and total consumption increases. For a while, this gap can be filled with higher levels of investment. However, over time, this increased investment will only aggravate the excess supply of goods even further. Eventually, excess supply will necessitate large cuts in production and a recession or even a depression. This recession will reduce savings and get production back in line with consumption—for a while. Ultimately, income and inequality will rise again and the whole process will start all over. The solution to this conundrum is to redistribute income from the rich to the poor who have higher propensities to consume. Also, increasing the level of government purchases within an economy is an effective way of generating higher and more stable labels of consumption. These solutions would be familiar to many as the cornerstones of Keynesian stabilization policy, which aims to minimize the impact of business cycles by using countercyclical fiscal policy to stabilize aggregate expenditure and output growth.

In Chapter 3 we talked about Keynes' theory that inequality actually stimulated productivity and economic growth by concentrating capital in a small number of hands, allowing investments to be made at the scale needed to sufficiently finance industrialization and new technologies. The fact that Keynes appeared to be of two minds about inequality—that it fueled growth but also created economic instability—captures the conflicted views that many economists have traditionally had about inequality. It is representative of this persistent belief in economics that there is a tradeoff between efficiency and equality when it comes to economic outcomes—a belief that the research and ideas presented in this chapter have tried to challenge.

Other economists worry about the role of inequality in feeding the booms and busts that drive financial crises. An important link between inequality and financial crises is that inequality fuels the excessive accumulation of debt.[147] The connection between inequality and debt may have been identified by Adam Smith, Robert Frank, and Thorstein Veblen: inequality encourages the poor to try to keep up with the increasingly ostentatious consumption patterns of the rich, whom the poor emulate because of their higher social status. This is particularly true for the context sensitive goods that convey the most social prestige. Thus, inequality leads to more consumption (the opposite of what was argued by the underconsumptionists) and more debt, setting the stage for a costly financial crisis when these debt levels lead to a spike in defaults and financial panic.

The aggregate empirical evidence on the link between inequality and the frequency of financial crises is unclear.[148] There are tantalizing clues about the links between the two, however. For instance, there is strong evidence from behavioral psychology that our spending habits are highly influenced by those around us—referred to as "framing" in the psychology literature. In one interesting study, researchers found that people who had a neighbor who won the lottery were more likely to accumulate debt and increase their own consumption.[149]

In a review of macro forecasting models, the economist Mark Zandi found that inequality is likely to magnify the size of future recessions primarily through its impact on financial volatility. Inequality worsens business cycles because (1) the wealthy are hurt by falling asset prices that occur during a recession, cutting their consumption, and (2) the poor are exposed to default risk because they have high levels of debt.[150] In other words, the poor are vulnerable to financial shocks because they are credit-constrained, and the rich are vulnerable because most of their spending is sensitive to changes in the prices of financial asset markets.

There is solid evidence that growing inequality contributed to the Global Financial Crisis of 2008 in the US and elsewhere. More than 70 percent of the changes in US consumption between 2003 and 2013 came from the changing consumption of the top 10 percent, suggesting that the rich were driving overall consumption and debt accumulation leading up to the Global Financial Crisis.[151] The primary source of the 2008 crisis was the boom and bust in the subprime mortgage market, where low-income households were able to borrow at greater levels than ever before. The subprime boom was driven by two factors, both linked to inequality. One was financial innovation, specifically mortgage-backed securities that increased the supply of funds in the mortgage market while weakening the incentives for many investors to pay attention to the risks of the homes they were backed with. Investors were particularly blasé about default risk because of the false claim pushed by the sellers of these securities that mortgage-backed securities had diversified most of the default risk away—in other words, that diversification could offset the extreme inequality in income among people who were purchasing houses. The second factor was the financial deregulation of mortgage markets. The subprime boom was intentionally encouraged by government policy and supported by members of both parties in the US as a way to benefit the struggling poor and middle-class without the need to raise taxes or increase social spending.[152]

One final link between inequality and macroeconomic instability is through its impact on political stability, which we talked about in the previous section.

There is evidence that countries with more inequality have a harder time sustaining growth because of greater political instability and the macroeconomic instability it unleashes. Inequality fosters conflict and tribalism that can fuel violent swings in economic policy from election to election depending upon the interest group that wins. Or, inequality and class conflict can lead to less effective macroeconomic management. For example, if inequality increases the political power of the rich, it then becomes harder to conduct countercyclical stabilization policy. Under the Keynesian conception of stabilization policy, governments should conduct expansionary fiscal policy during recessions by cutting taxes and increasing government spending. During expansions, governments should engage in contractionary fiscal policy and pay down the debt by raising taxes and cutting government spending. Unfortunately, growing inequality and the rising influence of the rich turn policies that are economically beneficial into policies that are politically untenable. Because of the influence of the rich, it becomes extremely difficult to ever raise taxes. As a result, we get lots of expansionary policy, little contractionary policy, and accumulating government debt that threatens financial stability.

IN CONCLUSION

The idea that inequality does not matter for our society or our economy is based on three faulty beliefs. The first is that "individual productivity" is something that exists; that we are all independently productive, homogeneous inputs that can be moved from production point to production point. This is nonsense. We know that our ideas and efforts leak and match in ways that make "us" much more productive than just a simple sum of our own individual efforts. While it is a complete cliché, there is no "I" in "economy" (but there is in economics—go figure). What we produce is determined by networks, not our individual network.

The second reason why inequality matters is that we know that fairness and respect inherently matter. Once again, an individual worker is not something separate from the society they work in. Instead, we know that *relative wages* impact our effort and our productivity, that it impacts our educational attainment, and that it impacts our public health. Inequality also plays an important role in shaping trust and cooperative social norms, which play a fundamental role in reducing the frictions of life as well as in providing the foundation for general peace and social stability. In fact, because we as individuals are so closely tied together, there are many ways in which inequality can feed vicious cycles and poverty traps. When our needs for money and esteem are not being met, we have fewer incentives to work hard and invest in ourselves and in our children; we have less reason to trust others; and we have more incentives to rent-seek, discriminate, and steal from those we can take advantage of. In other words, in many ways, we make others around us less productive when we make ourselves less productive, both now and in the future. In less equal and more tribal societies, we create cracks and clashes, not leaks and matches.

Finally, inequality impacts our institutions, which influence our ability as a society to function effectively and productively. Society is not just a collection of people. It is a network of social norms, shared history, ethical principles, traditions, and codified and uncodified laws that become the rules by which we can live together and work cooperatively. More unequal societies become less cooperative societies, and are more likely to suffer from political dysfunction, lower public health, worse educational outcomes, less intergenerational mobility, more rent-seeking, fewer public goods, more discrimination, conflicts such as crime and war, and greater macroeconomic and financial instability.

All of these problems are a lot to lay at the feet of inequality alone. But once again, the key point to be made is that we are all connected to each other, and inequality is connected with other determinants of what makes for a good and efficient society. When excessive inequality becomes the norm, its corrosive effects trickle down, in obvious and non-obvious ways, throughout our economic and social systems, creating the possibility of an endless variety of feedback effects and poverty traps. Likewise, the potential is there for greater egalitarianism to create virtuous circles that allow for more trust and cooperation, for people to be more motivated because they feel more valued, for larger and deeper networks of people to create more leaks and matches, and for efficiency to expand as equality expands.

It would make economics much easier if providing for freedom of choice and guaranteeing equality of opportunity made for societies that are both fair and productive. But unfortunately, freedom of choice and equality of opportunity are simply not enough to create a just society—outcomes also matter, and so does status. We are social beings, and it is wrong to ignore community when it comes to determining what is just and fair, and also when it comes to determining what is efficient and economic. It is shoddy economics to think that sociology, psychology, history, politics, ethnicity, gender, morals, ethics, and culture do not matter when we are making economic decisions. These things do matter, and this is why inequality matters.

NOTES

1. Bentham (1781).
2. Diamond and Saez (2011).
3. Jefferson (1813).
4. Johnson (2012).
5. Watson (2009).
6. Jargowsky (2015).
7. Reardon and Bischoff (2011).

8. Rothwell et al. (2013).
9. Bettencourt et al. (2007).
10. Chetty et al. (2014b).
11. Payne (2018).
12. Kalma (1991) and Payne (2018).
13. Emerson (1860).
14. Clark and Oswald (1996).
15. Fliessbach et al. (2012).
16. Russell (1930), p. 90.
17. Blanchflower and Oswald (2004) and Easterlin et al. (2010).
18. Mencken (1916).
19. *Thymos* is an important part of the ethical systems of many philosophers when it comes to examining what constitutes a fair society. Amongst them is Immanuel Kant and his universal maxim: "Act only on that maxim whereby you can at the same time will that it should become a universal law." The implication of the universal maximum is that you must treat people as ends in themselves. All ethical actions involve treating other people as a person worthy of self-respect in ways that enhance their *thymos*, not as an object of your own self-interest.
20. Rawls (1971).
21. Michael Sandel (2012) has argued that inequality is more and more a deterrent to equality of opportunity as a "market mindset" has grown increasingly prevalent in society. Money allows people to jump the queue at amusement parks and at airports, more easily immigrate to places such as the US, get premium healthcare, and get into the best colleges. In Sandel's opinion, when everything can be bought and sold, money means more and egalitarianism means less.
22. Rawls (1971, p. 101).
23. Mankiw (2013).
24. Barth et al. (2016).
25. In fact, one reason for the increased outsourcing and subcontracting of jobs by firms is that by moving workers outside of a firm, the boundaries of the workplace norms for fairness change. When fairness becomes less of an issue, firms can more easily reduce wages without harming morale (Weil, 2017).
26. Shapiro and Stiglitz (1984).
27. Card et al. (2012).
28. Akerlof and Yellen (1990).
29. Cohn et al. (2014b).
30. Cohn et al. (2014a).
31. Rouen (2017).
32. Veblen (1899).
33. Frank (2007).
34. Stiglitz (2011).
35. Chetty et al. (2014a).
36. Reeves and Howard (2013).
37. Reardon (2011).
38. Ibid.
39. Putnam (2015).
40. Hoxby and Avery (2013).
41. Corak (2013).
42. Putnam (2015).
43. Altintas (2015).

44. Hoff and Pandey (2004).
45. Chetty et al. (2014a).
46. Cullen et al. (2012).
47. Wilkinson and Pickett (2009).
48. Case and Deaton (2015).
49. Wilkinson and Pickett (2009) and Bourguignon (2015).
50. Bosworth et al. (2016).
51. *British Medical Journal* (1996).
52. Kaplan et al. (1996).
53. Adler et al. (2000) and Kawachi and Kennedy (2002).
54. Ferrer-i-Carbonell and Ramos (2013).
55. Callan et al. (2011).
56. Payne et al. (2017).
57. Singh-Manoux et al. (2003).
58. Corak (2013).
59. Chetty et al. (2016).
60. Bowles and Gintis (2002).
61. Heckman (2012).
62. Ibid.
63. Solon (2016).
64. Chetty et al. (2018).
65. Palomino et al. (2019).
66. Autor (2014).
67. Traub et al. (2017).
68. Wolff (2014).
69. Clark (2014).
70. Putnam (2015).
71. Ager et al. (2019).
72. Bivens and Mishel (2015).
73. *The Economist* (2018b).
74. Bivens and Mishel (2013).
75. Galbraith (1979, p. 79).
76. Kaplan (2012) and Kaplan and Rauh (2013).
77. Bebchuk et al. (2011).
78. Bertrand and Mullainathan (2001).
79. Kaplan and Rauh (2013).
80. Philippon and Reshef (2012).
81. Short (2019).
82. Kaplan and Rauh (2013).
83. Bakija et al. (2012).
84. Philippon and Reshef (2012).
85. Taplin (2017).
86. *The Economist* (2018c).
87. Thiel (2014).
88. Becker (1971).
89. The legal measure of discrimination in the US is not exactly the same as the definition used by Becker. One legal standard for discrimination is the "disparate treatment" standard, meaning anyone who applies different rules to people in a protected group is guilty of discrimination. The second discriminatory standard is "disparate impact", meaning practices that impose disadvantage on one

group more than on others, even if they appear to be neutral, are deemed to be discriminatory.

90. Bertrand and Mullainathan (2004).
91. Fix and Struyk (1993).
92. Blair et al. (2004).
93. Eberhardt et al. (2006).
94. Goldin and Rouse (2000).
95. Chetty and Hendren (2018).
96. Krosch and Amodio (2014).
97. Payne (2018).
98. Gilens (2009).
99. Arrow (1972, p. 357).
100. Putnam (2000, p. 135).
101. Rainer and Siedler (2009).
102. Smith (1759).
103. Zak and Knack (2001).
104. Beugelsdijk et al. (2004) and Henrich et al. (2001).
105. Putnam (2001).
106. Wilkinson and Pickett (2009).
107. Jordahl (2009), Knack and Keefer (1997), and Zak and Knack (2001).
108. Rothstein and Uslaner (2005) and Easterlin et al. (2010).
109. Putnam (2015).
110. Knack (2003).
111. Putnam (2000, pp. 358–9).
112. Lofstrom and Raphael (2016).
113. Wilkinson and Pickett (2006) and Kawachi et al. (1999).
114. Kaplan et al. (1996).
115. DeCelles and Norton (2016).
116. Bourguignon (2015), Fearon and Laitin (2003), and Collier and Hoeffler (2004).
117. Baten and Mumme (2013).
118. Bircan et al. (2010).
119. Scheidel (2017).
120. Smith (1776).
121. Acemoglu et al. (2014).
122. Besley and Kudamatsu (2006) and Edenbrandt (2010).
123. Quoted in Gilens (2012, p. 1).
124. Quoted in Bartels (2010), p. 270.
125. de Tocqueville (1835).
126. Sitaraman (2017).
127. Brown-Iannuzzi et al. (2015).
128. McCarty et al. (2016).
129. Taylor (1814).
130. Quoted in Milanovic (2016, p. 190).
131. Bonica and Rosenthal (2015).
132. Drutman (2015).
133. Ibid.
134. Schlozman et al. (2012).
135. Ansolabehere et al. (2003).
136. Sinclair, U. (1994), p. 109.
137. Bertrand et al. (2018a).

138. Bertrand et al. (2018b).
139. Bartels (2010).
140. Gilens (2012) and Gilens and Page (2014).
141. Richter et al. (2009).
142. Jayadev and Bowles (2006), Trounstine (2015), and Fournier and Johansson (2016).
143. Page et al. (2013).
144. Epp and Bourghetto (2018).
145. Milanovic (2016).
146. Ostry et al. (2014).
147. Morelli (2017).
148. Morelli and Atkinson (2015).
149. Agarwal et al. (2016).
150. Zandi (2017).
151. Bakker and Felman (2014).
152. Friedman and Kraus (2011) and Calomiris and Haber (2014).

5. Why has domestic inequality risen, and fallen, and risen?

Over the course of human history, inequality has been cyclical, slowly growing and then rapidly contracting over the very long run. In the broadest sense, there have been three "long cycles" of inequality within societies across the globe. The first was the rise in inequality associated with the Neolithic revolution, which began in the Near East at around 9,000 BCE and which ended with the spread of the plague across the globe in the mid-fourteenth century. The second long cycle of inequality began during the industrial revolution and ended with the "Great Compression", during which inequality fell between 1920 and 1980. Finally, the latest cycle of growing inequality within countries began in roughly 1980 and is still ongoing. As we discussed in Chapter 2, this modern upswing in inequality shows no signs of tapering off, and is occurring within most countries across the globe.

The objective of this chapter is twofold. First, to examine theories of why within-country inequality is cyclical and what drives broad-based expansions and contractions in inequality. These theories will then set the stage for the second objective of this chapter, which is to examine the seven primary reasons behind our current trend towards increasing inequality; reasons that are not mutually exclusive. The factors that are driving growing within-country inequality today are the result of the changing nature of production in modern, information-based economies, and the impact that these economic changes are having on our social norms. Changes in our economics—such as the growing importance of education-intensive labor, intangible capital, the role of globalization, and the creation of economic superstars and winner-takes-all markets—have changed the ways that we organize ourselves in our work, but also the ways that we organize our families, our broader society, and our politics. All of these factors are contributing to the growing domestic inequality we are experiencing today.

HYPOTHESES OF WHY INEQUALITY FLUCTUATES OVER THE LONG RUN

In the most general and simplistic view of economic history—one that also has a fair amount of truth in it—inequality can be viewed as the price of growth and improved standards of living. As the philosopher Jean-Jacques Rousseau noted, there was little inequality before the Neolithic revolution, when men lived in a "state of nature" and at subsistence levels of income.[1] The Neolithic revolution is where inequality began because it is also where economic growth started; intensive agriculture created food surpluses at a scale unknown to migratory hunter-gatherers. The invention of surplus food also demanded the invention of property, property rights, and the creation of laws and governments to protect these rights. Intensive agriculture and the domestication of animals led to an improved ability to produce and store food, while at the same time creating unequal wealth and institutional power that shaped the allocation of these resources. Social hierarchies were created, leading to changing political and economic structures in a feedback loop. To get an idea of the extent of inequality in early civilizations, anthropologists estimate that the Gini coefficient at the beginning of the Neolithic revolution was only .2 in 8000 BCE in Jerf el-Ahmar (today's Syria) but .5 in 79 AD in Pompeii, Italy.[2] Most economic anthropologists agree that the most influential pre-modern societies—from Babylonia to Egypt to Rome—were almost as unequal as they could possibly be, and many were close to the maximum feasible Gini (see Chapter 1) of .75. In these societies, the vast majority lived at subsistence and a few elites owned everything else.

As the economic historian Walter Scheidel has documented in his book *The Great Leveler*, the only factors that have significantly reduced inequality in long-lasting ways are catastrophic events that have also significantly reduced standards of living and created massive amounts of human misery. The big-picture summary of the rise and fall of economic inequality is growth versus disaster. Violent shocks (such as revolution, total war, state failure) or pandemics (such as the Black Death) are the only factors that have widely and significantly reduced inequality for long periods of time. But once growth returns, inequality begins to rise once more. The plague (which first appeared in the mid-fourteenth century in Europe and periodically reappeared there until the seventeenth century) killed nearly 40 percent of the population in some countries. But as tens of millions died, wages rose, compressing incomes and wealth, which created a miserable form of egalitarianism. However, once the industrial revolution began and standards of living as well as population growth rates began to rise, income inequality rebounded as well, with particularly large differences between urban (manufacturing) and rural (farming) areas.

Inequality gradually rose from 1650–1929 across countries that were participating in the industrial revolution, particularly in North America and Europe. However, the "Great Compression" of income began during the outbreak of World War I and continued though the Great Depression. The compression in incomes accelerated during World War II, which killed millions and destroyed trillions in wealth for everyone—but only for those who had wealth to destroy. World War II was then followed by violent communist revolutions in Russia, China, and in the third world that led to the repression of markets and expropriation of private property. By the end of World War II, income shares of the top 1 percent had fallen by two-thirds in Japan, one-half in France and the UK, one-third in Germany and the US, and by even greater amounts in Russia, China, and Korea.[3]

During the first three post-war decades, many countries evolved political structures that preserved the egalitarian income distributions that existed after the war, but which also allowed for economic growth. Representative democratic institutions were built that fostered broader inclusiveness in economics and politics by a greater proportion of the population. The most important examples of these increasingly inclusive institutions—such as the growth of social welfare states, progressive taxation regimes, and the removal of many formal discriminatory racial, gender, and class-based economic policies and political participation barriers—sustained low inequality in most industrialized democracies. By the time the Great Compression had run its course by the 1970s, inequality in both the developed world and in the most populous developing countries of Asia had plunged to levels that had been unknown since the Neolithic revolution thousands of years before.[4] However, as we have discussed in Chapter 2 and will analyze extensively in this chapter, these trends have now reversed themselves and economic inequality has been steadily rising within most of the world's countries since 1980. When placed within the context of this history, one interesting way to think about today's rising inequality is to ask the following: Is inequality rising to new highs, or just regressing to its long-run mean?

Within these "long-wave" cycles of rising and falling inequality identified by Scheidel and other economic historians, there are four other theories about why inequality rises and falls over shorter, more transitory periods of time. Each of these four theories has played an important role in shaping how economists think about rising and falling inequality within countries.

The first, and most well-known, theory of how economic inequality evolves as economic development proceeds was offered by Nobel Prize winner Simon Kuznets, and is often referred to as the *Kuznets curve*.[5] Kuznets predicted that inequality would first rise, but then fall, as countries moved through the early stages of industrialization to become developed economies. In pre-industrial societies, Kuznets argued that low incomes also meant low inequality among relatively egalitarian farmers living in rural areas. But industrialization requires urbanization. As growth and wages in urban areas boom, inequality grows in society, particularly between urban and rural areas. However, as more people move to urban areas and enjoy higher wages, inequality eventually declines. In other words, Kuznets believed that the relationship between aggregate income and inequality was an inverted U—inequality rises when countries are poor but growing, and falls as they join the ranks of the richer countries.

While Kuznets' hypothesis is intuitively appealing, there is a small problem: it does not appear to fit the data very well. Only 5 of 49 countries have exhibited inequality patterns that have followed Kuznets' inverse U-shaped curve.[6] As can be seen in Figure 5.1, the US experience is almost the exact opposite of what Kuznets predicted, with a U-shaped, not inverse U-shaped, relationship between GDP and the Gini coefficient. The Kuznets curve in the UK looks similar to the US, while the Kuznets curves in Spain, Italy, Germany, Netherlands, and Japan look different than the US and UK, but still do not exhibit the inverse U-shaped pattern predicted by Kuznets.

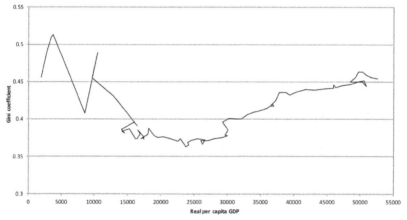

Source: Gini for 1774, 1850, 1860, and 1870 from Lindert and Williamson (2011). The Gini coefficient for gross household income 1918–2015 is from the US Bureau of the Census (2015). Real GDP per capita from the Maddison Project (2018).

Figure 5.1   *The Kuznets curve in the US*

What is the problem with Kuznets' theory? In part, agricultural societies were not nearly as egalitarian as Kuznets believed (e.g. the American South during slavery), meaning that early industrialization did not always increase inequality. But a larger problem is that while Kuznets might have been right to focus on the structural shifts that occur during development, he might have had the wrong sectors in mind. Kuznets focused on the agriculture/rural vs. industrial/urban divide as the primary source of income inequality. But today, the real divide that is driving growing income inequality in countries that have long-industrialized is the increasing divide between those with higher levels of education and those without.

This idea that structural shifts drive economic inequality was formalized in the second theory of how economic inequality evolves over time developed by another Nobel Prize winner, Jan Tinbergen, in what is known as the *skills-based technological change hypothesis*.[7] Tinbergen focused on how technological change in evolving economies shapes the supply and demand for certain skills and jobs, and how this creates a "race" between education and technology. When new technologies and jobs are created, Tinbergen argued that the supply of people that have the proper training and education to do the new jobs related to this new technology is very slow to respond. As a result, there are often skills for which supply is far short of demand and wage premiums are created (wages greater than marginal products) that increase income inequality. Over time, Tinbergen argued, the supply of workers to do these high-wage jobs will catch up as more people invest in the proper education and training. However, constantly evolving technologies will create skill premiums in other areas. When technological change is outpacing educational investments, technology is "winning" and inequality increases. When educational investment is "winning", inequality will decrease.

Tinbergen believed that as countries become richer, the race would eventually be won by education and all skill premiums would go to zero, eliminating a primary source of inequality. Tinbergen believed this because he thought that the quality of education training would improve over time, labor markets would become more efficient, and unnecessary regulations would be eliminated as countries developed economically. However, in today's world we are not seeing skills premiums go to zero. In fact, just the opposite, as more-skilled workers have increased their wages relative to less-skilled workers, meaning that education is losing the race with technology. We will talk more about the evidence regarding education and rising skill premiums later in this chapter.

There are two additional theories of how inequality evolves that have been influential among economists. The *political economy hypothesis* was introduced in the previous chapter. This theory focuses on the fact that political campaigns are often fought over the distribution of income, and the public policies that are adopted as a result of who wins and loses these campaigns impact the distribution of income over time. As a result, there are not really any long-run trends in inequality, just short-term fluctuations in political realities. Different political conditions change the public policies that shape the distribution of income, such as changes in progressive taxation, land and debt reform, economic crises, economic growth, democratic reforms, social welfare programs, education, labor unionization, and rent-seeking behavior. According to the political economy hypothesis, the Great Compression in the US and Europe occurred because of the rise of progressive political victories that imposed high tax rates on the rich, created more generous social welfare systems, encouraged unionization, and nationalized many industries. The upswing in inequality that began around 1980 did not occur the same everywhere, but coincided with a cross-country conservative political movement that focused less on equality, encouraged globalization, reduced the progressivity of taxes, discouraged unionization, and privatized state-owned industries.

Politics don't just determine economic policy, but they also influence social institutions that play a role in influencing economic inequality. Political institutions impact the degree of economic mobility that exists between groups. As we discussed in Chapter 4, when inequality exists, it also changes society by weakening the middle-class, encouraging political polarization, increasing racial and gender discrimination, and creating plutocracies. When this happens, inequality creates political changes that lead to more inequality in a vicious cycle. This vicious cycle is most likely to exist in representative democracies that fail to protect political institutions that ensure egalitarian and non-discriminatory participation in the political process.

Political institutions also impact group-level endowments, particularly when one group actively changes the rules to extract resources from another person or group. For this reason, the impact of changes in politics on political and social institutions can have long-lasting impacts on inequality. For example, consider slavery. Even when the institution of slavery was outlawed and formal political institutions changed, endowments (such as a lack of wealth, education, and access to social networks) persisted. As a result, so did inequality between blacks and whites, but also between former white slaveholders and white non-slaveholders. During the Reconstruction era immediately following the Civil War, wealth in the South became much more egalitarian: only about one-third of wealthy Southerners from 1860 remained wealthy in 1870.[8] However, political ties and unequal power remained, which led to the eventual reversal of Reconstruction and the implementation of Jim Crow laws that enabled many former slaveholders (and non-slaveholders) to use their political power to subjugate anew. Jim Crow laws favored whites in general, but former slaveholders in particular. For example, former slaveholders were much more likely to start a new business than non-slaveholders during the Jim Crow era.[9] According to one study, sharing a surname with a slaveholder was correlated with higher income in 1940 across more than 40,000 surnames.[10]

The final hypothesis for how inequality evolves over time was posited by Thomas Piketty in one of the best-selling books on economics in a generation, *Capital in the Twenty-First Century*.[11] As his title suggests, Piketty ties income inequality to the existence of long-standing wealth inequality, what he calls "*patrimonial capitalism*". In brief, Piketty makes the argument—using historical data on wealth from many different sources and countries—that financial assets are highly concentrated in only a few hands. As a result, if the returns to these assets (which he denotes as "r") rise faster than overall growth of income (denoted as "g"), then inequality will necessarily increase. In other words, inequality rises whenever r>g, or when the wealthy are reinvesting their wealth at rates faster than the overall growth rate of income in the economy. During the Great Compression, r<g held because of the expropriation and destruction of wealth due to two World Wars, the establishment of extremely progressive taxation and welfare systems during and after the two World Wars (which lowered r), and fast post-war economic growth (a higher g). However, based on his historical data, Piketty argues that there is a long-run trend towards greater inequality because the long-run values of these variables (which do change over time, and might change in the future) are r=5% and g=2%. This simple fact that r>g over the long term has created the inequality that we observe today.

Later in this chapter, we will evaluate the empirical evidence related to Piketty's patrimonial capitalism hypothesis in more detail. For now, I will say that the data does not clearly indicate that r>g holds under the broadest definitions of these concepts. In addition, it is not always the case that the richest people yesterday will be the richest tomorrow. While intergenerational mobility is low at high levels of wealth (meaning that rich families generally stay rich), when looking at the wealthiest people today, their wealth is most likely to be gained by entrepreneurial success and labor income, not inheritance and capital income.[12]

Using these four hypotheses as a framework for understanding how inequality evolves over time, let's now turn our attention to the factors—many of them related, and none of them are mutually exclusive of each other—that economists have identified as the primary factors driving rising inequality today within most countries across the globe.

Reason #1: Skills-based technological change and information and communication technology (ICT).

Tinbergen's idea of a "race between technology and education" has encouraged many researchers to identify the sources of technological changes and the barriers to developing the skilled workforce needed to maximize the benefits of these new technologies. The biggest source of technological change since 1980—when inequality generally began to rise—is the remarkable advancements in ICT. Consider that in 1805, it took 62 days for news about the Battle of the Nile to cover the 2,073 miles to London (at a speed of 1.4 miles an hour).[13] The invention of the telegraph in the mid-1800s allowed information to travel more than 100 times faster than it could previously. Landline telephone service in the 1900s once again doubled the speed in which information traveled. And today, with the internet and mobile phones, the speed with which information travels is primarily limited by our mental abilities to process it, not by our ability to gain access to it.

Every job requires a certain amount of *human capital*, meaning durable skills and attributes that earn a return in the market. Human capital can't be bought and sold like physical capital because it is tied to a particular person. One of the important differences between technologies of the past—such as the internal combustion engine, public sanitation, and petrochemicals—and the new technologies associated with ICT is the fact that ICT only changes the productivity of workers that possess high levels of extremely specific human capital. As a result, not everybody enjoys the same ability to access and benefit from ICT. Vaccinations made almost everyone more productive and increased wages across the board, regardless of their human capital. But big data, robotics, and artificial intelligence only increase the productivity of a few people with very specific skill sets. This is what economists refer to as "skills-based technological change": new workers with new human capital are needed to use a new technology most productively.

Skills-based technological change associated with ICT has put an increasing premium on specific types of human capital that are not going to be attainable by everyone. Because human capital is so specific, not easily transferable, and scarce, its returns are very high. To get an idea of how valuable, one meta-study reviewing 1,120 studies across 139 countries concludes that the average return to a year of schooling is 8.8 percent a year.[14] This means that a four-year college education increases your yearly income by 40 percent a year—year after year. And it appears that the returns to schooling are increasing over time. The data indicates that the returns to raw labor have fallen significantly relative to the returns to human capital since the 1980s.[15]

ICT places the largest wage premiums on jobs that are non-routine and highly cognitive, and has reduced relative wages for jobs that are routine and less cognitive. In general, the demand for jobs involving routine tasks has fallen the most, whether cognitive or not. For example, bank teller jobs are cognitive, but because they are routine, they can be replaced with computers. Jobs such as hairdressing or fitness instruction are less cognitive, but also less routine, meaning labor demand has stayed relatively strong for these jobs.[16] To be even more specific, computers and artificial intelligence currently do not threaten jobs that involve creating new ideas, communicating complex ideas, or which involve large-scale pattern recognition (particularly when it pertains to qualitative, not quantitative, data).[17]

Figure 5.2 presents wage growth data for full-time male workers, clearly illustrating the growth in college and graduate wages, but the flat and even declining wage growth for everyone else. During the period 1963–2008, the wage gap between college- and high school-educated workers doubled (from less than 50 percent to more than 100 percent greater for college grad-

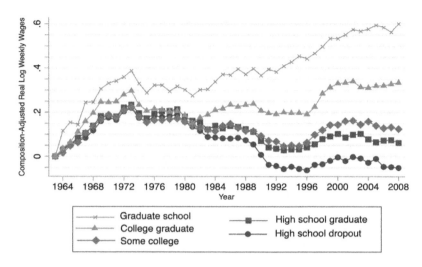

Source: Acemoglu and Autor (2011).

Figure 5.2   Changes in wages for full-time male workers

uates).[18] While the wages for low-skilled jobs are flat, the demand for these jobs has remained strong. As a result, advanced economies increasingly have a wage distribution that has a growing hole in its middle: lots of low-skilled, low-paying jobs and lots of high-skilled, high-paying jobs, but little in between. This has significantly increased income inequality, even among those who are not at the top end of the income distribution.[19]

This growing wage gap between high-skilled and low-skilled wages indicates that ICT is not only increasing the productivity of the highly educated, but also that the supply of high-skilled workers is not keeping pace with growing demand—i.e. that technology must be "winning the race" with education. This could mean that we as a society are not investing enough in education, or it could mean that we are educating our workforce badly. There is lots of evidence to support both of these conclusions. First, in terms of not investing enough in education, it is clear that the costs of higher education in many countries such as the US have increased rapidly, in part because of falling support from governments. Since 2000, the cost of community colleges in the US has risen by 28 percent (by $3,000) and of public universities by 54 percent (by $10,000). These rising costs are not primarily because of tuition increases, but because of increases in the overall costs of living (particularly for housing in more urban areas), declines in government subsidies, and difficulties in finding student employment.[20]

Second, higher costs have not only discouraged the overall level of educational attainment, but they have aggravated inequality because higher college costs impact the poor more than the rich, creating a vicious cycle between a lack of education and being poor. Mean family income has been largely stagnant in the US since 2000 and actually fell by 8 percent for the bottom 20 percent between 2003 and 2013. As a result, the net price of college for the bottom 20 percent has risen to 84 percent of family income (up from 44 percent in 1990). However, for the top 20 percent, the net price of college is only 15.4 percent of family income (up from 10.4 percent in 1990).[21] Because of this and other factors, only 21 percent of high school sophomores from the bottom 20 percent earned a bachelor's degree during the 10 years following their high school graduation, while 74 percent of those from the top 20 percent earned a degree.[22]

There is also evidence that the US is not providing the consistent quality of education students need, particularly in their early years and particularly to poorer students. The math and reading gap between rich and poor students is already large by the time children enter school, and public education does little to narrow this gap for most students.[23] Part of this is due to a lack of enrollment in pre-school; only 80 percent of children in OECD countries are enrolled in pre-school (only 54 percent of US children are enrolled).[24] Once they get to school in the US, poor children lag three-to-four grades behind high-income children, and lag two grades behind middle-income children.[25] Once in college, poor students with high test scores are about as likely to graduate from college as richer students with low test scores.[26] Income also impacts the kind of college a student gets into. Only 9 percent of students in the most highly selective colleges in the US come from the bottom 50 percent, while 74 percent of students at elite schools are chosen from the top 25 percent.[27]

Thus, it appears that technology is winning and education is losing, at least in the US. Robert Rycroft summarizes the situation as follows:

> The "normal" working of the market should lead to greater investment in human capital, a reduction in the returns to education and, eventually, a decrease in inequality. This "normal" response does not, however, appear to be taking place. The expected increase in educational attainment appears to be stalled. There has not been a significant decrease in the proportion of students who drop out of high school, nor has there been a significant increase in the proportion of high school graduates who go on to college or college students who complete their degrees.[28]

Looking to the future, the increasing importance of robotic automation and artificial intelligence will place increasing pressure on jobs that are neither creative, nor variable, nor highly cognitive. According to one study, robots are responsible for up to 670,000 lost manufacturing jobs between 1990 and 2007, and that number will rise because the number of industrial robots is expected to quadruple in the long run. Studies estimate that each robot per thousand workers decreases employment by 6.2 workers and wages by 0.7 percent, which is an impact on the labor market that far exceeds that of globalization.[29] Looking to the future, some studies have concluded that half of all jobs could be replaced by existing technology, and almost all jobs will be significantly disaggregated and re-bundled into tasks that machines can do and tasks they can't do.[30]

Before moving on, it is important to make clear that skills-based technological change is not the only thing driving within-country inequality. We know this because among people with similar education levels and in similar jobs, there is still high inequality. Wage variation between people with similar jobs in different firms has played an important role in rising inequality.[31] In other words, individual variation in human capital is not the only thing that is driving inequality higher. Which leads us to the next reason that within-country inequality is rising.

Reason #2: The increasing importance of intangible capital.

Technological change has not only changed the nature of human capital and labor, it has also changed the nature of capital. Typically, when you use the word "capital" you think about physical capital—machinery, equipment, structures, factories, and vehicles. But increasingly, capital no longer is physical—it is not tied to a particular place or person. Instead, many forms of capital are *intangible* and based upon ideas, networks, organizations, product platforms, supply chains, and training procedures. Intangible capital is the value of intellectual property (patents, copyrights, and trademarks), software, databases, research and development, creative materials and design, branding, decision systems, and business production processes. In the words of Diane Coyle, we are living in an increasingly "weightless world".[32]

The rise of intangible capital has been closely linked to the evolution from manufacturing-based economies that primarily relied upon the production of physical goods with tangible capital, to service-intensive economies that rely heavily on human and intangible capital. However, the growth of intangible capital has changed every business and every job—not just those in the service and ICT industries. While many forms of intangible capital are related to ICT, many are not. For example, the investments that firms make in producing brands and creative materials, such as trademarks and product design, are investments in intangible capital that are not necessarily related to the digital revolution. Perhaps the best examples of how intangible capital is impacting every business across the world can be found in retail. Consider two modern business giants: Amazon and Starbucks. Amazon's business is clearly driven by ICT. But Amazon is not just a technology company. Its value is also related to its branding, operations and delivery systems, production of original creative content, marketing analytics, and many other things that are only tangentially reliant on ICT. Amazon is largely about the synergies that can be created when all of these factors are integrated into one platform. Amazon has no place; it is a complex network of leaks and matches.

On the other hand, while Starbucks is in a much different business, in many ways it follows a similar model. Starbucks has more of a physical existence than Amazon—you are probably in or close to a Starbucks as you read this. But in reality, these coffee shops and the coffee that is served in them are a small part of the overall value that Starbucks creates for its customers. Starbucks is primarily about providing services linked to ideas: a level of quality and consistency of product, a certain atmosphere in their stores, a robust system for training and developing employees, lifestyle branding, and creative marketing that has built a clear picture of "Starbucks" that jumps into each of our heads when we hear that word. Starbucks' business is largely based upon ideas that are embedded in many different forms of intangible capital.

The value of intangible assets across firms can't be as easily measured as the value of physical capital. However, the best estimates suggest that the value of intangible assets in overall investment is skyrocketing. In the US, the value of intangible assets has been greater than the value of tangible assets since the mid-1990s. While tangible assets have been holding steady at 12 percent of value-added (value-added meaning how much is added to the value of a good or service at each stage of production), intangible assets have risen from 4 percent of value-added in 1948 to almost 14 percent of value-added in 2008.[33] Across all countries, the tangible capital share in value-added has fallen from 13.5 percent to 11 percent between 1995 and 2014, while the intangible capital share has risen from 10.5 percent to over 12 percent. The US, UK, and Nordic countries are the most intangible-intensive countries.[34]

The economics of intangible capital are different from those of tangible capital in four important ways. First, intangible capital involves large *fixed costs*. In other words, the costs of making and using intangible assets are almost entirely incurred up front. This is because intangible assets are primarily about ideas. As a result, the costs of producing ideas are often large in terms of research and development. But once you have an idea, it can be inexpensively used and shared. For example, computer software is costly to develop and implement, but cheap to actually use.

Second, because intangible capital is largely about ideas, intangible assets are *scalable*, meaning that they can easily be used in one place, a thousand places, or a million places. Think about Starbucks—the ease of creating an additional Starbucks explains why they are so ubiquitous. The intangibility of Starbucks makes each store non-rival, because opening a new Starbucks doesn't mean that other Starbucks can't exist (although when you see two

Starbucks across the street from each other, you have to wonder if Starbucks is testing how non-rival two coffee shops actually can be). In fact, the ease of creating a new Starbucks is part of its appeal because it creates networking effects: the more Starbucks is used, the more valuable Starbucks becomes because people become more familiar with it (Uber and many other digital service companies share similar networking benefits).

Third, because intangible capital is based upon ideas, it creates *positive spillovers* (which we discussed in Chapter 4). Because intangible capital is non-rival, it is easily transferred, duplicated, and imitated. Intangible capital creates leaks and matches that benefit everybody, not just the buyers and sellers of intangible capital. In other words, intangible capital is similar to a public good, and only stays a private good with the protection of intellectual property laws and, to the extent possible, secrecy.

Fourth, intangible capital creates *synergies*. In other words, it leaks and it matches through networks, making networks larger and the people in them more productive. The more ideas that exist, and the more people working on them, the larger networks become and the more intangible assets that are produced. As with ideas in general, intangible capital is likely to be highly concentrated geographically, particularly in densely populated urban areas. But intangible assets can also be increasingly shared using ICT that keeps the costs of information low and creates the platforms for massive networks of people and ideas. It is for this reason that the urban/rural wage gap for educated workers is growing, but it has disappeared for those without a college education.[35] It appears that less-educated workers don't get the same boost from moving to urban areas, likely because they cannot take the same advantage of intangible assets and idea networks.

Understanding these four properties of intangible assets—fixed costs, scalability, positive spillovers, and synergies—are crucial to understanding their complex implications. One important implication of intangible capital is also true for the production of ideas in general: there is an inherent tension between the public and the private nature of intangible assets. The creation and protection of intellectual property rights increases the private value of intangible assets and encourages research and development to create more intangible assets. However, intellectual property laws also limit synergies, reducing the positive spillovers and the value to society of intangible assets.

Intangible capital is also complex because determining the ownership of intangible capital, even with extensive intellectual property rights law, is always going to be difficult because of its innate synergies and spillovers. Who creates intangible capital, and who owns it, is usually unclear because many different people are making related intangible capital across many networks at the same time. As a result, companies that rely heavily on intangible capital are likely to be highly litigious. Just ask Apple and Samsung, who are constantly suing each other for patent infringement in the making of quite similar products that—while neither company can admit it—rely in large part upon the innovations of the other company.

Finally, intangible capital is complex because it has highly uncertain future benefits but large and immediate fixed costs. As a result, it is very hard to value, and investing in intangible capital is risky with huge upsides but large potential downsides. This makes intangible capital very hard to finance and, as a result, to invest in.

The connections between the rising importance of intangible capital and rising inequality are obvious. The scalability of intangible capital creates winner-takes-all markets. Many firms that rely upon intangible ideas will fail because they are risky. But those that succeed can become extremely profitable. If the ideas that they are built upon become successful, the business is quickly expandable at rates previously unimaginable. For example, Starbucks created more than 13,000 new stores in the US in the 10 years between 2007 and 2017.[36] These winner-takes-all markets are even bigger today because of globalization, and firms with large amounts of intangible capital are best positioned to take advantage of larger, global markets. A new Starbucks is opening in China every 15 hours, and 3,000 stores have opened there in less than 10 years.[37] Intangible capital also creates network effects in the sense that the more people use them, the more attractive they become. The fact that everyone knows Starbucks—that Starbucks has become part of our global cultural capital—can be leveraged to create huge profits. This leads to a very small number of coffee brands that are successful globally, and bigger gains for Starbucks as the global market leader.

When businesses win, then the workers within them win as well. This helps explain the fact about inequality I mentioned in the previous section: wage variation between people with similar jobs in different firms has played an important role in rising income inequality. If you work at a winning firm, all wages in that firm are driven higher. This is because actual productivity is higher in more profitable firms. But it also reflects the social nature of wage setting, where firms worry a great deal about relative wages and perceptions of fairness, even across workers who do different jobs in a company. Roughly 80 percent of the increase in earnings variability for all workers from 1997–2007 came from differences in the wages of similar jobs across firms, not differences in wages across different jobs within the same firm.[38] In other words, it matters as much *who* you work for as *what* you do. Because wages within firms tend to be relatively equal, in winner-takes-all markets workers take some of the winnings (or losses) of the company they work for, creating more overall inequality.

Intangible assets also contribute to inequality because intangible assets are more likely to be created and operated by those individuals who are already wealthy, in regions that are wealthy, and by countries that are wealthy. In other words, intangible assets contribute to the virtuous and vicious circles that generate inequality. In general, people who are richer also have more human capital, access to larger networks, and more intangible assets. Urban areas with a higher concentration of educated people and larger idea networks are also more likely to benefit from an increasingly intangible economy. The same holds for countries as well, particularly those that are open and integrated into international global markets. Where these things do not exist, the rising importance of intangible capital creates another pitfall for a poverty trap.

Intangible assets also increase inequality by driving up housing prices. Geography matters when it comes to scalability and synergies, and housing is an asset with a set location and fixed supply. The uneven growth in residential housing wealth has been a significant factor in growing wealth inequality in the US and many other countries. The fastest housing wealth accumulation in the US and UK has been in urban areas, particularly where there is an intangible-intensive economic base such as London, Silicon Valley, Southern California, and New York. These are also regions with the fastest-growing wealth inequality.[39]

The last way that the rising importance of intangible capital contributes to inequality is that it is very difficult to tax and, as a result, it is very difficult for governments to redistribute the profits from intangible capital. Because intangible capital is easily transferable, because it is everywhere and nowhere, and because it is very difficult to accurately measure, tax evasion is common. In practice, intangible assets are often taxed at assessed values that are much less than their true value, and the profits from intangible capital are easily moved to low-tax regions or countries. As a result, the poor—who primarily rely on labor that is easily taxed—often pay higher effective tax rates than those who earn most of their income from intangible assets.

Reason #3: Globalization.

International trade is a way of turning what you have into what you want, and what you are good at producing for what you are not as good at producing. Trade is a technology—it's a process for converting corn into running shoes, and aircraft engines into cars. In fact, it is hard to separate the impacts of technological change from the impacts of globalization—consider them complementary. Increasingly, technological change encourages globalization, and globalization encourages technical change. As a result, increasing trade can increase inequality in the same way that skills-based technological change can. In other words, the race between education and technology has gone global.

Economists traditionally have thought about the costs and benefits of trade within the context of David Ricardo's theory of comparative advantage.

According to Ricardo, countries can increase the productivity of their labor force by specializing in the products that they are most productive in making. Every country has certain natural advantages, technological advantages, or just large populations with low wages. As a result, they can specialize in producing goods that make the most of these advantages, and then trade for other goods that they are less productive at making.

International trade not only allows countries to take advantage of comparative advantage, it allows them to take advantage of technology transfer through leaks and matches, it allows them to attract foreign capital investment (both tangible and intangible), and it allows countries to take advantage of scalability by gaining access to larger global markets. As a result, international trade is a key channel through which labor productivity, employment, and standards of living increase over time. The aggregate benefits of international trade are clear from the data. To highlight just one result, countries that were always open to international trade between 1965 and 2000 have an average per capita GDP of roughly $23,000; those that were always closed during this time only $5,000.[40] This relationship between openness to international trade and higher income is one of the strongest empirical regularities that explain why some countries are rich and others are poorer.

In rich countries, a simple application of comparative advantage would suggest that international trade should increase the demand for human capital-intensive goods with higher wages (these are the goods that rich countries are better at producing), but decrease the demand for less-skilled work at lower wages (which rich countries are relatively worse at producing). As a result, international trade will also increase income inequality in richer countries. While international trade is good in the aggregate—it allows us to trade higher-paying jobs for lower-paying jobs, and increases aggregate productivity—it also creates winners and losers. The data indicates that most of the increases in productivity and wages in the US have been in human capital-intensive industries.[41] These high-skilled workers already had relatively high wages, while the less-skilled, poorer, and more vulnerable workers have seen their productivity and wages remain stagnant.

The same effect happens within poor countries as well. While poorer countries are more likely to specialize in less-skilled work, it is the most skilled workers within less-developed countries that have the most to gain because their skills are relatively scarce. In addition, international trade is strongly correlated with faster growth, and growth is most likely to benefit higher-skilled workers, particularly in the early stages of industrialization. As a result, international trade tends to increase inequality within both rich and poor countries. According to one study, greater international trade contributed to greater within-country inequality across a sample of 80 countries.[42]

International trade has often been blamed for the relative decline in manufacturing in developed countries. The rich G7 countries saw their share of global manufacturing fall from roughly 70 percent in 1970 to less than 50 percent in 2010, while the share of global manufacturing of the six fastest-growing emerging market economies went from 2 percent to 25 percent. The rest of the world saw its share of global manufacturing remain unchanged—Latin America and Africa were bypassed in this transfer of manufacturing—so that essentially all of the movement in global manufacturing went from the seven richest to the six fastest-growing emerging market economies. This has contributed to a fall in global inequality (as we will discuss in the next chapter), but it has also contributed to a rise in within-country inequality.[43] In the US, its share of global manufacturing has fallen at the same time that the number of jobs in manufacturing has tumbled. But, somewhat surprisingly, the level of manufacturing output in the US has actually risen. This means that manufacturing productivity is higher, which generates faster growth and higher wages—for those who still have jobs. Once again, the gains from international trade are not shared by all.

However, Ricardo's theory of comparative advantage does not explain the full impact of globalization on inequality today as well as it has done in the past. That is because ICT has changed the nature of globalization. In the past, countries specialized in goods based on their comparative advantages, and knowledge and labor was tied to specific locations—it was localized. Today, the cost of moving physical goods has fallen because of cheaper transportation through the use of technologies such as cargo container shipping. The costs of moving knowledge have become cheaper because of ICT. And the costs of moving people (virtually) have fallen because of increased virtual immigration (telepresence) and remote-controlled presence (telebotics). All of these forms of lower transportation costs have led to what Richard Baldwin calls "the great unbundling": location matters less than ever before. Location matters less for physical production, it matters less for knowledge, and it matters less for people.[44]

The result is that comparative advantage has become denationalized and now production is increasingly organized by multinational firms using global supply chains. These global supply chains allow for increased specialization at the "task" level, not the product level. In the old days, capital, people, and knowledge were centralized and products were made where these things were. Today, production has become unbundled and broken into more and more tasks, each completed where the proper specialized knowledge, physical capital, human capital, and intangible capital are located to most efficiently complete each stage of production. Or sometimes, the knowledge, capital, and human capital can even be moved virtually to where the product is. Regardless, the flexibility and complexity of modern global supply chains demands a much higher level of coordination in production than was possible before dramatic improvements in transportation and ICT.

What does this new era of global supply chains mean for the future of within-country inequality? On this question—as in most questions in economics—making definitive predictions is dangerous. The impacts of this new globalization are much messier than when trade could be thought of in terms of simple national comparative advantage across final products. Today, competition is taking place across different stages of production, not across industries or between countries. As a result, firms are increasingly thinking about what and where to complete each task most efficiently. Multinational firms have truly become multinational—decisions that will impact their profitability will be less and less correlated with what benefits their "home" country, because they essentially have no home anymore.

This said, overall, it appears that the biggest winners in the age of global supply chains have been, and will continue to be, the highly skilled and creative workers in rich countries and the low-skilled workers in poorer countries. It has been the medium-skilled workers in rich countries that have lost the most in the era of global supply chains because they had relatively high wages that were not competitive on global markets. This is exactly the pattern of income growth across the globe that was observed in the "elephant curve" in Figure 2.6. Overall, the elephant curve points towards decreasing global inequality. But at a national level in developed countries, it points to a reality that, once again, it is highly skilled workers that benefit the most from globalization, while less-skilled workers are the most likely losers. To the extent that global supply chains drive future advances in productivity and higher aggregate incomes, inequality in skills between people will be amplified into even more within-country inequality and greater disparity in incomes between the workers inside and outside of these networks.

Reason #4: The economics of superstars.

So when you take the first three reasons for rising inequality that we have talked about—technological change, intangible capital, and globalization—and put them all together, you get the possibility of winner-takes-all markets in the extreme: the economics of superstars.[45] This is not an explanation for changes in the overall distribution of income, but for what is happening at the top 0.1 percent and top 0.01 percent of the distribution. The fact is that ICT, globalization, and the scalability of intangible capital have created much larger markets than were ever possible before. And it is the size of the market that determines the wages of the top performers in these markets—individuals with unique attributes who can perform jobs where even small differences in skill level can lead to large differences in outcomes. Examples of winner-takes-all markets that reward superstars in the extreme include entertainment, sports, technology, law, and finance. These industries have outcomes similar to those of a footrace: only one gold medal is awarded and, as a result, even a small difference in ability makes all the difference in the outcome. For the people that have the distinctive skills to sell movies globally, draw viewers to games, design unique financial products, win important legal cases, or develop social networking applications, the possibility of turning a small advantage in ability into a huge fortune has never been more possible.

The superstars in these areas have one thing in common: they produce valuable intangible capital. As a result, their creations are increasingly scalable due to ICT and globalization, and their output can be used and sold over and over again. From an artistic viewpoint, I do not think that Tom Cruise is worth $30 million per movie. But from an economic perspective, Tom Cruise movies sell in China, his movies sell on Amazon, they can be streamed profitably on Netflix, and his movies can be cross-branded with everything from McDonald's to Apple products—all options that never existed for Humphrey Bogart. The number of people that can create such creative intangible capital is small, and those who are able to do it are able to earn more and more—and justifiably, from a market perspective.

Economic superstars are also born because of the nature of the networks created by ICT, globalization, and intangible capital. When networking effects are important, a small number of firms will get a disproportionate share of the entire market because "platform effects" dominate. By platform effects, I mean that there are positive spillovers associated with more people using a shared network (more leaks and matches), so that a little success breeds more success because more people create a more useful product. For example, a large part of what makes Facebook so popular is that everyone else uses it and is familiar with using it. The benefits of networks and the platforms that they use tend to be distributed via what is called the *power law*: the top social media platform accounts for the same share of the users in the top 10 as these top 10 platforms do in the top 100 platforms, as do the top 100 account for the same share in the top 1,000 platforms, and so on.[46] A bell curve no longer accurately captures the top of the distribution, where extreme inequality exists. This power law does not just hold in social media, but in book sales, movie sales, and even sports salaries. In baseball, the average salary is three times the median salary, meaning that baseball salaries are the opposite of the well-known Lake Woebegone effect, because relatively few players are paid above average.[47] But most importantly, the power law seems to capture what is happening in the top 10 percent of the aggregate income distribution in countries like the US: salaries of the top 1 percent are ten times those of the remaining 9 percent in the top decile, despite the fact that there are no observable differences in education and experience between these groups.[48] Most of the people who comprise this top 1 percent have not come from inherited wealth, but have earned their income across a wide variety of occupations that are education-intensive and in scalable industries such as finance, mass retail, entertainment, and particularly ICT.[49]

The superstar effect also plays a large role in skyrocketing CEO pay—a large proportion of the people in the top 0.01 percent are high-level executives—and small differences in perceived quality between different potential CEOs can be used to justify huge compensation packages. CEOs have what is called "decision leverage": at the top ranks of any organization, the consequences of a decision maker's actions become more important to the firm's profits.[50] As a result, even a small perceived difference between the top contenders for any CEO position can lead to dramatically higher compensation offers for the first choice than for the second best candidate, even when the actual difference in ability is very small. Likewise, performance pay incentives such as bonuses and stock options are common at the highest executive levels. These performance pay incentives are actually cheaper from a tax perspective for firms to pay than salaries, creating leverage for further increases in CEO pay.[51] Performance bonuses also create incentives for CEOs to focus on short-term gains and encourage excessive risk-taking, neither of which are good for the long-run performance of the companies they lead.[52] The salaries of the CEOs of technology companies are also likely to reflect the platform effects discussed above. Data suggest that the ICT intensity of a company is a strong predictor of CEO compensation and explains differences in CEO compensation across industries.[53] Finally, bigger companies tend to do better in superstar markets, and CEOs get rewarded for this. The 600 percent increase in market value of the largest corporations between 1980 and 2003 was matched by a 600 percent increase in CEO pay over the same period.[54]

Another factor driving superstar economics is our psychology. If I asked you to name your favorite musicians, you would probably be able to readily name only six or seven acts. Most people have a limited ability to process and remember large amounts of information, and the number of examples they can readily call up at a moment's notice typically is six or seven.[55] What this implies is that a relatively small number of names (or brand names) will dominate many industries and earn disproportionate rewards, even when they are only marginally better—or no better—than everyone else. Because of the elite power of superstar brand names, superstars often serve as social status symbols: brand names impress our family and friends and are an important part of Veblen's conspicuous consumption.

Reason #5: A vicious circle between the power of elites and inequality.

As we discussed in Chapter 4, democracies are vulnerable when power is unequally distributed across society and when elites can use their outsized influence to seek rents in ways that benefit them now and ensure that their power persists into the future. Plutocracy, populism, polarization, and cynicism are the potential consequences of concentrating economic and political power in too few hands.

What is the evidence that there is a vicious cycle between economic inequality and political inequality? First, as we discussed in the previous chapter, the rich are playing a larger and more influential role in the political process. Voter participation is closely correlated with income: the richer you are, the more likely you are to vote. Campaign contributions have also become more correlated with income over time, particularly among the wealthiest voters. The top 0.01 percent in the US contributed 40 percent of campaign funding in 2012.[56]

Second, polarization and political dysfunction are increasing as inequality increases. Measures of political polarization in Congress have closely tracked trends in income inequality, and both have been growing rapidly since the 1980s. In fact, it appears that polarization is a leading indicator of income inequality, and not the other way around.[57] This suggests that elites are able to exploit political dysfunction to gain rents, and that these rents play an important role in growing economic inequality. In other words, it appears that it is changes in government policy that are driving inequality, not vice versa.

Third, as inequality has increased, public policy has focused less on income redistribution and poverty alleviation. There is ample evidence that this is happening in the US, and also across many developed democracies. According to the US Congressional Budget Office: "The equalizing effect of transfers and taxes on household income was smaller in 2007 than it had been in 1979."[58] While the overall levels of transfer and taxes have remained approximately steady, government taxes are less progressive and government transfers are more equally distributed across everyone so that less actual redistribution of income and wealth is occurring.[59] In fact, most countries are seeing proportional rises in both their market income and disposable income Gini coefficients, suggesting that tax and transfer programs are not large enough to offset the economic factors that are driving market income inequality higher.[60]

The changing nature of government redistribution can be seen most clearly when looking at the decline in the top marginal tax rates across countries. During World War II, top marginal tax rates reached peaks of more than 90 percent across most industrialized countries. Maximum tax rates at this level almost certainly were on the right side of the Laffer curve and might have reduced growth and efficiency. However, top income rates have fallen since then in all but two of 18 OECD countries. For example, the top marginal tax rate in the US fell from 80 percent in 1970 to 39.6 percent today, while the capital gains tax also declined from 35 percent to 15 percent (remember that the top 10 percent get 90 percent of the capital gains). As a result, in the US, the *average* income tax rate for the top 0.1 percent has fallen from 42 percent to only 27 percent![61] Figure 5.3 shows the average tax rate for the entire population, the top 1 percent, and the bottom 50 percent in the US between 1914 and 2014. Clearly, these average tax rates have gotten much closer together, meaning the tax code has become less progressive. And for the wealthiest Americans, the current tax code even becomes regressive. In 2007, the average tax rate on the wealthiest 400 wealthiest Americans was only 16.6 percent, which is less than the average tax rate on all Americans of 20.4 percent.[62] Similar declines in top marginal tax rates have occurred in the UK, Canada, and Japan, while little change has occurred in Denmark, Germany, Spain, and Switzerland. Those countries with the largest declines in the top tax rates have seen the biggest income gains among their top 1 percent.[63]

Source: Piketty et al. (2018), data available at http://gabriel-zucman.eu/uswealth/.

Figure 5.3   *Average tax rate in US by pre-tax income group*

Taxes on inheritance and estates, meaning taxes on transferring wealth inequality across generations, have also fallen. According to Adam Smith, the "power to dispose of estates forever is manifestly absurd". But it has become increasingly less absurd to policymakers. In the US in 2013, only 3,800 estates paid taxes—1 out of every 700 people who died, or 0.14 percent of all estates.

(In 1976, it was 139,115 estates, or 7.6 percent of all estates, that paid estate taxes.) In 2013, the top estate tax rate was nominally 40 percent in the US, but because of exemptions, the average estate tax for the small number who had to pay it was only 17 percent.[64] Across other countries there is a great deal of variability in estate tax rates, from 55 percent in Japan and 38 percent in Europe, to only 4 percent in Brazil and zero in China, Australia, Russia, Canada, South Africa, Norway, and India.[65] Among OECD countries, the proportion of government revenue created by inheritance taxes has fallen by more than half since the 1960s to less than 0.5 percent of total revenue.[66]

The impact of lower tax rates on the rich is magnified by an additional factor: increasing tax avoidance. Because of the mobility of intangible and financial capital, wealth and profits are increasingly offshored in tax havens. OECD countries lose $240 billion annually (between 4 and 10 percent of global tax revenues) to tax havens.[67] In the US, roughly 20 percent of all corporate profits of US corporations are recorded in tax havens, which has reduced the effective corporate tax rate by about one-third.[68] And new tax havens are being developed all the time. For example, only 0.7 percent of Bitcoin investors are paying taxes on their investments, despite the fact that 7 percent of Americans own cryptocurrency.[69]

Fourth, the increasing influence of elites is also changing labor and industrial policy in the US, creating more inequality. In regards to labor, regulation has become increasingly unfriendly to collective bargaining. Setting aside the impact that unions have on efficiency—a matter of intense debate among economists—there is considerable evidence that less collective bargaining leads to higher levels of inequality by reducing the wages of middle- and lower-class workers. Unionization rates have fallen in every OECD country except Spain since 1980. In the US, unionization rates of males fell from 34 to 6 percent of the labor force, and from 16 to 6 percent for women, between 1973 and 2007.[70]

Unionization has fallen for many reasons, not all of them related to government policy. One reason is the decline in manufacturing and the rise of employment in the service sector, where jobs are more heterogeneous, wages are more variable, and workers are harder to unionize. The increase in skill-intensive employment has also reduced unionization because of the heterogeneous nature of these jobs with more variable wages. Subcontracting and outsourcing have also undermined union jobs by moving workers to subordinate businesses that operate in highly competitive markets with lower wages and fewer worker protections. In addition, by outsourcing and subcontracting jobs, firms are able to move workers outside of the firm, where the boundaries of workplace norms of fairness change. When fairness becomes less of an issue, wages are inevitably pushed downward.[71] In fact, some observers have argued that the decline of unionization and the rise of outsourcing have begun to fundamentally change our social norms regarding fairness, and that society is increasingly willing to accept CEO wages that are 50 times that of the average worker as "fair", but union wages that pay more than non-union wages as "unfair".[72] Finally, it is also clear that government policy has played a role through the passage of "right to work" laws that prohibit unions from requiring all workers at a firm to pay union membership fees.

Looking across countries, there is empirical evidence that OECD countries with higher unionization rates have less inequality.[73] Lower unionization is associated with higher incomes for the top 10 percent, and is responsible for between 15 and 30 percent of the rise in male income inequality across countries (the US is at the high end of this range).[74] In turn, higher inequality and lower rates of unionization impact workers' quality of life in many other ways. For instance, the fact that US workers work three-to-four more weeks a year than their German counterparts each year can be explained by differences in unionization and inequality between the countries, as workers in the US have to work harder and longer to keep from falling down a much steeper domestic income ladder.[75]

In regards to industrial policy, in theory government regulation should aim to protect workers' safety, while antitrust regulation and competition policies should aim to protect consumer welfare and market efficiency by breaking up monopolies and minimizing rent-seeking behavior. In practice, however, government regulation has become less about limiting the power of elites and more a tool for elites to leverage their power. There is considerable evidence that US special interest groups use their political power through organized lobbying (in the face of unorganized and uninformed consumers) to change regulations, manipulate accounting standards, and get preferential treatment in the evaluation of mergers and acquisitions.[76] One study found that money spent on lobbying politicians and regulatory agencies has a stronger impact on stock market valuations than spending on research and development.[77]

Reason #6: Assortative mating.

One of the biggest secrets about inequality is that it is largely voluntary, in the sense that we as a society are increasingly self-selecting for inequality in terms of whom we marry, whom we choose to have children with, and the strategies we use to raise these children. In other words, it appears that we are making family choices that not only increase household inequality now, but also create the conditions for perpetuating inequality far into the future.

As we discussed in Chapter 1, economists typically define income in terms of household income. As a result, the number of adults in the household, the number of adults earning a wage in the household, and the overall size of the family will be important factors in the overall level of inequality between different households. Since the 1950s, most people know that there have been a growing number of dual-income households as women have entered the workforce in larger numbers. But less well known is the fact that there has also been an increasing correlation between the incomes of married couples. Prior to the late 1970s, rich husbands were more likely to marry lower-earning wives, and vice versa, as many households tended to be more traditional, with the women working at home. The boom in women entering the labor force initially reduced household income inequality because it was women from the poorest households that went to work first. Beginning in the 1970s, as the number of college-educated women skyrocketed, the correlation between the earnings of men and women entering a marriage became positive and has increased over time, with higher-earning husbands tending to marry higher-earning wives.[78]

These same phenomena are not just true for income, but for wealth as well. Today, the correlation of the wealth between two people getting married is .4, which is similar to the intergenerational correlation of wealth between parents and children. In other words, people tend to marry and raise children in the same wealth class they were raised in. To put this in perspective, this correlation in wealth between the partners in a marriage is marginally smaller than the correlation between the heights of parents and their children of .5.[79]

One root cause of this higher correlation in income between the two partners in a marriage is the fact that the educational attainment of partners has also become more closely related than ever before. To understand how big this change has been, consider that in 1960, only 3 percent of marriages had two college graduates. By 2012, 22 percent of marriages had two college graduates. In fact, for the first time, the number of marriages where the wife has more education than the husband is larger than the number of marriages the other way around.[80] The convergence of income and education levels of the individual partners in a marriage has contributed to growing household income inequality.[81] According to one empirical study, between 10 and 15 percent of the rise in overall household inequality can be attributed to the increased correlation of the education levels of partners in a marriage alone.[82]

What about those men and women who have not attended college? Increasingly, less-educated women are not getting married at all and become the head of single, poorer households. Less-educated men, on the other hand, find themselves with fewer responsibilities and contribute less to household income and the raising of their children. Back in 1950, about 80 percent of female high school graduates aged 30–44 were married, while only 70 percent of college graduates were married. By 2010, women's marriage rates had fallen across the board, but the educational gap had reversed: 69 percent of college graduate women were married, but only 56 percent of those with a high school degree were married (these numbers are similar for males). Marriages in which one partner does not have a college education also have much higher divorce rates.[83]

Changes in assortative mating are also having profound impacts on the ways that children are raised, not only by changing current levels of inequality, but future intergenerational mobility as well. The children from households led by non-college-educated parents are much more vulnerable to poverty in part because they have lower incomes, but also because they are more likely to be raised in single-parent households. A woman without a college degree is roughly five times more likely than a college graduate to be a cohabiting or an unpartnered mother. Also, mothers that do not have a college degree spend a lot more time working, and, as a result, mothers with children under the age 13 spend 30 minutes less per day in primary childcare than mothers with college degrees. On the other hand, marriage among college graduates supports intensive cooperative time investments in their children by both parents.

College-educated parents also engage with their children in more developmentally appropriate ways that help them in school. For example, high-income, high-educated parents talk with their children three more hours a week than low-income, lower-educated parents.[84] In other words, there are "diverging destinies" between children raised by married, college-educated parents with intensive, developmental styles of parenting, and those children who are not.[85] Variations in parenting styles explain 40 percent of the income-related differences in cognitive abilities of 3- to 5-year-old pre-school children.[86] As the philosopher Adam Swift put it, "What one's parents are like is entirely a matter of luck. What one's children are like is not."[87]

The diverging destinies between children are particularly stark along racial lines in the US. Half of all African American children are raised by unmarried mothers (this is true for only 20 percent of white children), and African American students are twice as likely as white students to fail to complete high school on time.[88]

The failure to maximize the potential of every child is, in the words of Nobel Prize winning economist and education expert James Heckman, "the biggest market failure of them all".[89] In the "normal" workings of markets, under-utilized resources become more valuable when they are invested in. What prevents us from undertaking these same investments in disadvantaged children? It's the simple fact that human capital is not physical capital—children can't be traded to someone who will use them more efficiently by investing in them more (and, of course, they shouldn't be). According to another Nobel Prize winner, Gary Becker, "The answers to these and related questions lie partly in the breakdown of the American family, and the resulting low skill levels acquired by many children in elementary and secondary school—particularly individuals from broken households."[90] In other words, there is a feedback loop between skill-based technological change and skill-based social change. The higher demand for more educated workers, and the relative decline in the demand for less-skilled workers, has also changed what people look for in a marriage and how they parent their children. Educated people put a premium on finding educated partners and raising educated children who will be successful in the world they are familiar with. Those families from less-skilled backgrounds place less of a premium on these things for the same reasons: because we all value what is known and familiar. As a result, families are re-sorting and reorganizing themselves as the result of skills-based technological change. The inevitable outcome is assortative inequality, which, while in the broadest sense is voluntary, has profound ramifications for future economic inequality and also efficiency.

Reason #7: Patrimonial capital.

Finally, we come to Thomas Piketty's "patrimonial capital" theory of why inequality is growing. Piketty's basic insight is well expressed in the well-worn adage that it's easier to make money when you have money. Piketty's model of why this is the case relies upon two basic facts. The first fact is that physical capital and financial wealth are more unevenly distributed than human capital and labor income. For example, in the US between 1970 and 2012, the wealth of the top 1 percent doubled, the top 0.01 percent tripled, and the top 0.01 percent quadrupled. Simultaneously, the share of total capital income going only to the top 1 percent went from one-third to two-thirds.[91] In terms of financial wealth specifically, the top 1 percent claims three-quarters of all dividends and taxable interest. The interest earned by the top 1 percent of households went from 2.1 percent of all interest income in 1970 to 27.3 percent of the total in 2012. By 2007, 38 percent of all stocks in the US were owned by wealthiest top 1 percent and 81 percent by the top 10 percent, while the poorest 50 percent owned almost zero (the same distribution holds for bond wealth).[92]

The second part of Piketty's theory is that the returns to physical capital and financial wealth (r) are higher than the overall rate of economic growth (g). If r>g, then the income from wealth (the primary income source of the rich) is compounding at a faster rate than the income from labor (the primary income source for the poor).[93] This creates an upward trend towards growing inequality in the levels of wealth that persists until some intervening factor—political shocks that change the nature of public policy, or one of Scheidel's "big four levelers"—interrupts this process. Of course, any small changes to the rates r or g that are sustained over time will have huge impacts on the level of wealth because of the compounding effect of wealth accumulation. A 1 percent difference between r and g that is sustained for 70 years will lead to a doubling in the difference between the levels of wealth accumulated through capital income and the wealth accumulated through labor income. A 2 percent difference will lead to a doubling of the difference in only 35 years.[94]

Does the return to capital (r) exceed overall economic growth (g) over the very long run? This is a complicated empirical question because even if the historical data was available and reliable (it is often not), it is hard to account for differences in taxes, inheritance laws, consumption (that reduces savings), government expropriation, inflation, changes in income definitions, who marries who, and the fact that many estates are broken up between children as the population grows (if the rich have more children than the poor, this could reduce wealth inequality over time). Piketty (and others) argue that the evidence suggests that r is greater than g. In their view, the best evidence that r is greater than g can be found in the rising share of total income that goes to capital (which he refers to as α). α has increased in 42 out of 59 countries between 1975 and 2012 by an average of 5 percent a year.[95] In the US, α rose from .35 to .4 between 1980 and 2013.[96] Piketty argues that this is due to the rise in intangible capital, globalization that favors capital over labor, labor-saving technological change (i.e. robots), lower unionization, higher rents, and the decline in progressive taxation of wealth—all the things that we have discussed in this chapter. Second, Piketty believes that there is evidence that growth in developed countries has slowed, reducing g and making it even more likely that r>g.

It is also possible that r is higher than g only for the wealthiest, who are able to earn higher than market returns—economic rents—on their capital because of the privileges their wealth creates. Many holders of capital are what have traditionally been called "rentiers"—they hold unique and privileged capital and rent it at rates that earn them a higher-than-average market return. Rentier capital is often "context sensitive", as discussed by Robert Frank in the previous chapter, whose fixed supply and privileged position bid up its value over time. Prime urban real estate is a classic example of rentier capital—for those who own this real estate, ownership alone is sufficient to guarantee an elite income. Because of the growing wage premiums in urban areas—which has increased the value of living in major metropolitan cities—owning well-placed urban real estate has increasingly generated huge returns for its owners (supported by a host of new "not in my back yard" regulations aimed at making it harder to build new housing). Since the 1980s, the premium for location in real estate has increased dramatically. For example, between 1975 and 2016, the value of real estate in Washington, DC increased by 78 times, while housing prices in Alaska remained unchanged. As a result, residential wealth has increased by 75 percent since the mid-1970s, but only a relatively small group of people that own urban real estate have received the vast majority of these gains.

For these reasons, according to one estimate, the richest 10 percent earn roughly 30 percent returns a year on their wealth, while the poorest 10 percent earn returns of approximately zero.[97] This also explains why some families have wealth that is more vulnerable to shocks than other families. In the aftermath of the Global Financial Crisis of 2007, the wealth gap between white and black households rose significantly. More than three-fourths of the increase in this wealth gap could be explained by the fact that black families have a much larger percentage of their wealth tied up in their homes, which suffered disproportionately when housing prices collapsed.[98] On the other hand, white families have more of their wealth in financial assets such as stocks and bonds which, while they initially suffered losses, rebounded much more quickly and strongly after the crisis passed.

Of course, r and g are such broad concepts that it is an ongoing debate as to whether r is actually greater than g over long periods of time. Others argue that it is not at all clear that r has risen because it is not clear that the share of total income going to capital, α, has really risen. There is evidence that the estimated rise in α is only due to changes in real estate prices, not a broad increase in the returns to capital more generally.[99] As a result, the rise in capital has been highly variable and tied to booms in local real estate markets. In other words, r>g plays less of a role than location.

The two most comprehensive studies of this question of whether r is greater than g suggest, however, that it is, but conditionally. One study by the US Federal Reserve, aiming to look at "the rates of return to everything", finds that between 1870 and 2015 in 16 developed countries, the rate of return on capital was equal to 6 percent while growth only averaged 3 percent. In fact, r fell below g only during the Great Compression period.[100] Likewise, Edward Wolff focuses on 150 years of US wealth data and concludes that while there is not convincing evidence that r>g broadly, it does appear that the rates of return that the rich get on their capital are greater than the rates of return that the middle-class and poor get on their capital. This means that it is more true that r (rich)>g, which would still lead to rising inequality, particularly at the upper reaches of the income distribution, which is exactly what we are observing in many countries.[101] The rich earn a higher return on their wealth primarily because, as we just discussed, the rich have more of their wealth tied up in high-end real estate and financial assets such as stocks, which have had the highest rates of compounded return over the long run.

There is an important limitation to Piketty's patrimonial capital theory, however. While the compounding of capital does appear to play a role in growing wealth and income inequality, it cannot be the only factor driving income inequality. Increasingly, those who earn high levels of capital income also earn a great deal of labor income. In 1980, of the top 1 percent in capital income, only 17 percent were also in the top 1 percent of labor income. By

2000, 27 percent of the top 1 percent in capital income were also in the top 1 percent in labor income. Today, the probability of being in both the top 1 percent of labor income and the top 1 percent of capital income is now over 50 percent in the US.[102]

In other words, this is not the old days when only the poor worked and the rich were a leisured class that earned income as rentiers. The rich of today may earn higher returns from their wealth, which contributes to income inequality. But today's rich also are highly educated and work long hours for which they are paid well because they have invested in skills that are highly prized in today's education-intensive, intangible capital-reliant, and globalized markets. In a real sense, the rich today are more "meritocratic" than they have been in the past, although this also illustrates the myth of meritocracy. The rich are highly productive, but they are highly productive because they have had the highest endowments of wealth, access to the best educational opportunities, and have the most productive social networks.

IN CONCLUSION

There is no simple answer as to why within-country inequality is rising. The causes of inequality are synergetic and complicated. But at the highest level, inequality is changing because our economics are evolving, societal norms are changing as a result, and our civic interactions and values are responding accordingly. The powerful economic consequences of skills-based technological change, globalization, ideas-intensive intangible capital, and the power of compounded wealth have changed who we are as a society, creating superstar winners, an increasingly affluent and educated upper-class, and a large group of "others" that see themselves as undifferentiated labor in a less rewarding world that is much different than the world they grew up in. We have become increasingly specialized, particularly along educational lines—education is the new basis of class distinctions between people. This has changed our society because it has led to changes in our families: it changes who we marry, where we want to live, who we network with, our parenting styles, and our political beliefs. Assortative mating is leading to assortative child-rearing, assertive socialization, assortative networking, and assortative inequality. The polarization of our politics, coupled with the increasing concentration of wealth and political power, has led to changes in our public policies that are doing less to address the growing inequalities in market income and accumulated wealth, and in many ways now serve to magnify these inequalities.

In Chapter 7 we will turn to the question of what can be done to offset this growing trend in within-country inequality. But after reading this chapter, I believe that you will agree that the origins of inequality are complex, that they involve complicated economic phenomena and even more complicated societal and political trends, and that the origins of economic inequality are rooted in many voluntary personal decisions that are not simply the result of impersonal market interactions. Given all of this complexity, there can be no simple answer to how we address the growing phenomena of economic inequality within countries.

NOTES

1. Rousseau (1775 [1985]).
2. Kohler et al. (2017).
3. Scheidel (2017).
4. Ibid.
5. Kuznets (1955).
6. Deininger and Squire (1998).
7. Tinbergen (1974).
8. Dupont and Rosenbloom (2016).
9. Gonzalez et al. (2017).
10. Derenoncourt (2016).
11. Piketty (2014).
12. Kopczuk (2015).
13. Gleik (2011).
14. Psacharopoulos and Patrinos (2018).
15. Krueger (1999).
16. Acemoglu and Autor (2011).
17. Brynjolfsson and McAffee (2014).
18. Autor (2014).
19. Bussolo et al. (2018).
20. Goldrick-Rab (2016).
21. Ibid.
22. Kena et al. (2015).
23. Conti and Heckman (2012).
24. National Center for Education Statistics (2018).
25. Reardon (2011).
26. Hoxby and Avery (2013).
27. Stiglitz (2012).
28. Rycroft (2009, p. 345).
29. Acemoglu and Restrepo (2016).
30. Manyika et al. (2017) and Brynjolfsson et al. (2018).
31. Schmitt et al. (2013).
32. Coyle (1998).
33. Corrado and Hulten (2010).
34. Haskel and Westlake (2017).
35. Autor (2019).
36. Statista (2018).
37. LaVito (2017).
38. Barth et al. (2016).
39. Bonnet et al. (2014).
40. Wacziarg and Welch (2008).

41. Tyson and Spence (2017).
42. Bourguignon (2015).
43. Baldwin (2016).
44. Ibid.
45. This phrase was first used by Rosen (1981).
46. Jones (2015).
47. Brynjolfsson and McAffee (2014).
48. Ibid.
49. Kaplan and Rauh (2013).
50. Frank and Cook (1995).
51. A 1993 US tax law limited to $1 million the deductibility of executive compensation unless it is performance-based.
52. Lemieux et al. (2009).
53. Brynjolfsson et al. (2013).
54. Brynjolfsson and McAffee (2014).
55. Miller (1956).
56. Bonica et al. (2013).
57. Atkinson (2015).
58. Congressional Budget Office (2011).
59. Piketty (2014) and Causa and Hermansen (2017).
60. Milanovic (2016).
61. Alvaredo et al. (2013).
62. Pollack and Thiess (2011).
63. Scheidel (2017).
64. Hanlon and Steinberg (2013).
65. Piketty et al. (2018).
66. *The Economist* (2017b).
67. OECD (2016).
68. Zucman (2014).
69. *Fortune* (2018).
70. OECD (2011).
71. Weil (2017).
72. Rosenfeld (2014).
73. Checchi and Garcia-Penalosa (2008).
74. Jaumotte and Buitron (2015) and Western and Rosenfeld (2011).
75. Bell and Freeman (2001).
76. Hacker and Pierson (2010) and Atkinson (2015).
77. Bessen (2016).
78. Schwartz (2010).
79. Charles et al. (2013).
80. Wang (2014).
81. Greenwood et al. (2014).
82. Burtless (2007).
83. Lundberg et al. (2016).
84. Phillips (2011).
85. McLanahan (2004).
86. Waldfogen and Washbrook (2011).
87. Swift (2005, p. 267).
88. McLanahan and Jencks (2015) and DePaoli et al. (2015).
89. Reeves and Venator (2014).

90. Becker and Murphy (2007).
91. Alvaredo et al. (2013).
92. Wolff (2017).
93. You can think of Marxist economics in terms of it being a special case of Piketty's model, but where r>g because g=0.
94. This can be determined through the use of the "rule of 70": anything that grows at a compounded rate of x percent a year will double in levels every 70/x years.
95. Karabarbounis and Neiman (2014).
96. Elsby et al. (2013).
97. Lee (2019).
98. Wolff (2019).
99. Bonnet et al. (2014).
100. Jordà et al. (2017).
101. Wolff (2017).
102. Atkinson and Lakner (2017).

6. Why are the three most important factors in global inequality location, location, and location?

On a day-to-day basis, most of us tend to think about inequality at the local and national level. We compare ourselves to our neighbors and to our fellow citizens. Sometimes we will make the mental leap to compare the average citizen in one country to the average citizen in other countries, but this usually feels like a somewhat abstract thought experiment.

Up to this point in this book, our analysis has been primarily focused on countries. We have examined inequality at the national level, and inequality between different groups of people within countries. But in this chapter we want to look at inequality from a global perspective and examine differences in income across the entire world's population, regardless of country. We want to understand why the global income distribution is as unequal as it is, and also how and why this global income distribution has changed dramatically over the last 25 years.

However, as we examine the global distribution of income, we will see that it is almost impossible to set country and nationality aside when talking about inequality across the world. There is a familiar saying in real estate that the three most important things in the real estate business are location, location, and location. Well, the same holds when we talk about global inequality. The vast majority of inequality across people can be explained by one simple fact: which country you live in. In other words, "where" is much more important than who you are or what you do. The accident of which country you were born into is the single biggest determinant of what your lifetime income will be. When we treat the world as one population, we come back to the fact that global income is largely a function of nationality, a fact that simply cannot be dismissed.

The significance of location has important ramifications for both comprehending and addressing global poverty. The biggest insight that comes from understanding the geography of income is that the social determinants of productivity are much more important than the individual determinants of productivity. In other words, the societies we live in play a bigger role in determining our income than how hard we work or our innate skills. As a result, the data tell us that the easiest and most effective way for individuals to move towards the top of the world's income distribution is to simply move. This explains the huge incentives that most of the world's population has to migrate—an incentive not easily discouraged by borders and immigration restrictions. In this chapter, we want to understand all of this by explaining why "where" plays the biggest role in global inequality, and why inequality, poverty, and wealth are so persistent across place and time.

GLOBAL VERSUS DOMESTIC INEQUALITY ACROSS THE GLOBE

Consider the world's population as a whole, where everyone is ranked from the poorest to the richest. This distribution captures what we will call *global inequality*. Figure 6.1 presents the global income distribution (in terms of dollars per person per day) in 1800, 1975, and 2015. Figure 6.1 is the happiest figure in this entire book. In 1800, the vast majority of the population lived in extreme poverty (defined as those living on less than $1.90 a day in 2016). In 1975, much of the world lived in extreme poverty. But by 2015, the vast majority of the world now lives above the extreme poverty line. Global inequality has declined at a remarkable rate and reflects dramatic improvements in the quality of life of billions of people across the globe. The dominant factor driving these changes in the global distribution of income has been rapid economic growth in Asia, particularly in India and China. This is the result of the changes captured in the Elephant Curve in Figure 2.6. Unfortunately, almost all of the improvements in poverty have occurred in Asia, with little improvement in poverty in Africa.

To add some concrete numbers to Figure 6.1, consider that these changes in the global income distribution mean that the number of people living in extreme poverty has fallen by 1.1 billion people since 1990, at the same time that the world's population has increased by more than 2 billion people. In fact, the number of people living in extreme poverty fell from 40 percent of the global population in 1980 to 14 percent in 2008, and only 10 percent today.[1]

It is hard to fully appreciate the profound impacts that this remarkable decline in global inequality has had on the lives of billions of people across the globe. One area where the benefits of reduced poverty and higher incomes are most evident is in public health. The simple fact is that higher incomes mean longer lives. Every country in the world has seen its infant mortality rates fall since 1950, and nearly every country in the world has increased its average life-expectancy. Many countries have seen their average income rise to a point where they have made what is known as the *epidemiological transition*. In countries that have not made this transition, almost half of all deaths occur as the result of preventable infectious diseases, many of these deaths

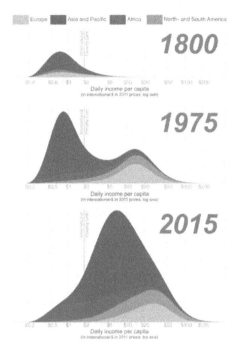

Source: Roser (2018), used with permission.

Figure 6.1   Global income distribution in 1800, 1975, and 2015

among children under 5 years of age resulting from malaria, tuberculosis, and influenza. These are the diseases that people in rich countries were dying from 200 years ago. But for those countries that have seen their income levels rise above the epidemiological transition point, most deaths are now among older people and are the result of chronic, less preventable diseases such as heart disease and cancer. This epidemiological transition point is approximately at per capita GDP levels of $10,000 a year: roughly where Egypt and Indonesia are today. Since 2000, global deaths from malaria are down 40 percent, HIV by 50 percent, pneumonia by 40 percent, diarrhea by 40 percent, and measles by 60 percent.[2]

While life-expectancy gains have been the largest in poor countries, it is still a fact that low income is closely related to poor health. Life-expectancy in sub-Saharan Africa, for example, remains 26 years below that of rich countries. More than one-fourth of all children in sub-Saharan Africa die before they reach 5 years of age; these are worse health statistics than the US had in

1900 before the changes in public health and sanitation associated with the discovery of germ theory were implemented.[3] The good news for countries below the epidemiological transition point is that dramatic improvements in health are achievable because the most common causes of illness are preventable with existing medicines, improved public health, and more vaccinations. A dollar spent on health in countries below the epidemiological transition point has a much bigger impact on public health outcomes than a dollar spent on health above this point. The bad news is that these dollars are hard to come by in poor countries. Per capita health expenditure in sub-Saharan Africa is $100 a year, compared to England and the US where they are $3,470 and $8,300 a year, respectively.[4] Such vast inequalities in global public health are the direct result of inequalities in global income.

Despite reductions in global inequality, dramatic differences remain between the incomes of people across the world's population. How do we explain these differences in income across the globe? One factor is the amount of inequality that can be attributed to what country you live in, because we see that, in general, people from Sierra Leone are poorer than people from Thailand who are poorer than people from China who are poorer than Canadians. We call this type of inequality *between-country inequality*, which is directly attributable to nationality. The remainder of global inequality can be attributed to *within-country inequality*, meaning inequality within countries such as Sierra Leone, Thailand, China, and Canada. The question is, if we can break down global inequality and separate it into these two sources, which will be more important: within-country inequality or between-country inequality?

If we measure global inequality using the Gini coefficient, we can't do this decomposition between these two sources of inequality. But as we talked about in Chapter 1, we can use Theil's statistic to measure global inequality, which allows us to break world inequality into what is caused by variation within groups and variation between different groups. If we define our groups as countries, then we can separate global inequality into that determined by who you are within a country (within-country inequality) and that determined by which country you live in (between-country inequality).

Figure 6.2 presents the decomposition of global inequality into within- and between-country inequality. The biggest takeaway is the one we already revealed in fact #6 in Chapter 2: "where" and not "who" is the biggest story in global inequality. Three-fourths of global inequality can be explained by between-country inequality and only one-fourth by within-country inequality. In other words, which country you live in matters much more than who you are and what you do within that country. Place matters three times as much as person. The accident of where you are born is the most important factor in determining your lifetime income potential.

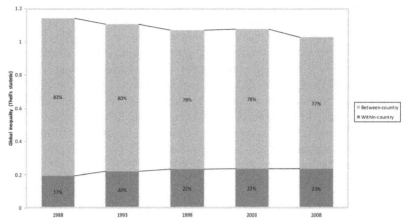

Source: Lakner and Milanovic (2013).

Figure 6.2   Global inequality decomposition

One implication of the power of location is the *citizenship premium*, which was first identified by Branko Milanovic.[5] For 118 countries in 2008, Milanovic ranked people across the globe by their household incomes (using PPP data) into 11,800 categories. Using regression techniques, he then estimated the effect of location on each group relative to living in the Congo (the poorest country in the group). His results indicate that if an average Congolese person migrated to the US, they would see their income rise by a factor of 92; migrating to Sweden would increase income by a factor of 71, to Brazil by a factor of 13, but to Yemen only by a factor of 3.[6] These premiums become even larger if you make the comparison between the poorest 10 percent in the Congo and the poorest 10 percent in the destination country, because the poor in rich countries do relatively better than the poor in poor countries.

These incredible returns to migration illustrate two important points. First, there are huge economic incentives for the poor to migrate to rich countries, because location plays such an important role in income. However, it remains a fact that 97 percent of the world's people live where they were born. As a result, the luck of birth remains the dominant factor in explaining global inequality. Second, we cannot explain the citizenship premium—and global inequality—until we understand why place matters more than who you are, your education levels, or how hard you work.

We can also see in Figure 6.2 that it is not only true that overall global inequality has declined between 1988 and 2008, but the share of between-country inequality is also falling, from 83 percent of the total to 77 percent. But this is a marginal change, and so while within-country inequality is rising in relative importance, it appears that "where" will dominate "who" in the global inequality story for a long time into the future.

WHY IS THERE SO MUCH INCOME INEQUALITY BETWEEN COUNTRIES?

You will not be surprised to learn that a variety of factors play a role in making place such an important factor in influencing global inequality. However, many of the tools that we have already learned that help us to understand within-country inequality also provide us important insights into why so much inequality exists between countries on a global scale.

Let's begin to answer this question at the beginning. When did inequality between countries, regions, and different human societies begin to exist? Historically, significant between-country inequality began with the advent of economic growth. Throughout the Middle Ages and into the seventeenth century, there was relatively little between-country inequality because the vast majority of the populations in any country were living at incomes that were only slightly above subsistence levels. In fact, until the Middle Ages, what we think of today as the developing world of Asia, the Middle East, and Northern Africa was slightly richer than Western Europe.

The industrial revolution changed everything when it comes to global inequality. While standards of living slowly increased in the non-industrialized world throughout the eighteenth century, they boomed in countries that fully participated in the industrial revolution, particularly in Western Europe and North America. In the year 1700, what today constitutes the "developed world" was about 20 percent richer than what we can call the "underdeveloped world". By the year 2000, the developed world was about 700 percent richer than the underdeveloped world.[7]

This big-picture boom in global inequality obscures the fact that there are really two underlying economic trends across the globe that have been occurring simultaneously. The first is that amongst the richest and poorest countries there is divergence between those at the very top and the very bottom. Rich countries are growing faster, and pulling away from the least developed and slowly growing countries that are primarily in sub-Saharan Africa, the Middle East, and Latin America. The ratio of per capita income in the 15 richest to 15 poorest countries in the world has risen from roughly 40 in 1990 to approximately 60 today (all 15 of the poorest countries in the world today are in sub-Saharan Africa). However, at the same time, there is also convergence of income going on between rich countries and the emerging market countries that have been poor but are catching up with the developed world: primarily China, India, and other East Asian countries.

How do we explain convergence and divergence in income occurring across the globe at the same time? These two competing trends are being driven by two competing phenomena. The first is that different countries started to grow at different points in time. Western Europe and the US started in the early 1700s and got a huge head start on the rest of the world. Japan and South Korea started in the 1950s, and China in 1979. This is the primary source of divergence across countries. As time goes on, the income gap between the countries that are growing and those that are not growing is getting larger and larger.

But at the same time, countries that are richer tend to grow slower than countries that are poorer but have begun to grow. This somewhat counterintuitive result occurs because of what economists refer to as the *law of diminishing marginal returns*. Understanding diminishing marginal returns is one of the most powerful ideas in refuting lazy economic thinking about why different countries grow at different rates. The law of diminishing marginal returns says that everything else being equal, as the amount of capital used in production increases, the productivity gains from adding more and more capital begins to fall. This concept is quite intuitive: the first tractor that a farmer buys is very productive, the second and third tractors less and less so. At some point, adding more and more capital to production, keeping the other inputs to production the same, will lead to fewer and fewer benefits in terms of increasing productivity and income. And what holds for a single farmer holds for a country as well, only at a different scale.

The crucial implication of the law of diminishing marginal returns is that while a country might be able to increase income for a period of time by adding more capital alone, it can't do it forever. Eventually, diminishing marginal returns kick in and the importance of capital in production begins to slow. While the law of diminishing marginal returns says that differences in physical capital are not the most important determinant of differences in *income levels* across countries, differences in capital investment rates can play a large role in explaining differences in *income growth rates*. This is because, according to the law, the first units of capital should be much more productive than the last units of capital within a country. In a poor country with relatively little capital, increasing capital investment will increase productivity and growth more than it will in a rich country that is already saturated with capital. This is why the fastest-growing countries in the world are also some of the poorest—they are growing because they have been able to increase their investment rates and rapidly expand upon their extremely low levels of existing capital, quickly increasing productivity and creating a growth boom. However, as these countries obtain more capital and become richer, new capital will become less productive and their income growth rates will necessarily decline.

As a result, high growth rates are not so much a sign of great economic success as they are signs of past economic failure; likewise, growing more slowly over the long term is one of the consequences of being rich, and it is a small price to pay. To the extent that differences in income reflect differences in physical capital, the law of diminishing returns says that these differences should disappear over time; in other words, there should be convergence in income. This is, in fact, what we observe among developed countries: developed countries that were the poorest 50 years ago have grown the fastest since that time, narrowing the gap between the income levels of rich countries. But when we compare rich countries to poor countries that have not started growing because they have not yet participated in the industrial revolution, we see no convergence, only divergence.

The vast dispersion of income levels and growth rates across countries can be best understood using a footrace analogy in which the runners start at different times, and when they start running they sprint out of the gate but slow down the longer they run (diminishing marginal returns). Overall, there is a great deal of dispersion amongst the runners because they started running at very different times, and the gap between the leaders and those still standing at the starting line is increasing. But among those that are running, there is convergence because those that have just started running are running the fastest. If the race is long enough, all of the runners will eventually end up catching up with the leaders.

Understanding convergence and divergence, growth takeoffs, and diminishing marginal returns helps us understand why there is so much inequality in income levels across countries today. But it does not get us to a deeper understanding of why some countries are growing and others are not growing, and why it is that some countries are able to sustain faster long-run rates of growth than other countries. In other words, to move beyond the footrace analogy and towards a deeper understanding of economic growth, we need to think about why some runners find it easier to get started, and are better runners once they do. To do this, we need to think more carefully about the fundamental determinants of economic growth.

What determines the level of aggregate income in a country? In a word: productivity. It is a simple fact that wages and income are low when workers are unproductive, and high when they are productive. When workers do not produce very much when they work, then firms cannot afford to pay them very much either. This is the reason why skilled labor pays more than unskilled labor. The productivity of labor increases as the result of the accumulation of incremental changes in business practices such as the purchase of new capital and equipment, incorporating new methods of organization, adopting new technologies, and using accrued knowledge to produce more with less. The primary driving force behind these incremental changes is competition. Because of competition, firms are constantly forced to adjust their production processes and become more efficient over time in order to stay profitable in the face of competition from other firms making similar changes.

So productivity is foundational to determining income levels. In the Classical view of the world, productivity is fundamentally based on three factors: the quantity and quality of labor (human capital), the quantity of equipment, tools, and infrastructure (physical capital), and how we combine inputs to make output (technology). Countries that have more human capital, more physical capital, and more technology should be richer. In the big picture, it is just that simple.

Or is it? This "helicopter view" of economic growth obscures many important realities. If getting rich were simply a matter of accumulating more human capital, physical capital, and technology, then there would be more rich countries. This is because, as we talked about before, in the long run diminishing marginal returns predicts convergence across the globe. The fact that physical capital, and human capital as well, exhibit diminishing marginal returns means that countries that begin to invest in education and capital should grow quickly, eventually beginning to converge (although maybe never actually catching up) with rich countries. And this convergence should take place more rapidly if human and physical capital are capable of moving—through migration and foreign investment—because poor countries should become magnets for human and physical capital because their returns will be highest where they are most scarce. Likewise, most forms of technology are transferable. Ideas leak and match. The vast majority of good ideas that have been created in rich countries are not subject to patent and copyright laws; they should be transferable to poor countries, allowing them to catch up and converge fairly quickly with rich countries. However, as we have just talked about, convergence is not the whole story when it comes to understanding the evolution of global inequality. While convergence is happening in some areas of the world—think China and East Asia—this is obviously not happening elsewhere—think sub-Saharan Africa and South Africa. What is our simple "helicopter view" of economic growth missing?

THE IMPORTANCE OF INSTITUTIONS

Economics is fundamentally the study of how people respond to incentives to further their own self-interests. This is at the heart of what Adam Smith had in mind when he said: "It is not from the benevolence of the butcher, the brewer, or the baker that we expect our dinner, but from their regard to their own interest."[8] The economic focus on incentives does not mean that the only incentives that matter are financial rewards or penalties. They could also be social incentives, such as the approval or the condemnation of peers, or physical incentives, such as avoiding punishment or gaining comfort. The key is that these incentives are rewards or punishments in forms that people care about, and as a result, influence behavior.

When we think about economics across the globe, we have to recognize that different people live in different environments and face a diversity of incentives that vary across time. These diverse incentives motivate different actions between people and even in the same person over time—not just economic behaviors but social and personal as well. So when economists study incentives, we are not only interested in how certain incentives encourage certain actions, but we are also interested in how governments and societies shape incentives in ways that encourage people to behave in ways that benefit both themselves and society as a whole. For instance, one of the primary challenges of economics is to develop policies, laws, and enforcement systems that incentivize people to produce their own goods (where everyone stands to benefit) and not just steal the goods of others (where someone benefits only at a cost to others).

Economists use the term *institutions* to refer to the political, economic, and social structures created by societies, families, and governments that shape incentives and influence individual behavior. While the word "institutions" has a number of meanings in general conversation, economists use the word institutions to specifically refer to the laws, rules, practices, and beliefs that shape incentives and which, in turn, influence behavior. Because society, culture, and government can change over time, so do institutions. And as institutions change, so do the incentives and behaviors they encourage or discourage.

To describe this perspective in another way, economics operates under a fundamental assumption (often unspoken among economists) that people are innately very similar. Human nature is universal, and the incredible varieties of human behavior that we observe across different groups of people are not created by our inherent dissimilarities, but are the result of the diversity of our social environments. Poor countries are poor because they live under a set of institutions that do not incentivize people to engage in productive behaviors that, over the long run, increase income. The people in poor countries do not sufficiently invest in education, or save to accumulate capital, or invest in creating and adopting technologies, or start businesses. They do not do these things because these options are blocked and the proper incentives (such as societal pressures or financial payoffs) to get people to do these things are lacking. Likewise, rich countries are rich because they have developed, or inherited, a set of institutions that create incentives that encourage their people to engage in productive behaviors. These productive behaviors—such as investing in education, physical capital, and particularly technology—have led them to increase their productivity and incomes over time.

At our very essence, we are all entrepreneurs. We are all trying to earn an income to provide for the wants and desires of ourselves as well as our families. Both Jeff Bezos and Napoleon were trying to accumulate wealth and gain the respect of their peers. But for one, the institutions that existed in society rewarded those who had financial, computer programing, and operations management skills. For the other, the institutions that existed at the time ensured that the rewards went to powerful men that could organize armies and thrive at warfare. Entrepreneurs are not innately "good", but are pushed into constructive or destructive behavior based on the institutions that are in place.

Institutions are one of the primary reasons why there is no such thing as individual productivity. As we discussed extensively in Chapter 4, we know that our ideas and efforts leak and match in ways that make "us" much more productive than just a simple sum of our own individual efforts. Understanding the ways that our individual productivity is really a function of the networks we belong to and the people we work with goes a long way towards explaining why there are no true "just deserts" for our work. There is something profoundly unknowable about how much of our income any of us can legitimately claim to have earned, because so much of it depends on things out of our control. The primary thing out of our control is the institutions that fundamentally determine the economic environment in which we live and work. The institutions around us not only our influence our behavior, but influence the behaviors of the people around us—the people who determine how productive we can be (or fail to be).

In many ways, the question of what drives between-country inequality and what makes some countries rich and other countries poor can be rephrased in the following way: To what extent do governments and society create rules that favor makers—and, as a result, increase the productivity of everyone in society—and in what way do these rules favor takers, reducing aggregate productivity?

WAYS THAT GOVERNMENTS SHAPE INSTITUTIONS

To get a better feel for what economists mean by institutions, let's talk about some of the ways that institutions differ between countries. Let's begin by focusing on a number of ways that government policy shapes institutions.

Law Enforcement and Corruption

Working in an organization, operating in a market, or being a productive member of society requires cooperative behavior. The functioning of markets, of businesses, and of good government requires that everyone follows the same rules of the game. Society needs confidence that information that is shared is truthful, that property will not be stolen, and that there is a process of reasonable compensation and punishment when someone does break the rules. Productive countries find ways to consistently punish those who disobey the rules—either through legal or through social sanctions—even when such punishment requires other people to incur costs as well (such as the expenses associated with law enforcement). However, when members of society lose confidence that other members will enforce the rules and incur the costs that come with punishing those who violate cooperative behavior, then people turn to thinking only about their own short-term self-interests, and society as a whole begins to suffer. In other words, people are conditional cooperators.[9] When no one punishes rule-breakers, there is no enforcement of communal values, and people can quickly begin to see "taking" and not "making" as the easiest way to get ahead.

The most obvious way to make sure that people play by the rules and cooperate is to maintain law enforcement and judicial systems that are efficient, fair, and honest. In too many countries, law enforcement is often indiscriminate and, as a result, the law is indiscriminately followed. Also, in many countries, the judicial systems proceed so slowly that they become almost irrelevant. Finally, when firms and entrepreneurs lose confidence that contracts will be honored and promises can be relied upon, they become reluctant to start businesses and stop engaging in the kinds of long-term investment in physical and human capital that drive employment and wage growth.

The worst way that law enforcement fails to create productive institutions is through the corruption of government officials: bureaucrats, police officers, and judges. Corruption is more costly than thievery because it reduces the perceived legitimacy of the law and provides an easy justification for disobeying the rules because "everyone else is doing it". Corruption first limits opportunities to get ahead, but then comes to be seen as the best way for the victims to get ahead themselves. It is this violation of the basic notion of fairness that makes societies with rampant corruption more accepting of illegal behavior and of diversion over creation.

Another way to think about the broad role of government in encouraging productive institutions is that good governments find ways to reduce conflict, either external conflict with other countries or internal conflict between its citizens. Reducing conflict requires political structures that encourage stability and cooperation among the population, regardless of the income, ethnicity, ideology, or special interests of any particular group. For example, having a legal system that does not discriminate against people based on their race, gender, or class is one important mechanism for minimizing conflict.

As a result, countries that are rich tend to have more efficient and fair legal systems, lower corruption, and stable political systems that encourage cooperative and productive behavior, and discourage getting rich through thievery and breaking rules.

Balancing the Tradeoff between Protecting Property Rights and the Dangers of Inequality

One of the most important tools that governments have for mitigating conflict is to maintain a system of well-defined property rights that help to avoid conflict over questions related to who owns what. Property rights are also at the heart of incentivizing investment. When property rights are not sufficiently protected, people have no reason to make the sacrifices and take the risks associated with investing in physical and human capital. When a government, a bureaucrat, a mobster, a soldier, or an entrepreneur can take what is yours without recourse, no one will create things worth taking.

Nobel Prize winner Douglass North has argued that the spark that ignited the industrial revolution was not new technology, but a single idea: that individual property rights should be respected and protected. It is no coincidence that the industrial revolution began in England, the place where the first limits on the government's ability to expropriate personal property were adopted. The Declaration of Independence, the French Universal Declaration of Human Rights, the Bill of Rights, Adam Smith's *The Wealth of Nations*, David Hume's *A Treatise on Human Nature*—each of these seminal documents from the mid-eighteenth century record a change in the mindset of the population in Western Europe away from vesting power and ownership rights in the state and towards vesting power and ownership rights in individuals. This seemingly simple idea about the primacy of property rights in incentivizing individuals to accumulate wealth helped transform unproductive institutions into productive institutions, starting countries on the race to economic development.

But as we talked about earlier, not all countries joined this race to economic development at the same time, and some countries have yet to begin it. Often, the failure to grow is a direct result of the lack of protection of individual property rights for a host of political, sociological, and historical reasons. For example, the economist Hernando de Soto argues in his book *The Mystery of Capital* that the fundamental cause of underdevelopment in many places is that the poor cannot cheaply obtain legal title to the assets that they informally own.[10] De Soto documents just how extreme some of the obstacles to obtaining legal title can be. In the Philippines, obtaining legal title to untitled urban land involved completing 168 bureaucratic steps that take between 13 and 25 years to complete. In Haiti, purchasing government-owned land involved 176 steps that would take 19 years to navigate. Without legal title and formal ownership, this land and capital cannot be used as collateral in order to gain access to finance. It also reduces the incentives to improve upon this land in an effort to make it more productive. This "dead capital" cannot be used to increase labor productivity, employment, and wages in the same ways that it could if it existed under a legal system that more effectively assigned ownership rights to it.

On the other hand, property rights enshrine inequality. As we have seen in Chapters 4 and 5 of this book, there are good reasons to think that economic inequality harms growth and that governments have a responsibility to reduce inequality for the betterment of society. However, when governments intervene in markets to reduce inequality through regulation and taxation, governments are also violating people's property rights to keep what they create. When governments become excessively involved in markets—often with the objective of reducing inequality—the negative impact on growth from the weakened protection of property rights can begin to outweigh any positive effects that come from lower inequality. This is at the center of the conservative critique of taxation and of other government interventions in markets.

As an example of how government regulations aimed at protecting workers and reducing inequality can become counterproductive, consider the matter of registering a business so that it can legally hire workers. Advocates of government regulation argue that this process needs to be lengthy and exacting because workers can be exploited by businesses with more power and information. However, reasonable regulation can quickly grow into excessive red tape that gets wrapped around the neck of job creation. According to the annual World Bank publication *Doing Business*, in the US it takes an average of 6 days to complete and process the paperwork to start a small business at a cost equivalent to roughly 1.4 percent of per capita GDP. In India, it takes 29 days at a cost of 50 percent of per capita GDP; in Nigeria, 34 days and 63 percent of per capita GDP.[11] The harder it is to open a business or close a business, hire a worker or fire a worker, change a wage or resist wage changes set by the government, or avoid paying a bribe, then the less likely it is that businesses will hire new workers in the first place. Similarly, unemployment benefits are intended to serve as a safety net for workers who lose their job, but unemployment benefits can become so generous that workers often stay out of the job market, or work under the table, so that they can continue to collect unemployment benefits.

Likewise, in the name of promoting equality, governments often provide legal protections, financial support, or even nationalize certain firms or industries in an effort to save jobs. However, oftentimes these jobs are at risk because of technological innovation, and saving these jobs means blocking the benefits of new technology. Saving specific jobs and blocking "the perennial gale of creative destruction" often stunts innovation and economic growth in the process.[12] Queen Elizabeth I's ban on knitting machines in 1589 and the Luddites smashing sewing machines in 1793—both in an professed effort to "help the poor"—are two classic examples of how labor interests often try to protect existing jobs at the expense of future jobs. Many populists claim that equality can be promoted by blocking technological innovation because they believe that capital and technology are substitutes for labor. Instead, history has shown us that technology is a complement to labor: by making labor more productive, technology not only increases wages but it actually increases the overall demand for labor, raising wages for everyone and reducing global inequality.[13]

Probably the most insightful economist on the dangers of promoting equality over the protection of property rights is the Austrian economist Friedrich Hayek.[14] In his book *The Road to Serfdom*, Hayek warned of the dangers of intrusive government intervention into the economy, particularly in regards to the dangers of central planning. As we talked about in Chapter 3, Hayek's critique of government planning focused on the role of information. In markets, vast quantities of information are conveyed through prices. Prices reflect the cumulative knowledge of large groups of people and send signals about where resources can be used most productively. A small number of government bureaucrats can never know as much as a market, and, as a result, governments will make less efficient investment decisions and be guilty of malinvestment. According to Hayek, focusing too much on redistributing income in the interest of promoting equality will likely create inequality of the worst kind: one where everyone is poor.

Hayek's observations provide powerful insight into exactly why governments in so many countries fail to establish productive institutions in the interest of creating equality of outcomes. At one extreme, you have the failure of centrally planned communist economies such as the USSR, China (pre-1980), and North Korea. Consider a brief history of the USSR. In the interest of promoting equality, the communists eliminated private property, collectivized agriculture, and labor and capital were forcibly moved into manufacturing. Nearly 6 million people died of starvation between 1928 and 1933, and what little manufacturing growth occurred was the result of increasing inputs, not from increasing efficiency. There were no incentives to innovate or to become more productive (outside of being sent to Siberia) in a country where most everyone was always destined to be equally poor and unproductive.

Today, there are few economies left that are completely centrally planned, but there are many economies in which the government plays an extensive role in the economy, often in the interest of reducing poverty and inequality. State-owned enterprises in many countries often dominate natural resource industries or agriculture in the interest of protecting "the people". In agriculture, a common way this is done is through the creation of marketing boards, where the government becomes the sole customer for farmers. The stated rationale for marketing boards is that the government is protecting the interests of poor farmers by serving to provide predictable demand, stable prices, and higher incomes. The actual rationale is usually to exploit farmers and serve the interests of the urban elite—it is no coincidence that most of the hungriest people in Africa are farmers. With little profitability in farming, farmers have few incentives to invest in technology or engage in other ways of increasing their productivity. This leads to the counterproductive result that policies aimed at keeping food prices low in Africa actually result in food prices being much higher than they are in countries where markets are allowed to function and the incentives to increase productivity are much higher.

As a result, as in most things in economics, there is a balance. On one hand, protecting property rights and allowing people to keep the "fruits of their labor" incentivizes hard work that increases growth. However, property rights set the stage for growing income inequality that can threaten future growth. Government intervention in markets through income redistribution and market regulation can reduce inequality, but can distort economic incentives and threaten the growth that creates higher incomes for rich and poor alike. There is no simple answer for where this balance lies, other than to say that some countries are clearly doing a better job of getting close to it than others.

Historical Path Dependence

Another reason why institutions differ across countries and societies is that current governmental institutions reflect the long-lasting effects of the different historical legacies of these societies. In the words of William Faulkner "The past is not dead. It's not even past."[15] Events from the past influence today's institutions and social norms because institutions and norms are very slow to change.

In a widely cited study on the long-lasting impact of colonization on global inequality, Daron Acemoglu, Simon Johnson, and James Robinson argue that the wide variety of institutions and income levels in former colonies today reflects the different colonization strategies that were followed in different places hundreds of years ago.[16] Where the climate and health environment was conducive for the permanent settlement of immigrants, colonization strategies focused on establishing institutions that encouraged productive, cooperative behavior and the rule of law, just like the colonizers had back home. This includes establishing representative political systems and building equitable and effective legal systems. This was most likely to occur in colonies within temperate climate zones, such as in North America, Australia, and New Zealand. However, in many other colonies, immigrant mortality was so high that few colonizers could risk living there permanently. In Nigeria in the mid-1800s, roughly 2,000 deaths occurred each year to sustain a constant level of 1,000 settlers in the country! In these high-mortality countries, primarily in Latin America, South East Asia, and sub-Saharan Africa, European immigrants established extractive colonization policies, such as slavery and discriminatory legal systems. In fact, these authors find that the settler mortality rates that existed in the mid-1800s are closely related to various measures of productive institutions that still exist in former colonies today, including the risk of government corruption and autocratic political systems. This is evidence of the persistence of institutions over very long periods of time.

And why were some countries colonizers and other countries colonies in the first place? Jared Diamond argues that this occurred because of the "Guns, Germs, and Steel" advantages which resulted from natural ecological advantages.[17] Because of superior climates for food production (more land in temperate zones), foodstuffs (wheat and potatoes), and animals that were more easily domesticated (such as having horses and not zebras), the Neolithic revolution began in Eurasia and set the conditions for the race to development to begin there first by facilitating faster population growth, political organization, and technological development. As a result, Eurasians were slightly more advanced than the rest of the world when they first came into contact, setting the stage for their initial domination that allowed them to impose their self-serving institutions in the Americas and Africa that continue to influence institutions and global inequality today.

Opening or Closing Markets to International Trade

Countries can increase the productivity of their labor force by specializing in the goods that they are most productive in making. International trade is one of the greatest technological advances of all time—it is a way of turning what you have into what you want. As a result, international trade is a key channel through which productivity, employment, and incomes increase over time. But many countries deny their citizens the benefits of international trade because of an economically confused belief that by blocking imports, a productive domestic industry will necessarily develop in its place. Almost always, this is not the case.

The fact of the matter is that international trade is crucial to accumulating the things that make countries rich: physical capital, human capital, and technology. International trade increases the amount of physical capital within an economy. With trade in goods come the inflows of international capital in the form of factories and equipment. Also, access to larger foreign markets allows countries to increase the scale of their production beyond what they could produce for their own smaller domestic markets. Producing for a global market is often a prerequisite to being efficient. A computer manufacturer cannot afford to make 50,000 computers a year and still afford to invest in the technology and equipment needed to stay at the cutting-edge of productive efficiency. A firm needs to be making a million computers to justify these huge investments, and that would be impossible without access to global markets.

International trade is also crucial to attracting and improving human capital and technology in countries. International trade does not simply involve trading goods and services, it also facilitates the exchange of ideas, knowledge, and expertise—the leaks and matches—that directly make everyone in a country more productive.

The benefits of international trade are clear: countries that were open to international trade between 1965 and 2000 had an average per capita GDP that was more than four times that of countries that were mostly closed.[18] This relationship between openness to international trade and higher incomes is one of the strongest empirical facts that explain why some countries are rich and others are poor today.

Many people would be surprised to learn that the large differences in income that exist today between growing Asian economies and largely stagnant sub-Saharan African economies are a relatively new phenomenon. In 1900, Africa as a whole was actually about 25 percent richer than East Asia. However, today East Asia is close to being three times richer than Africa. One of the starkest differences in economic policy followed between these two regions is in their approaches to international trade. There is a history behind these different approaches. In the fifteenth through nineteenth centuries, large parts of both Asia and Africa were subjected to painful and exploitive colonization. However, as many Asian and African countries gained their independence in the 1950s and 1960s, the lingering after-effects of slavery and the most severe forms of expropriation led many African countries to reject foreign trade and adopt "import substitution" policies that established trade barriers and tariffs aimed at protecting domestic businesses at the expense of foreign competition. While the goals of import substitution are understandable, the results have been disastrous. The relatively small countries that make up Africa found themselves blocked from global markets and unable to access global technology or take advantage of economies of scale. Because they were protected from competition, there were few incentives for African firms to increase the productivity of their labor.

The independence movements in Asia, on the other hand, have gradually created governments that have adopted outward-orientated approaches to economic development, or "export promotion". Focusing on exports has allowed Asian firms to increasingly specialize, take advantage of economies of scale, attract foreign investment, access new technologies, and maximize the leaks and matches of knowledge. This approach has also sparked economic growth throughout Asia that has raised more people out of poverty in a shorter period of time than during any other period of human history.

However, despite its costs, protectionism has an undeniable political appeal. Protectionism is the classic example of a special interest policy: the benefits of protectionism are enjoyed by a small number of people—those who see their monopolies protected, their unproductive but politically connected firms allowed to remain in business, and their jobs saved at the expense of other people's jobs—at the costs of higher prices and lower incomes for the rest of the population. The journalist Tom Friedman has suggested that anti-globalization groups would be more accurately referred to as "The Coalition to Keep the Poor Poor".[19] Protectionism is often framed in populist appeals to "protecting the little guy", and as a method of promoting economic equality. However, the best evidence suggests that international trade reduces global inequality by increasing incomes across the globe, but by the most in the poorest countries.[20]

Macroeconomic Policy Management

Bad governments kill growth through bad macroeconomic policy. Bad governments spend beyond their means and accumulate debt that they can't repay, often because of corruption and political patronage that leads to excessive spending and inadequate tax collection. If excessive debt is the root cause of many economic crises, inflation is the cure that is worse than the disease itself. Inflation is always an appealing option in the short term for governments to pay their bills because, in the words of Federal Reserve Chairman McChesney Martin, "inflation is a thief in the night".[21] Without levying any explicit new taxes, inflation allows governments to surreptitiously eat away at the value of money and deposits in bank accounts in ways that are often not immediately obvious to the public.

Inflation not only destroys financial wealth, but inflation kills financial systems because trading money now for money later is never a good deal when it's losing value rapidly. Inevitably, high inflation rates are associated with bank failures, dysfunctional financial markets, and a lack of access to financial services for the poor. Without a means to borrow or save, the poor are made more vulnerable, even long after the inflation has diminished.

The boom and bust cycles associated with debt accumulation and inflation in many poorer countries mean that economic crises are so common that risk avoidance becomes as important as creating income. In other words, the focus shifts from creating jobs and income to protecting what you already have. Macroeconomic calamity is a regular fact of life in many countries: debt crises, hyperinflations, currency crises, banking crises, repressed financial systems, and expropriatory tax rates to name just a few disasters. By creating risky macroeconomic environments, some governments eliminate any incentives for people to make risky investments in physical capital, human capital, and innovation.

Quality Educational Systems

When labor is labor, it is destined to be cheap and workers will be poor. When labor becomes specialized, it is no longer the quantity of labor but the *human capital* that is in this labor that matters. It is human capital that gets paid a premium.

One of the largest and most persistent differences between rich countries and poor countries is in the quality of their educational systems. The value of human capital in the US is four times the value of its physical capital.[22] Those who live in rich countries spend almost twice the amount of time (12.4 years vs. 6.7 years on average) in school as compared to poorer countries.[23] These differences in schooling are not caused by differences in school access, or the supply of education. Today, 99 percent of the world's population has access to public schooling. Instead, the biggest problem is the demand for schooling, which in turn reflects a lack of perceived value. In some countries, the quality of schooling is so poor that it is not worth the fees or the time. In other countries, extreme poverty and the need for even the meager wages children earn encourages child labor over schooling.

History has shown that the most effective way to reduce child labor is to increase the overall productivity of labor. More productive labor decreases the demand for child labor, which is unproductive and low-skilled, while increasing wages for those adults in the family that are of working age, reducing the need for child wages. But this will only occur when the overall institutions in a country improve and incentivize investment in the things that make labor more productive and incomes higher: more education and human capital, more physical capital, and more technology.

THE ROLE OF CULTURE IN SHAPING INSTITUTIONS

Culture is a commonly offered answer to so many questions regarding why some countries are rich and others are poor. There is no doubt that cultural differences play a role in shaping institutions. This is particularly true in regard to how culture determines social norms, or commonly accepted beliefs about how people should behave. Culture can play an important role in shaping institutions and making them either productive or unproductive. For example, in cultures that glorify crime, thievery, or war, it should not be surprising that many people actively engage in these activities and many other people are accepting of it. Culture can also play a role in limiting the opportunities to get an education or for workers to specialize. Many societies have cultural beliefs that encourage racism, sexism, tribalism, and caste systems that have historically been used to justify systematic discrimination. Finally, there are cultural beliefs that limit pluralism and participation in the political or economic system, such as the ways that women are discriminated against based on religious beliefs.

However, there are strong reasons to be skeptical of cultural determinist arguments that insist that most of the differences in institutions and income can be boiled down to variations in culture. The problem with cultural determinism is that cultural explanations can often be used to argue either side of any debate. As we will discuss, countries have moved from poor to rich, and sometimes back to poor again. However, culture changes much more slowly than income. A country like China has seen vast swings in its relative prosperity over the last 1,000 years but has been one of the most stable cultural environments in the world. Chinese culture was blamed for China being poor when it was poor ("Chinese culture encourages authoritarianism and creates people that only obey rules and cannot be creative") and for China becoming rich ("Chinese culture eliminates the need for the messiness of democracy and encourages hard work and following rules"). Both of these cultural arguments seem plausible, but they are also contradictory. The fact is that culture matters in economics, and while culture shapes institutions, institutions are about much more than just culture. The idea that culture predetermines a society's path, or that there is a single "best" culture for development, is contradicted by too many examples to the contrary.

GEOGRAPHY AND INSTITUTIONS

Location matters. Income is clearly related to place. But is it geography itself—the natural resources, location, climate, and landscape—that determines which countries are rich and which are poor? In other words, is global inequality natural?

The idea that the natural environment determines income is the basis of Malthusian economics. Thomas Malthus lived in England in the late 1700s when England still was primarily an agricultural economy. Malthus believed that the land-to-population ratio was the primary determinant of productivity. However, while population was growing, the amount of land was fixed. As a result, more people would lead to a lower land-to-population ratio, which would reduce income per person as well. In the long run, the only constraint on population growth was a brutal one: famine. Human populations would have to adjust to the amount of land available, so that income levels were permanently stuck at subsistence levels, no more, no less.

A more modern proponent of natural determinism is the *Guns, Germs, and Steel* author Jared Diamond who, as we discussed earlier in this chapter, argues that ecological advantages led to an earlier Neolithic transition in Eurasia, creating more surplus labor and also supporting a greater population that allowed for more complex societies and faster technological development.

There are a number of other hypotheses about how geography contributes to global income disparities, wealth, and poverty. One is that geography influences the transportation costs associated with trade. Access to ocean ports and navigable rivers reduces the costs of moving goods and people while also facilitating trade and the leaks and matches of ideas and technology. Interestingly, only 17 percent of the world's land is within 60 miles of an ocean or a navigable river connected to the ocean, yet this relatively small area produces nearly 70 percent of the world's GDP and is home to 50 percent of the world's population.[24] Unfortunately, access to water is not shared equally across the globe, and this likely contributes to global inequality. For example, despite Africa being about eight times the size of Europe, Africa has half the amount of coastline, few deep-water ports, and a very limited number of navigable rivers. In fact, half of the world's landlocked countries are on the continent. Compounding this problem, most of the African coast is arid because of weather patterns, so most of Africa's population lives in the interior that has few navigable rivers.

Geography also plays a role in determining climate. As you move away from the equator, temperatures decrease and incomes increase. Per capita GDP in tropical countries is less than one-fourth of what it is in temperate countries north and south of the tropics. This is true not only across countries, but within countries and regions as well (e.g. the colder parts of Europe, Africa, Italy, the US, Mexico, and Brazil are richer than the warmer parts).

Why does climate matter in determining income? First, warmer temperatures in the tropics reduce agricultural productivity by an estimated 30–40 percent, which is a huge problem given that half of all employment in the tropics is in agriculture.[25] The reasons for this are complex, but are related to more frequent droughts, poorer soils, and monsoon flooding. Second, warmer tropical climates are also associated with increases in parasitic diseases such as malaria, sleeping sickness, dengue fever, river blindness, and hookworm. According to the World Health Organization, adults in malaria-free Latin America earn 50 percent more than adults living in malaria zones.[26] Disease not only makes it difficult to work and go to school, but it also serves as an important barrier to technology and knowledge transfer. Finally, warm weather makes it hard to work hard. It simply takes more energy to work when it is hot, reducing labor productivity.

However, there are good reasons to question just how important geography is in explaining global inequality. The most persuasive argument against the importance of geography is that the causation is often reversed: it is poverty and inequality that makes geography critical, not the environment that is creating inequality and poverty. Without the proper institutions to create the incentives to invest in more physical capital, human capital, and technology, many poor countries find it hard to generate enough income to escape from the geography trap. For example, infectious disease is partially attributable to climate, but disease is also related to simply being poor. Spain and India have roughly the same malarial ecology based on their climates and geography. But Spain has no malaria because of effective implementation of parasite eradication programs, while 66 percent of India's population is at daily risk for malaria.[27]

Likewise, government-created barriers to trade can be as imposing as any mountain or distance from water. Bad governments create bad institutions that reduce agricultural productivity in ways that are as damaging as any climate challenges. Even the role that warmer temperatures play in discouraging hard work can be seen as a failure of economic development, given modern power grids and air conditioning. Huge parts of the world have migrated to hotter climates (e.g. the US sunbelt, Dubai, and Singapore) without a loss in labor productivity, but only when institutions and incomes are attractive enough to draw them there.

The fact of the matter is that there is a lot more variability in income than there is variation in geography. The geography in countries such as China has not changed, but its income levels there have. Today, we are seeing more growth in the tropics than we have ever seen before. While the natural environment may be a contributing factor in global income inequality, it is not the determining factor.

WHY IS GLOBAL INEQUALITY FALLING TODAY?

Global inequality is falling because the factors driving convergence across the globe are stronger than those of divergence. Simply put, institutions in many countries have become more productive, and with that, many more countries have been able to take advantage of the power of diminishing marginal returns to grow quickly and catch up with richer countries. In addition, many countries have been able to take advantage of the powers of globalization to attract physical capital, human capital, and technology transfers to further boost their economic growth to rates that were never possible in a less globalized world.

The popular press often talks about "growth miracles"—such as China—and "growth disasters"—such as the Congo—as if the things happening in these countries are somehow random, unexplainable phenomena. However, there is little about growth miracles that are miraculous, and growth disasters are not natural disasters. Instead, history in many ways is the story of how institutional change has led to fundamental changes in the incentives and behaviors of people, causing the economic power and affluence of societies to rise and fall.

In *Why Nations Fail*, Daron Acemoglu and James Robinson provide historical accounts of how political institutions interact with economic institutions to create economic success and failure.[28] In brief, they argue that political institutions shape economic institutions. Political institutions are shaped by "big events", such as wars, colonization, or the rise and fall of democratic or dictatorial leaders. These sorts of historical events shape political systems, and once they are in place, path-dependence means that political institutions persist for long periods of time and only change slowly until the next big event occurs. While Acemoglu and Robinson are not suggesting that economic growth is random, they are suggesting that there are critical junctures in history when if historical events had played out in a different way, the shape of global inequality would have looked much different than it does today.

Big events are important because of path-dependence, but their importance is magnified by vicious and virtuous cycles. When countries are able to establish pluralistic governments that are inclusive and do not centralize power in too few hands, they are also able to establish productive economic institutions that encourage productive behavior. Productive economic institutions lead to general prosperity, which encourages more pluralistic politics and further enhances productive institutions, on and on, in a virtuous circle. But when countries slip into dictatorship, kleptocracy, or anarchy, political institutions quickly get twisted towards the interests of a small number of elites and the cynical mindset of "grab while the getting is good" takes hold. This undermines productive economic institutions and leads to growth-killing behaviors that are more focused on taking rather than making. Lower growth means that elites are even more likely to see theft as the primary means of getting rich, encouraging them to build more barriers to political participation that further worsens growth in a vicious circle.

The fact that some countries have failed to join the race to economic development illustrates the importance of thinking about poor countries not as growth disasters, but as the victims of poverty traps. The poor are trapped in poverty because they are trapped in institutions that do not reward productive behavior, and they interact with those who are poor and cannot share knowledge and technology. The rich are rich in large part because they live in environments where productive behavior is rewarded and interact with those that are rich and knowledgeable.

Can we more clearly identify exactly why institutions have generally improved in many countries, leading to the recent trend in falling global inequality? Four general trends have been important across the globe over the last 30 years.[29] First, the fall of many communist and totalitarian governments in the 1990s has led to a rise in the number of more market-oriented economies, China and the Soviet bloc countries being the best examples of this. Communist countries suffered from the dangers of central planning discussed by Hayek, including a lack of specialization, little innovation, malinvestment, and an inability to access global markets and take advantage of leaks and matches.

Second, many communist and totalitarian governments have been replaced by more democratic governments with humanistic leaders that have prioritized individual rights over establishing kleptocracies or nationalist interests. Democracies also generate buy-in and cooperation from their populations by fostering broader political participation. When governments think about individual incentives when setting policy and encourage cooperative outcomes, they are much more likely to create productive institutions that foster growth. The average per capita GDP in countries that are classified as democracies by the World Bank is four times that of non-democracies. Countries that have transitioned to permanent democracies—including free elections and constraints on executive power—were 20 percent richer after 25 years than countries that have not adopted democracy, a result that holds whether the country was rich or poor to begin with.[30] The empirical evidence strongly suggests that democracies have less corruption, are better at breaking up monopolies, are more effective at protecting property rights and enforcing contracts, are better at providing public health and education, and are more stable—all important factors in creating productive institutions.[31]

The third trend driving improved institutions and the decline in global inequality is that the end of the Cold War has also led to a decline in war, particularly civil war. As the economist Paul Collier has said, "War is development in reverse."[32]

Finally, as we have talked about, increasing globalization has increased economic growth, particularly amongst the poorest countries. Declines in tariffs and reduced trade barriers have synergized with technological innovations such as reduced transportation costs and ICT to create an explosion in specialization, global supply chains, greater access to international capital, and more leaks and matches of ideas and technology.

What is to be done about the countries that are not following these trends, are not growing, and are falling farther and farther behind as time goes on? While it is easy for economists to say "change your institutions and make them more productive", how you actually do that in a real-world context is not always clear. Economists can provide no simple answers on exactly how to orchestrate changes in institutions. What we do know is that institutional changes that are imposed from the outside are unlikely to work on the inside, regardless of the good intentions behind them. Building the right government and laws for any specific country must reflect the social norms, culture, and the history of that country. There are intricate feedback loops between these factors, political institutions, and economics institutions that mean that specific policies that work in one place may not work in another. The free-market ideologues who thought that the legal and political systems that have been productive in the US would work just fine if imposed in Iraq were ignorant of both history and economics. Similarly, critics who argued that China's government-led market economy could never foster growth because it did not meet Western standards of private property protection were thinking with the wrong mindset. It is not what Western economists believe that matters in China, it is the incentives that the Chinese citizenry face in practice, and how they respond to these incentives.

As a result, the impact of externally imposed institutional change is highly unpredictable. Some problems cannot be solved by outside experts, and creating productive institutions is not some engineering project. The problem is the human factor: people are not easily designed. Humans—our societies, our cultures, and our economies—evolve, they are not created. Economists can play a role in helping people understand the role that institutions play and use history to help give tentative recommendations about potential courses of action, but we are less successful at prescribing how people will act in reality.[33]

MIGRATION AND GLOBAL INEQUALITY

Far and away, the most important determinant of your lifetime income is what country you were born in.[34] While 97 percent of the world's population lives in the country they were born in, the remaining 3 percent—roughly 230 million people, which is a population that would amount to the fifth largest country in the world—are migrants. A sizeable majority of these migrants move from poor to rich countries despite the many barriers, legal and otherwise, in doing so. And the number of migrants has been growing, rising from only 1 percent a year in the 1990s to 3.2 percent a year by the mid-2010s. According to one survey, 10 percent of the world's population would like to migrate if they had the opportunity.[35]

The financial incentives for cross-country migration are massive. We have talked about the citizenship premium at many points through this book, which is couched in terms of a citizen from the poorest country in the world—the Congo—migrating to another country. A Congolese would see their income rise by a factor of 92 by immigrating to the US. Migrating to Sweden increases income by a factor of 71, to Brazil by a factor of 13, but to Yemen by only a factor of 3.[36] But even from middle-income countries, the incentives to migrate to richer countries are huge. The average Mexican increases their wages by 2.5 times by migrating to the US, the average Indian by 6 times, the average Haitian by 10 times, and the average Nigerian by 15 times.[37]

The clear and obvious benefits of migration are the single best example of the power of institutions, and of the importance of leaks and matches. It is an obvious statement of fact that when a migrant from a poorer country places their foot onto the ground of a richer country, their productivity and their wages instantly rise. This is true for all migrants, regardless of their personal qualities and characteristics. It illustrates an important point that I have been making throughout this book: that there really is no such thing as personal productivity. Each of us is only as productive as the environments that surround us and the people with whom we share the leaks and matches of our talents.

Because of this, there is no single policy that has greater potential for reducing global inequality and improving global human welfare than adopting free and open migration. If motivated workers from poorer countries were allowed open access to the institutions and networks of richer countries, then the potential gains in global income would be staggering. Migration allows for economic development without the constraint that you can only enjoy development in the place where you were born. And while open migration seems like a radical suggestion, we have seen that the increased flow of capital across borders has played an important role in increasing global income by allowing capital to move to where it is most productive. Why shouldn't people enjoy the same opportunities as capital? Why is it that only capital is allowed to benefit from free-market thinking in terms of freedom of movement and low taxation? A global system that values human rights would seem to demand it.

In this sense, it is useful to compare and contrast expanding migration with cutting taxes. In both cases, aggregate productivity is likely to be increased because resources can more easily move to their most productive uses without the distortions of taxes or borders. On the other hand, both taxes and migration will change the distribution of income. Tax cuts will likely favor the rich over the poor. Migration—for reasons we will talk about in a moment—likely favors the global poor over the global rich. As a result, free-market proponents are being hypocritical when they argue that the primary focus of policy should be on productivity and enlarging the size of the pie, but favor only tax cuts and not increased migration.

Of course, migration has the potential to improve *aggregate* income and welfare. But this is a book about the distribution of income, and while migration can increase the size of the pie, it also means that this pie will be divided differently than before. While both skilled and unskilled workers in poor countries have incentives to migrate in terms of absolute income, skilled workers from poor countries could see their relative income decline (meaning they might fall to a lower decile on the income distribution) after they migrate because of the greater supply of skilled workers in rich countries. However, unskilled workers are in relatively short supply in rich countries, meaning that they are more likely to improve their relative income than skilled workers. As a result, the incentives for unskilled workers to migrate are greater than those of skilled workers. And, in fact, we observe that migrants that want to migrate to countries such as the US are disproportionally unskilled.

In other words, by increasing the supply of labor, migration could reduce domestic wages for all types of workers already in the destination country, but the pressures will be particularly intense in low-skilled jobs. As a result, migration could exacerbate within-country inequality in rich countries while reducing global inequality at the same time. This is really at the heart of the debate over migration within rich countries. Whether migration helps or hurts the poor depends upon whose poor you are talking about: the poor of rich countries or the poor of the world.

However, while migration *could* increase within-country inequality, it doesn't have to. The simple story I just told about the supply of skilled and unskilled workers misses an important part of the bigger story: New immigrants also create new leaks and matches that have the potential to raise the wages of all current residents. Even the countries from which people are leaving may benefit from migration if it encourages more people to get an education and invest in the skills that will help them migrate in the future. Some of these more educated people will migrate, but not all. If enough of these people stay behind—and over time are supplemented by immigrants who return home and become instruments of technological diffusion—then it is possible to reach a tipping point where enough ideas are leaking and matching in domestic networks to turn a poverty trap into a virtuous circle. As a result, immigration has the power to become a technology for sharing ideas and expanding networks of leaks and matches. It can make everyone better off. However, the key for this to happen is that immigrants must be allowed to integrate themselves into society and into the social networks of the countries they move to. The more that immigrants are discriminated against, blocked from accessing education and other public goods, and socially shunned, the more likely it is that immigration will worsen domestic inequality while failing to deliver any growth benefits.

There are ideas for allowing a broader share of society to share in the benefits of migration, not only the migrants themselves. One idea is to permit discriminatory migration. One method of discriminatory migration is to require migrants to purchase residency or citizenship. In the US, if a foreigner invests $1 million or more in US companies or $500,000 in a rural or high unemployment area, they are given special access to a green card residency permit. However, by only allowing the richest people to migrate to the US, this policy is not only elitist, but adds to global and within-country inequality. A second method of discriminatory migration is to allow temporary guest worker visas, which is common in many places such as the Gulf countries, where hundreds of thousands of foreign workers live at any one time. These guest worker programs do reduce global poverty, and economists have made the argument that discriminatory migration policies do more to help the poor than rich-world bans on migration.[38] However, the human rights concerns with these programs are real, as these temporary workers are often essentially living as indentured servants, receiving transportation and a stipend for their families back home in return for turning over their passports to their employers and working without recourse for prolonged periods of time.

Proponents of more humane forms of discriminatory migration have argued for granting migrants partial citizenship that requires them to pay more taxes, receive fewer public benefits, and that restricts their voting rights. However, this two-tier citizenship is a form of institutionalized discrimination and, as we just talked about, serves as a big barrier to immigrants from fully integrating into society and contributing to the leaks and matches that drive growth. However, it is also true that many migrants voluntarily choose to migrate under similar conditions when they migrate and live as undocumented immigrants.

One avenue of migration that is available to more people and that can be almost as effective in increasing the incomes of the poor in some countries is for rural people to move to urban areas. Today, roughly half of the world's population lives in an urban area, and by 2050 this number will be nearly 70 percent. Urban migration is most pronounced in poorer countries because this is where the gap between urban and rural wages is the largest. In China, the largest human migration in history has occurred since 1980, where more than 250 million Chinese have moved from rural to urban areas. This migration has been driven by the fact that urban areas have higher-paying manufacturing, private sector, and export-oriented jobs. In China, urban incomes—even after all of this migration—are still three times what they are in rural areas.[39]

Wages are higher in cities because cities are more innovative and, as a result, more productive. As we talked about in Chapter 4, one of the strongest results from the research on how ideas are created is that innovation is closely linked to cities.[40] Cities are places for people to congregate and diffuse new ideas, enlarge their networks, and make themselves and each other more productive. In the US, 63 percent of patents are developed in only 20 cities.[41] A city that is 10 times larger than another city is 17 times more innovative—a city 50 times bigger is 130 times more innovative.[42]

Cities have another quality that makes them more innovative, and it's that people enjoy more diverse and fluid social and professional networks in urban areas. One study finds that people with diverse backgrounds, diverse experiences, and diverse social groups are three times more innovative than those who do not enjoy such diverse interactions.[43] This not only explains the benefits of living in urban areas, but the costs of discrimination and other legal and social barriers that prevent certain groups of people from maximizing their ability to share their abilities.

THE INTERPLAY BETWEEN BETWEEN-COUNTRY
INEQUALITY AND WITHIN-COUNTRY INEQUALITY

Domestic inequality is increasing within most countries, but inequality between countries is decreasing. This apparent contradiction is occurring because many of the factors that have contributed to increasing domestic inequality in middle-income and rich countries are also contributing to the decline in global inequality. Five factors that we have talked about throughout this chapter and this book are responsible for this contradiction: migration, technological change, globalization, geography, and institutions.

We just talked about how the migration of workers from poorer to richer parts of the world has lowered global inequality by raising the wages of the global poor. But it also likely puts downward pressure on the wages of those living in the bottom 50 percent of rich countries. This is at the heart of the Elephant Curve (see Figure 2.6) that we have talked about throughout this book.

Skills-based technological change and globalization are also contributing to the divergence between domestic and global inequality. ICT has made it possible for work to be divorced from physical location in ways that it has never been before, and globalized markets have allowed production processes to be increasingly broken into smaller tasks that can now take place wherever the necessary labor skills exist and costs are low. These global supply chains have placed large premiums on workers who are highly educated and have unique skills, while also increasing employment opportunities for less-skilled workers throughout the world. However, it has also placed increasing wage pressures on low-skilled workers in rich countries who now face more competition than ever before.

For these reasons, geography itself is playing a role in this divergence between domestic and global inequality. While location matters a great deal in explaining global inequality, it matters less than it did and, as a result, between-country inequality has fallen, as we see in Figure 6.2. However, location actually seems to be playing a bigger role in explaining within-country inequality. The growing divide between rural and urban wages within many rich countries illustrates this. The best way to take advantage of our increasingly knowledge-based economies is to live in a large urban area with lots of other idea creators, or to have the necessary ICT skills that allow you to virtually network with diverse groups of people so that you can take advantage of the leaking and matching of ideas. But less-skilled workers living in rural areas can quickly become trapped in situations where they cannot take advantage of knowledge-based jobs and feel the wage pressures created by increasingly globalized labor competition. In the US prior to the 1990s, regional disparities were declining as more people moved to urban centers—similar, but at a much smaller scale, to what is happening in China today. However, since 1990, regional disparities in the US have solidified because people are moving less than they did. In addition, not all urban centers are equal. Children born in the poorest 20 percent in Detroit have half the likelihood of making it into the top 20 percent than children born in the poorest 20 percent in San Francisco.[44] These regional differences are contributing to the increase in inequality within the US at the same time that many people across the globe are increasingly escaping their location-based poverty traps.

Finally, institutions matter not just for economic growth but also for global inequality. Government-created institutions impact within-country inequality in a myriad of ways that we talked about in Chapter 5. Fiscal policies, social policies, law enforcement systems, and institutionalized discrimination can create institutions that might facilitate economic growth, but also lead to higher levels of domestic inequality.

Brief case studies of Brazil, India, and South Africa illustrate the variety of ways that institutions can facilitate faster economic growth but also lead to greater within-country inequality at the same time.[45] Despite their very different histories, these countries demonstrate how the path-dependent nature of long-standing social hierarchies, discriminatory property rights, and unequal wealth and education create entrenched income inequality. India, Brazil, and South Africa have each moved towards much more market-oriented and productive institutions, which have increased economic growth. This faster growth has raised large segments of their populations out of absolute poverty and has contributed to falling global inequality. However, inequality within these countries has also risen because the gains from development have been shared unequally, largely as a result of legacies of discrimination and large differences in endowments between different groups of people. As a result, in all three countries, the top 10 percent earn more than half of national income. Despite faster economic growth, large populations in each country remain stuck in poverty and their middle-class populations remain small.

In India, beginning in the mid-1980s, the government deregulated markets and opened the economy to international trade, but at the same time reduced the progressivity of its tax code in the interest of "competitiveness". Also, the entrenched caste system in India continues to institutionalize social, legal, and political discrimination in numerous ways that have been difficult to eliminate. As a result, the top 0.1 percent in India saw gains in income that were as great as the entire bottom 50 percent. India continues to rely heavily on consumption taxes and not progressive income taxation, even in the face of growing inequality.

In South Africa, extreme inequality is one legacy of the Apartheid system. Until the early 1990s, a white minority of 10 percent of the population essentially comprised the top 10 percent of the income distribution. Today, despite a nominally non-discriminatory legal system, inequality between the black and white populations continues to increase because of unequal endowments between the two groups in terms of wealth, education, and social privilege. South Africa continues to rely upon indirect taxes (such as consumption taxes) and not progressive income or inheritance taxes. This lack of progressive taxation protects the interests of the rich and other elites.

Finally, Brazil was the last major country to abolish slavery in 1888, and large regional inequalities that stem from the colonial slave-owning era continue to contribute to economic inequality today. While the Brazilian economy has reformed, unequal access to land ownership, poor education systems, and regressive fiscal policies mean that most Brazilians have seen their incomes increase relative to their global peers, but the poor in Brazil have seen their relative incomes decrease relative to rich Brazilians.

IN CONCLUSION

To the extent that people see themselves as part of a global community, economic inequality is shrinking. There has never been a better time for the median person on this planet to be alive than right now. Gradually, institutions across the globe are becoming more productive as governments have adopted market-oriented reforms, political systems have become more democratic, fewer civil wars are occurring, and international trade has increased. As institutions improve, more and more countries have been able to jump-start their race to development because of the inherent advantages that diminishing marginal returns provide them. In addition, access to ICT and globalized markets have sped up the convergence process to be faster than ever before. Even the poorest countries can gain access to global physical capital, global human capital, and technology transfer through trade and the leaking and matching of ideas.

But improvements in global inequality and the decline in the number of people living in extreme poverty have also put pressure on other income groups. This is true of the global middle-class—which is the poorer citizens of rich countries—who now face increasing global competition in the labor market. It is also true of the poor in the poorest of countries, who are still stuck living in places with unproductive institutions and little growth.

As long as it is relative income that matters to people—and I have argued throughout this book that relative income is the most important determinant of how satisfied people are with their current economic situation—then the fact is that when there are relative winners, there will also be relative losers. This is at the heart of the matter with the growing concern about inequality. While it is the best of times for the world's median person, best of times for most of the global rich, and good times for many of the global poor, it also feels like the worst of times for some individuals on either side of that median person in the global income distribution who feel squeezed by the rising poor and discouraged by the rich who are pulling away and receding into the distance.

NOTES

1. World Bank (2018).
2. Deaton (2013).
3. Ibid.
4. Ibid.
5. Milanovic (2015).
6. Milanovic (2016).
7. Maddison Project (2018).
8. Smith (1776).
9. Experimental evidence in support of the claim that people are conditional cooperators can be found in Fischbacher et al. (2001).
10. de Soto (2000).
11. World Bank (2015).
12. Schumpeter (1942).
13. While technological innovation reduces global inequality, remember that its impact on within-country inequality is likely very different. In our ICT-intensive modern economies, the positive impact of technology will be most pronounced when workers have the skills, education, and proper institutions to use this technology effectively. Technology will contribute little to the demand for labor and higher wages when the labor force is raw, unskilled, and unproductive. It is for this reason that technology might, in the short run, contribute to domestic income inequality—particularly in rich countries—by raising the wages of skilled relative to unskilled employees.
14. Hayek (1944).
15. Faulkner (1951), p. 73.
16. Acemoglu et al. (2001).
17. Diamond (1997).
18. Wacziarg and Welch (2008).
19. Friedman (2001).
20. Urata and Narjoko (2017).
21. Board of Governors of the Federal Reserve System (1955).
22. Christian (2014).
23. Barro and Lee (2013).
24. Gallup et al. (1999).
25. Gallup and Sachs (2000).
26. World Health Organization (2010).
27. Kiszewski et al. (2004).
28. Acemoglu and Robinson (2012).
29. Radelet (2015).
30. Acemoglu et al. (2014).
31. Treisman (2000), Leblang (1996), and Acemoglu et al. (2014).
32. Collier (2007, p. 27).

33. For these same reasons, there are good reasons to believe that foreign aid will never raise vast numbers of people out of poverty. In part, because foreign aid typically follows a "one size fits all" approach that fails to consider the distinct institutions that exist on the ground, such as corruption.
34. Milanovic (2015).
35. Ibid.
36. Milanovic (2016).
37. Clemens et al. (2009).
38. Posner and Weyl (2018).
39. Wanli (2015).
40. Comin et al. (2010).
41. Rothwell et al. (2013).
42. Bettencourt et al. (2007).
43. Ruef (2002).
44. *The Economist* (2017a).
45. Assouad et al. (2018).

7.   Is inequality a problem we can solve?

There is an increasing sense that inequality is something akin to the weather: everyone complains about it, but nobody does anything about it. Up until this point in the book, we have spent a lot of time talking about the causes and consequences of inequality, but have spent little time discussing what governments and societies can or should do about it. In this chapter, we examine policies that could reduce domestic inequality, while keeping a keen eye on the potential costs of these policies in terms of reducing efficiency and production.

But before we begin, we must first ask this question: Do people really want more equality? This book has examined myriad reasons that people *should* want more equality, but do they *actually* want it? The answer appears to be yes. As we talked about at the beginning of Chapter 2, people across the globe underestimate actual inequality levels in their country. In a survey by Michael Norton and Dan Ariely, Americans believed that the richest 20 percent own 60 percent of wealth in the US, when in fact they actually own 84 percent of wealth. Following up on this, the authors then presented the same people in their study with a range of options about what inequality should look like in a perfect world. They found that a large majority of participants thought the wealthiest 20 percent should have roughly one-third of all wealth and the poorest 20 percent should have about 10 percent of wealth. In reality, these numbers are actually 84 percent and 0.1 percent in the US. But while these numbers don't look at all like the wealth distribution of the US, they do look quite similar to the wealth distribution of Sweden. In fact, 92 percent of participants preferred the income distribution of Sweden to that of the US, and this was consistent across political party identification.[1] It appears that John Rawls' "veil of ignorance" is correct: if we didn't know what our position was going to be in the income distribution of society, most of us would choose an egalitarian distribution. Some inequality at a level that incentivizes hard work and enhances aggregate productivity appears to be acceptable to most people, but more than that is not.

So, if people want more equality, how do we achieve it? When it comes to addressing inequality, we first must remind ourselves of one of the fundamental facts about economic inequality: historically, higher levels of income have been generally associated with higher levels of income inequality. The poorest societies are the most egalitarian—there is equality in general poverty. Inequality only became possible as overall standards of living rose. History has shown us that economic growth reduces absolute poverty and raises absolute standards of living for most people in the society, but that these aggregate gains will not be shared equally. Growth, almost by definition, necessitates some level of relative inequality. During periods when growth has declined—war, state failures, and natural disasters—inequality has declined along with overall standards of living.

However, note that I said that there is a *general* association. The relationship between growth and inequality is not deterministic. While economic growth does tend to lead to more inequality, the tradeoff is variable, unstable, and differs from country to country and over time. Some countries have seen dramatic increases in standards of living with only minimal increases in inequality. Other countries have experienced minimal growth that has gone almost entirely into the pockets of a very few elites. We have even seen some countries that have been able to turn the tradeoff on its head; once these countries reached middle-income status, they were able to become more egalitarian over time. In fact, today it is generally true that the richest countries have lower levels of inequality than middle-income countries.[2]

Why isn't there a strict tradeoff between growth and inequality? Once again, it's because economic institutions and public policy matter. Institutions and the incentives that they create change not just the size of the pie, but alter the way that the pie is distributed. As we talked about in the last chapter, differing institutions between countries create vastly different income levels between countries. And it is also true that differing institutions create vastly different levels of inequality between countries with similar income levels. Some rich countries have higher inequality (such the US) and some much lower levels of inequality (such as the Nordic European countries). Likewise, there are some middle-income countries that have high inequality (China) and relatively low inequality (Mexico); there are poorer countries that have higher (Namibia) and lower (Egypt) levels of inequality. And, of course, differing institutions not only impact the current level of inequality, but they also impact how inequality changes over time, as evidenced by the fact that inequality has risen faster in the US and in the UK than in other higher-income countries.

This chapter examines the efficacy of government policies that aim to fundamentally alter economic institutions and reduce inequality. This includes examining structural reform policies that change the workings of markets (such as changes in labor laws, creating more market competition, and improving education) and fiscal policies that transfer resources from the richer to the poorer citizens (such as increasing the progressiveness of taxation and providing universal guaranteed incomes). The purpose here is to understand the policy menu options that governments have to choose from when they set a goal to reduce inequality.

STRUCTURAL REFORMS TO REDUCE INEQUALITY

Structural reform policies change the structure of labor and goods markets in ways that equalize the power between firms, workers, and consumers when it comes to influencing wages, prices, and incomes. The idea is that when power is equalized within markets, then markets will become more competitive, wages and prices will not favor firms over workers, or capital over labor, or producers over consumers. Instead, prices and wages will more accurately reflect the true value of goods and the productivity of workers, not just the monopolist power of firms. Structural reform policies also focus on equalizing the power between individuals in terms of their natural endowments, particularly their access to equal education and protection from discrimination.

The argument for focusing on structural reform instead of direct transfers of income is that structural reform policies can, in theory, reduce the rent-seeking behaviors and unequal endowments that are the fundamental driving forces behind inequality. In other words, more equitable and competitive markets should lead to more equitable outcomes across society.

Minimum Wage Laws

Minimum wage laws (sometimes referred to as "living wage laws") set a price floor for wages. By increasing wages for the working poor, minimum wage laws aim to reduce poverty, moderate inequality, and provide stronger incentives for the poor to work and develop their human capital. Proponents of minimum wage laws argue that firms have too much power in many labor markets and use this power to suppress wages below the productivity of many low-skilled workers who have little bargaining power. Minimum wage laws impose some balance in labor markets by guaranteeing that low-skilled workers are not exploited by being forced to work at subsistence wages.

One interesting example of minimum wage laws working in practice to eliminate discrimination in the US was the Fair Labor Standards Act of 1966, which extended a federal minimum wage to many service jobs not previously covered by minimum wage laws: service jobs in agriculture, restaurants, and other areas that were disproportionately held by black Americans. According to recent analysis, this broader minimum wage led to the wage gap between blacks and whites that existed at the time being cut in half—leaving it close to the 25 percent wage gap that exists today—without any impact on the employment rates of either blacks or whites.[3]

Critics of minimum wage laws argue that government-enforced wage controls increase unemployment by raising wages above the productivity of many low-skilled workers, forcing employers to lay off these workers rather than pay them more than their work is worth. Minimum wages incentivize firms to operate with fewer workers, either by cutting production or replacing labor with capital through automation. As a result, the impact of minimum wage laws on inequality rests fundamentally on this question: Does the impact of higher income for the working poor outweigh the income lost through increased unemployment? Critics claim that it doesn't. On the other hand, proponents argue that minimum wage laws create little unemployment because wages are suppressed at levels well below their productivity and, as a result, firms will still find hiring existing workers beneficial even if wages are forced to rise.

The real-world impact of minimum wage laws on unemployment, poverty, and inequality has been a matter of intense debate and empirical study amongst economists. Some studies have found that variations in minimum wage laws across US states are not significant in explaining differences in the unemployment rates among these states.[4] However, the weight of the evidence from other studies suggests that higher minimum wages do reduce employment among low-skilled workers, particularly young workers in low-wage industries.[5]

However, there are still good reasons to think that minimum wage laws—at least at moderate levels—do not have large impacts on employment. The first is that minimum wage laws in many areas are not effective, meaning that they are still below market wages for the least skilled workers and, as a result, don't actually change wages. In many parts of the US this is currently true. Only when minimum wages are set at levels much higher than the market wage will they have a pronounced impact on unemployment. In other words, the impact of minimum wage laws doesn't depend upon how high the minimum wage is, but how different it is from the local market wage.

But an even more fundamental reason why minimum wage laws may not impact employment is that even amongst low-skilled workers, efficiency wages are an important factor in determining the true cost of wage increases. Remember that efficiency wages refer to the fact that wages don't just reflect labor productivity but they impact labor productivity. Higher wages can incentivize workers to work harder, stay in jobs longer, and invest in building their human capital. In other words, higher wages increase costs but also create benefits for firms, meaning that the net impact on the labor market and unemployment will be unclear, and could actually be positive for many firms and workers.

Antitrust Regulation/Competition Policy

Market power plays a role in creating economic inequality. Monopolists generate extreme profits that go primarily to the holders of capital, who tend to already be well off. Monopolies also create inequality by centralizing power and resources that are used to generate economic rents that flow primarily to economic elites. As we saw in Figure P.1, a growing wedge exists between productivity and pay. While workers are becoming more productive, their wages are not rising proportionally as they should in the Classical theory of economics. This gap is one measure of the growth of economic rents, and these rents create inequality because they primarily flow to those who already have endowment advantages. There is also evidence that growing market concentration is playing an increasingly large role in our politics, which has influenced government policies in ways that also increase rents and contribute to rising inequality.

Antitrust regulation and competition policy aim to protect consumers and enhance market efficiency by breaking up monopolies and minimizing rent-seeking behavior. There is strong evidence that across most of the world, market concentration is growing. For example, in the US, one company makes more than 60 percent of the world's cell phones (Apple), three companies control nearly 80 percent of the cellular networks, and four airlines control 70 percent of flights. Across all industries in the US, concentration has been rising in the majority of markets. The four largest firms in every US market today control, on average, more than one-quarter of the production in their markets of operation.[6]

The growth of monopoly power is particularly striking in the technology industry. Consider the growing importance of the technology giants Facebook, Google, and Amazon. Each of these companies is a rapidly growing monopolist in the primary markets that they operate in. Google has an 88 percent share of online search advertising and 60 percent of the browser market. Facebook (and its subsidiaries Instagram, WhatsApp, and Messenger) conducts 77 percent of mobile social traffic.[7] In 2017, Facebook and Google accounted for nearly 80 percent of news publishers' referral traffic and together claimed roughly 80 percent of every new online-ad dollar in the US. Meanwhile, Amazon controls some 40 percent of America's online retailing and 77 percent of book sales.[8] By these measures of market share, all three are clearly monopolies. This kind of market power reduces competition because new firms can't compete in terms of the size of their offerings or in terms of the size of their networks.

But just as importantly, each of these companies is also a growing information monopolist because of the consumer information and intangible capital they have acquired through their primary businesses. These companies now have assets that they can leverage to gain market power in many other markets, even markets not yet developed. For example, Google has used the information and intangible capital they acquired through the data collected in their internet search and advertising businesses to gain an advantage in developing artificial intelligence systems.

One possibility for creating more competition in the technology sector that would benefit more people—not just the shareholders of these companies—is to break these conglomerates up. For example, Google could be broken into its more than 200 subsidiary companies, including YouTube, Android software, Deepmind artificial intelligence, Nexus information services, etc. Of course, breaking up big companies reduces the advantages that they provide in terms of networking and economies of scale. Another alternative is to treat these big technology companies as natural monopolies, meaning that their advantages in terms of size and scale are important to retain, but the company should be regulated—like a public utility company—so that these companies cannot exploit their power to earn excessive profits or exert undue political influence. Of course, any regulation aimed at making these companies less profitable is sure to reduce these firms' incentives to innovate as well. One final alternative would be to force these growing technology monopolies to share their information and intellectual property with new entrants at reasonable fees—essentially nationalizing data and making it a public good.

In addition to their influence over consumer markets, monopolists can also use their clout to lower wages for their workers because workers have fewer alternative options for jobs in these industries with other companies. There is evidence that the growing power of monopolies is transforming labor markets as well as consumer markets. One recent study of 8,000 local labor markets in the US found that when local labor markets are dominated by a small number of firms, wages are 17 percent lower than in local labor markets that are less concentrated.[9] Many economists have argued that antitrust law should be reformed to consider the market power firms have in labor markets, and that firms should be broken up and mergers banned when labor market concentration exceeds a certain threshold.[10]

Collective Bargaining/Corporate Governance

As discussed in Chapter 5, there is considerable evidence that the decline in unionization has contributed to higher levels of inequality by reducing the wages of middle- and lower-class workers.[11] Unionization has declined for a number of reasons related to structural shifts in the economy, such as the decline in manufacturing and the rise in education-intensive employment. However, it has also fallen because collective bargaining laws have become more hostile to workers, including the rise of "right to work" laws that prohibit unions from requiring all workers at a firm to pay union membership fees. This makes it much more difficult for workers to unionize because each worker has an incentive to free-ride off union members by not contributing dues.

Creating environments more conducive to unionization can reduce inequality. But many economists worry about the potential costs of unions, particularly the fact that by aggregating the power of labor, unions have their own power to engage in rent-seeking behaviors that help union members but impose costs on non-union workers, in particular by driving up unemployment. However, proponents of unions argue that the best way to counteract the monopolist power and rent-seeking behavior of firms is to fight it by creating monopolist power among labor. This can be achieved through adopting laws that make it easier for workers to unionize, including laws that require all workers who work in unionized jobs to pay union fees.

Another set of legal reforms aimed at changing the ways that firms and workers do business is to reform corporate governance, specifically in ways that give corporate boards and workers more say over the wages in their firms, from the CEO on down. Corporate governance reform could include a number of different policy actions. It could include limits on executive incentive pay so that executives can only make a limited multiple more than the lowest-paid worker in the firm. It could grant corporate boards more informed and active oversight of CEO compensation by adopting requirements for larger corporate boards whose members are not all chosen by the CEO. Changes in corporate governance could also encourage incentive pay for lower-level workers as well as include requirements for boards to include more inside members who work in the firm (while limiting the number of outsiders on a board picked by the CEO, who are often less informed and obligated to the CEO). Corporate reforms could mandate that the largest shareholders for firms (who are most interested in making sure executives are not excessively compensated) would have the option to appoint members to serve on the corporate board.[12]

Finally—and perhaps most importantly—corporations should be encouraged to allow for more workers to hold an ownership stake in the companies they work for. Incentive pay (over and above an hourly wage) is seen as crucial for CEOs, but why not for all workers? One of the best ways to incentivize hard work and the creation of ideas is for every worker to be a part owner, and to have an investment stake in the ownership of the company they work for and an opportunity to share in its profits. Broader ownership of corporations creates the possibility that more people can share the benefits of capitalism, not just those who own the most capital. Broader ownership would also require that workers at all levels of a company, from the top to the bottom, would be allowed to serve as representatives on corporate boards. Such a system exists in Germany—referred to as the codetermination system—and it has been shown to be a key contributor to higher labor productivity and lower income inequality levels in Germany.[13]

Globalization

As previously discussed, increasingly globalized markets have helped the world's poor and the world's rich, but have squeezed the world's middle- and upper-middle-class, particularly low-skilled workers in richer countries. As a result, globalization has reduced global inequality, while at the same time increasing domestic inequality in richer nations.

One way to potentially limit the growth in domestic inequality in the US would be to erect barriers to imports (and exports) that would put an end to global supply chains and return the US and other developed countries to the economies that they had in the 1950s and 1960s. But the problem with going back to the closed markets of the 1960s is that this would also require a return to 1960s-level productivity and standards of living, which in the US were only about one-twentieth of what they are today.

There are other problems with thinking that putting an end to globalization will mitigate inequality. First, while there is evidence that globalization is contributing to growing domestic inequality, it is not the primary driving factor.[14] In Chapter 5 we pointed to a number of other factors that play a much larger role in trending inequality, particularly skills-based technological change. While international trade in the US has grown by about one-third since 1990—a big change—internet penetration has increased by over 600 percent.[15] The changes in our economics that have resulted from innovation and technology have dwarfed those from increased international trade alone.

Second, while globalization might contribute to higher inequality, it is not clear that taking the opposite approach and creating trade barriers will reduce inequality. History tells us that when selective trade barriers are imposed in the interest of "helping workers", the primary beneficiaries are almost always elites and the rich who use their wealth and political influence to protect their own interests, not necessarily the interests of workers harmed by trade. For example, protectionist barriers in the US have been reduced on lower-wage manufacturing but are higher in the most highly educated sectors of the economy, such as the market for healthcare. Likewise, workers who rely on intangible capital such as intellectual property and copyrights continue to be more protected from trade than those who work with physical capital, such as in manufacturing.[16] As a result, time and time again, protectionism as it is actually implemented typically favors capital over labor, the educated over the less-educated, and the rich over the poor.

Taken as a whole, there are very good reasons to believe that the costs of addressing inequality by adopting protectionist policies far outweigh its benefits.[17] Most economists believe that the most effective way to help those workers directly hurt by increased import competition would be to fund what are known as "trade adjustment assistance programs", which provide enhanced benefits to those workers hurt by international trade. These benefits include increased unemployment benefits, wage compensation for workers who are forced to move to lower paying jobs, enhanced disability and retirement benefits, job retraining, and other forms of government income assistance. However, when a worker loses their job in the US as a result of import competition, trade assistance programs currently offset only about 10 percent of the income loss to a household without children.[18] As long as the current situation exists where the costs of international trade are concentrated almost entirely on the relatively small number of workers who lose their jobs, globalization will continue to scare all workers and be an easy scapegoat for politicians to use to blame every economic ill upon, including rising inequality.

Are there other ways to rethink globalization in developed countries so that more of the gains from international trade are enjoyed by the middle-class? According to the economist Richard Baldwin, the most effective way to guarantee that the greatest number of people benefit from globalization is to invest in "sticky" factors of production that can't easily move to places where they could receive a higher return.[19] This means investing in human capital, so that our workforce can fill non-routine jobs because these jobs are the hardest jobs to outsource. It means investing in social capital, so that we create places where people across the globe want to live, work, and raise children. Finally, it means investing in cities, where most new ideas are created and which, because of leaks and matches, are essentially "modern information factories".

Education

The government program that is most closely tied to inequality—both in reducing it and in perpetuating it—is public education. Education is one of the fundamental endowments that propagate inequality: the children of highly educated parents also tend to be highly educated, and less-educated parents tend to have less-educated children. Any structural reform program that aims to change the nature of market income inequality has to deal with the fact that income inequality largely reflects education inequality.

We know that one of the fundamental reasons that income inequality has been rising is that education is losing the race with technology. The demand for education-intensive jobs is outpacing the supply of educated workers, driving up the wage premium on education and widening the income disparity between skilled and unskilled workers. One clear solution to inequality is to increase the proportion of workers who have the education and skills that are in demand in our modern ICT-intensive marketplaces.

On the surface, it appears that many countries are attempting to better prepare their children for today's changing labor market. For example, overall spending on public education in the US and most countries has risen as a percentage of GDP. In fact, at almost $15,000 per student, the US spends more on public education than almost any other high-income country.

The problem is that education spending in the US and many other countries is decidedly unequal. Most education resources in the US are spent on the children of educated and richer parents, meaning that education resources are not being spent to compensate for differences in endowments that children are born with, but are actually serving to magnify them. Unequal education spending in America primarily occurs in two ways. First, it occurs because the US spends less on public schools in poorer school districts. Elementary and secondary schools in the US are primarily financed through local property taxes. In areas where property prices are high, the schools are likely to be better off financially, and vice versa. As a result, the US is one of only three OECD countries that spend less on students from disadvantaged backgrounds than the average student; in fact, 33 out of the 50 states allocate less money per student to districts with higher levels of poverty. As a result, the best teachers are significantly less likely to work in disadvantaged schools in the US because of worse pay and worse working conditions, the opposite of what happens in countries with the best education systems.[20] One successful idea that has yet to be significantly funded in the US is the Talent Transfer Initiative, which pays teachers up to $20,000 extra to teach in high-poverty, low-performing schools. This program has been shown to improve student scores and retain good teachers in poorer districts, even after teacher bonuses expired.[21]

Second, inequality in education spending occurs because the US spends a great deal of money on its college and university educational system. For every dollar spent on primary education in the US, three dollars are spent on higher education, the highest ratio of all developed countries.[22] However, children from rich families are much more likely to go to college. Out of every hundred American children whose families are among the bottom 10 percent of income earners, only 20 to 30 will go to college. However, when parents are in the top 10 percent of earners, that number rises to 90 out of 100. Furthermore, 60 percent of higher education spending is financed through private sources, not the government, meaning that many students can't afford college even when they are admitted.[23] Unfortunately, the college-funding gap is getting larger over time as college costs rise (largely because of a drop in government subsidies to higher education) and median income has remained stagnant. Since 2000, the average cost of community college has risen by 28 percent (by $3,000) and the cost of public university has risen by 54 percent (by $10,000). This has occurred as mean family income has remained flat and the incomes of the bottom 20 percent actually fell by 8 percent. As a result, for the bottom 20 percent, the average net price of college has risen to 84 percent of annual family income (but only 15 percent of annual family income for the top 20 percent).[24]

Why is spending on education in the US so fundamentally unequal? There are many reasons, but two factors stand out. The first is that education spending is a political process, and in the US this political process is primarily one that occurs at the local level. Elites with money have more power, and use this power to their advantage, particularly in the interests of their own children. While many people are supportive of spending more on poor children in theory, they are decidedly less supportive when the resources have to come at the expense of their own privileged children.

Second, education is an example of how growing inequality is changing the fundamental nature of public goods. As the rich have become richer, they increasingly treat many public goods such as education as private goods. They purchase their own private education and are unwilling to spend tax dollars for general education for everyone. Higher-income families pay for private schools, private tutors, and private coaches, turning goods that were traditionally public goods into private goods. Increasingly, many rich want the government to "get out of" the education business and focus on public goods that are more difficult to privatize, such as national defense and policing. This change in the mix of public goods away from public investment goods and towards more public security goods has had a profound impact on our society (for example, the rise in incarceration rates in the US) and on economic inequality.

Improving education is not simply about spending more on schools and spending it more equitably. It is also about changing social attitudes about education. As we talked about in Chapter 5, schools do not create inequality in educational outcomes—it is there when children enter school, and unfortunately it remains when they leave. Educational inequality is a complex mixture of genetics, parental modeling, class status, cultural traditions, peer interactions, and early educational opportunities. What we observe in countries with schools that are better at generating greater intergenerational mobility is that they have social attitudes towards teaching and education that are inherently egalitarian. They tend to revere learning and teaching, and the occupation of teaching at any level is seen as a prestigious profession. As a result, they pay teachers well, they attract the best college graduates to teach, and competition for teaching jobs is highly competitive. Once teachers get a job, they are given a great deal of independence to teach students in ways that they think are best, and curriculums are flexible, not standardized. Finally, successful educational systems also tend to intensively invest in remedial education at early ages, focusing on getting younger students that are subpar up to standard.

The changes that would lead to the biggest improvements in education have to take place outside of schools and in the home. As previously discussed (Chapter 5), changes in family structure, such as assortative mating, have had a profound impact on intergenerational mobility, as have the differing parenting approaches adopted by high-income/high-education parents and those from lower socioeconomic classes. There is no simple public policy for changing these parenting and family dynamics.

Technological Innovation

If education is losing the race with technology, then one way to bridge the gap is to create a more educated workforce. Of course, this is expensive and slow and faces the real constraint that not every person is capable of working in a unique and highly skilled job. However, another way to bridge this gap would be to create new technologies that can be used by lower-skilled workers. As high-skilled labor gets more expensive, there are strong economic incentives to develop technologies that can more productively use low-skilled labor.

One way to achieve this would be to refocus public research and development spending, public investment, and entrepreneurship on creating more jobs and less on maximizing productivity. This means thinking about innovation from the perspective of making the workers in existing jobs more productive, not just automating jobs and replacing workers. It also means thinking about the human implications of technological progress and taking a more holistic approach to considering the social costs and benefits of new technologies. What such policies would actually look like and how they would be implemented is unclear, but in a world where artificial intelligence threatens to replace one out of every five jobs over the next 20 years, it is something that we need to begin thinking about now.

Discrimination

As discussed at greater length in Chapter 4, discrimination is a particularly insidious form of rent-seeking. It is not just explicitly unfair. It also changes people's incentives to make the necessary investments in human capital needed to improve the aspects of themselves that they can control because they know that the aspects of themselves that they cannot control will always be used against them (or to their benefit, in the case of a privileged class). In other words, discrimination is in some sense self-fulfilling and easily "validated" by the discriminator.

Reducing discrimination requires comprehensive anti-discrimination laws, and just as importantly, vigorous enforcement of these laws. It also requires reforming laws that may not be explicitly discriminatory, but have statically discriminatory effects because they disproportionally impact a group of people who lack the same endowments as other groups because of historical discrimination. For example, while today's criminal sentencing laws in the US are not explicitly discriminatory, they unduly impact people of color who are also disproportionally poor and less educated, in large part because of past discrimination. As a result, criminal justice reform in the US is an important part of any anti-discriminatory reform program (as is granting past felons the right to vote and to have their say in politics). Reducing discrimination also necessitates a whole range of changes in government programs, social norms, and even family interactions in order to effectively change the social attitudes and behaviors that propagate the unequal treatments of people simply because they belong to a certain group.

Politics

In a very real sense, any policy solution to reducing inequality is unlikely without political reform. The increasing power of money and social media has created influential elites that benefit from political polarization and special interest politics. As long as the political processes in countries such as the US are heavily weighted towards elites and biased against those who are poorer and less powerful, it will be almost impossible to adopt policies that seriously attempt to address inequality. Are there ways to reduce economic rent-seeking by returning to one person, one vote? This seems to be an increasingly crucial question for today's democracies.

Is campaign finance reform that is aimed at reducing the influence of money in elections sufficient to do this? Or are there other ways that we can engage more people in their communities and reduce the number of people who are "surfing the internet alone"?[25] The dominance of ICT in our social lives has contributed to increasing tribalism and extreme individualism. How do we find ways to interact and empathize with each other more? Answering these and other questions quickly takes us well beyond economics and the scope of this book. But these are questions that need to be carefully considered if the goal is to actually change policy in the real world, not just speculate about it in a book.

FISCAL POLICY: TAXES AND TRANSFERS

Probably the most direct, and most powerful, tool that governments have to influence the level of inequality is through taxation and transfers: taking money from some people and giving it to others directly in the form of cash or indirectly in the form of services that will enhance their standards of living, either now or in the future.

Governments tax and transfer for many reasons, but one of them has always been to redistribute income. Redistributing income in this manner is often done in the pursuit of fairness. But just as importantly throughout history, redistributing income was seen as politically practical and in the self-interest of elites. The poor were often too poor to tax, and providing some basic levels of services that were available to rich and poor alike was seen as important in promoting social stability and preventing uprisings against the ruling class.

Progressive Income Taxation

The tradeoff between efficiency and equity is fundamental to the imposition of taxes. Jean-Baptiste Colbert, finance minister of Louis XIV, is said to have made an analogy between raising tax revenue and "plucking the goose so as to obtain the largest possible amount of feathers with the smallest possible amount of hissing". The hissing is the deadweight loss of inefficiency, but in a democracy it is also the complaints of those who are being taxed and believe that their tax burdens are unfair. Until we are able to impose the tax revenue method suggested by Monty Python in their "Tax on Thingy" episode—to "tax all foreigners living abroad"—taxation will always create complicated streams of costs and benefits that must be weighed in the face of imperfect information about the future.[26]

All of this said, Adam Smith's maxims of efficient taxation still hold today when he observed that the best taxes are (1) efficient, (2) certain, (3) convenient, and (4) fair. The best taxes are efficient if they discourage productivity the least in order to raise a specific level of revenue. The best taxes are certain if people know in advance what they are going to pay and when they have to pay it so that they can plan for the costs (and mitigate the impact) accordingly. Next, the best taxes are convenient, meaning that there are not large transaction costs associated with paying the tax in terms of calculating how much you have to pay and in the method of paying it. Finally, the best taxes are fair, which, as we have discussed throughout this book, can mean very different things to different people. But Smith took a simpler view of fairness and argued that fair taxes are ones in which similar people with the same incomes and wealth should pay the same tax. Progressive income taxation—a tax in which those with higher incomes pay a higher tax rate (not just tax level) than those with lower incomes—can be justified based on Smith's four maxims of efficient taxation. Let's examine each of these four maxims in turn, beginning with the question of whether progressive taxation can be efficient. As discussed in Chapter 3, conservatives believe that all taxes are very harmful to growth, but they believe that progressive taxes are particularly costly because they require that richer taxpayers pay higher tax rates. According to supply-side economics, the rich are the most productive members of society and higher tax rates disincentivize working, saving, entrepreneurship, and many other sorts of money-making behaviors among the rich, the costs of which trickle down in the form of lower standards of living for everyone.

While the supply-side story is a convincing one to many, the problem with it is that there is not much evidence to support it. Numerous empirical studies have failed to find evidence that progressive tax rates (how you slice the pie) impact economic growth (how big the pie actually is), either across countries or across time.[27] Likewise, there is little empirical evidence for the Laffer curve assertion that higher marginal tax rates reduce total tax revenue, at least at the marginal tax rates that currently exist in most countries.[28]

Why don't higher progressive tax rates on the rich have much of an impact on productivity and growth? First, to the extent that higher taxes on the rich are replacing taxes on the poor, progressive taxation can be efficient because taxing the rich is less likely to distort behavior than taxing the poor, particularly in terms of their choices to work. Those in the top 10 percent and beyond earn enough to work less than the poor, but interestingly, there is little evidence that the rich choose to work less than the poor. A great deal of evidence suggests that the elasticity of labor supply (how responsive labor supply is to changes in wages) is very close to zero for men, regardless of income.[29] As a result, higher marginal taxes do little to reduce people's desire to work. However, taxes do seem to play a large role in labor supply decisions for two types of workers. The first are those who are working at or near the poverty line. For the working poor, higher tax rates may be enough to reduce their disposable income to the point that they are better off not working and instead live on public assistance, particularly considering childcare expenses that must be incurred when working outside of the home.[30] The other group are rich, high-skilled workers who can easily migrate to other countries. For example, there is some evidence that the choice of the top 10 percent in Europe as to which country to live in is influenced by differences in the top income tax rates across different countries.[31]

This said, there are other reasons why taxes do not have major impacts on productivity and growth. Behavioral economists have identified many reasons why taxes do not play an unduly large role in our economic decisions, and it is because of the ways that people perceive taxes as part of our budget. The fact is that many of us—even the richest of us—don't know the marginal tax rates that we pay because we don't have to know them. Instead, taxes are treated as a fixed cost in our general "mental accounting", in the words of the Nobel Laureate Richard Thayer. In other words, taxes are a price we are forced to pay "off the top" and kept separate from other consumption and working decisions.[32]

In fact, contrary to the claims of conservative tax policymakers, taxing the rich may improve efficiency because there is strong evidence that inequality is partially driven by rent-seeking behavior (see Chapter 4) such as the increasing power of monopolies, special interest politics, and discrimination. As a result, higher taxes on those who are receiving these economic rents can be efficient because it discourages these activities.

Finally, progressive taxation that reduces economic inequality can actually improve efficiency for all of the reasons we have talked about throughout this book. As we have repeatedly emphasized, productivity is not an individual phenomenon but a social one. Production is not just done in isolation, but conducted through networks where our work and our ideas leak and match. We are only as productive as the people around us, and when inequality serves to make the people around us less productive, it makes each of us less productive and harms all of our incomes. This is the reason that while it is difficult to identify a solid empirical relationship between higher taxes and lower growth, there is a strong empirical relationship between higher inequality and lower growth.[33]

In regard to Smith's maxims that progressive taxation must be convenient and certain, progressive taxation is no less certain than a flat tax that is not progressive. Whether there is a single tax rate or multiple tax rates, the calculation is simple math. When taxes are not convenient or certain, it has nothing to do with there being multiple tax rates and everything to do with the unnecessary complexity of the rules that determine what income is taxed and what income is not taxed, and the ways that governments make it difficult for people to actually pay their tax bills.

What about the question of whether progressive taxes are fair? According to Smith, a tax is fair as long as two similar people with similar incomes and wealth pay the same tax. This can be true under any sort of progressive tax system. However, given the complexities of our lives, our wealth, our incomes, our natural endowments, etc., it is easy to argue that no tax can be truly fair under alternative definitions of fairness. But to require complete fairness in our tax system is unreasonable. The relevant question to ask is whether progressive taxes create outcomes that are *more fair* than those that exist if the tax is not imposed at all. While no tax is perfectly fair, many taxes do contribute to greater fairness.

Figure 7.1 presents the Gini coefficients across countries for market income (before taxes and transfers) and for disposable income (net of taxes and transfers) across a group of countries. The data here includes the impact of both progressive taxation and social safety net spending programs. Countries are ranked in order of the percentage difference between their market and disposable income Gini coefficients, with those countries with the smallest difference (Taiwan) at the top and those with the largest difference (Poland) at the bottom. Countries that have the smallest percentage difference use fiscal policy the least to reduce inequality in disposable income; those with the largest differences use redistributive fiscal policy the most.

There are a number of important takeaways from Figure 7.1. The first is that the effectiveness of fiscal policy in regard to its impact on inequality is clear:

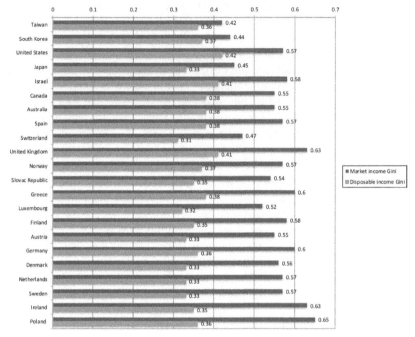

Source: Luxembourg Income Study database, available at https://www.lisdatacenter.org/, based on most recent data.

Figure 7.1   Market income vs. disposable income Gini coefficients across countries

across every country, disposable income after governmental intervention is more equal than market income before government intervention. In countries at the top of this list where the difference between the two is relatively small (such as East Asian countries and the US), the government is doing relatively little direct redistribution through fiscal policy. In countries at the bottom of the list where the difference is large (Germany, Sweden, Ireland, and Poland), government is more actively redistributing income through fiscal policy.

Another takeaway from Figure 7.1 is that there are multiple ways to achieve lower inequality. Some countries—particularly European countries—do it through aggressive fiscal policy redistribution, and there are larger differences between their market and disposable income Ginis. Other countries—such as Taiwan, South Korea, and Japan—achieve greater equality by having lower market income inequality in the first place. In other words, these countries rely less on fiscal policy and more on a mixture of structural reform policies.

The US is a particularly interesting case: as measured by the market income Gini, the US looks to be roughly in line with other developed countries. But its disposable income Gini is the highest because the US government does less redistribution of income using taxation and spending. Specifically, US redistribution policy focuses more on taking from the very rich and transferring to those at or near the poverty line, but does less to redistribute income among those in the upper- and lower-middle-class.[34] In fact, according to one comprehensive study, in the period before 1995, progressive taxation alone in the US offset roughly 60 percent of market inequality. However, in the last two decades since 1995, progressive taxation has had almost no impact on reducing inequality.[35] This is, in part, because the top marginal tax rate in the US fell from 80 percent in 1970 to 39.6 percent today, while the capital gains tax also declined from 35 percent to 15 percent (remember that the top 10 percent receive 90 percent of capital gains). As a result, the *average* income tax rate for the top 0.1 percent has fallen from 42 percent to only 27 percent.[36] Looking back at Figure 5.3, it is clear that the average tax rate of the top 1 percent has gotten much closer to that of the bottom 50 percent. And for the wealthiest Americans—the top 0.01 percent—the current tax code even becomes regressive. In 2007, the average tax rate on the 400 wealthiest Americans was only 16.6 percent, which is less than the average tax rate on all Americans of 20.4 percent.[37]

The US tax code has also become less progressive because it has become increasingly complex, with lots of loopholes that are most easily exploited by the rich. In other words, the US tax code is not only failing the fairness test, but it also fails to be certain or convenient. As a result, it is difficult to argue that the current US tax code meets any of Adam Smith's four maxims for an efficient tax system.

Overall, the cross-country data in Figure 7.1 can be seen as an example of the success of redistributive fiscal policy because levels of income inequality are being reduced because of it. Or, this data can be seen as illustrating the limits of redistributive fiscal policy, as significant levels of inequality in disposable income still exist across the world even in the face of redistributive policies adopted by governments. However, this data is *prima facie* evidence that governments can use fiscal policy to create a *more fair* distribution of overall disposable income, if not a completely fair distribution of income. This means that progressive taxation can be consistent with Smith's requirement that taxes must be fair.

Unfortunately, across most of the world there is a general trend towards less progressive taxation. Declines in top marginal tax rates like in the US have also occurred in the UK, Canada, and Japan, while little change in top tax rates has occurred in Denmark, Germany, Spain, and Switzerland. Those countries with the largest declines in the top tax rates have seen the biggest income gains among their top 1 percent.[38] Across all OECD countries, income redistribution has declined because of less progressive taxation and less redistribution of these tax receipts to the poorest citizens.[39]

An important reason for this decline in progressive taxation is that many countries have increasingly relied upon labor taxes tied to payrolls—which disproportionally impact the poor and middle-class—and less on taxes on corporate profits and capital—which disproportionally impact the rich. The reason for this gradual shift towards taxing labor and away from taxing capital is the increasing ease of avoiding capital taxes. Capital is more mobile than ever before, making the taxation of capital much more difficult than it has been in the past. Capital has become more mobile because of the three big changes in the nature of capital that we have already talked about. First, capital is increasingly financial in nature, meaning it is more fungible. Second, capital is more global, meaning that barriers have fallen and capital can more easily move across borders. Third, the boom in intellectual property has contributed to the overall explosion in intangible capital—more than half of all capital in many companies—which is difficult to value, easy to hide, and easily relocated to any tax haven across the world. Because of this, today over 40 percent of multinational profits are shifted to low-tax countries every year.[40]

Because governments are reluctant to tax profits and capital for fear of chasing it abroad, they are increasingly taxing what is harder to move: people and immobile capital (land and property). Of course, this reduces the ability of governments to use progressive taxation to promote greater equality because, as we talked about throughout this book, capital inequality (particularly inequality in intangible capital) has become an increasingly important factor in driving overall income inequality higher. Without the ability to tax capital, it is becoming harder and harder for governments to use progressive taxation to offset the unequal distribution of market income.

Wealth and Inheritance Taxes

Instead of focusing on income, a more effective method of dealing with inequality is to address unequal endowments in wealth by directly taxing wealth while people are alive, and taxing bequests to any heirs after their death.

The most influential proponent of an inheritance tax was Adam Smith, who argued that inherited wealth was unearned, and taxing it would eliminate dynasties, encourage charity, and incentivize entrepreneurship and hard work. In the US, the inheritance tax was first pushed in the early 1900s by the patrician Theodore Roosevelt, who argued it would stimulate individual initiative and hard work.

Of 24 developed countries in the OECD, 18 of them impose either an estate or inheritance tax.[41] However, many countries provide large exemptions, loopholes are generous, and tax avoidance/evasion is common. In the US, where the nominal tax rate on estates is high at 40 percent, very few households actually pay it; estates below $5.3 million are exempt and only 1 out of 700 estates pay any estate tax.[42] As a result, most inheritance tax systems raise little tax revenue—on average much less than 1 percent of total tax revenue. They also redistribute very little wealth—less than 1 percent of total inheritance wealth is reallocated. As a result, in the US almost half of total wealth inequality can be explained by inheritance alone.[43] On the other hand, the best evidence suggests that despite the lack of taxation, larger inheritances have played little role in rising rates of wealth inequality in developed countries such as the US.[44]

Wealth taxes are charged as a percentage of a person's assessed wealth every year. Currently, only three OECD countries impose a nationwide wealth tax (down from 11 in 1985). Wealth tax rates vary widely across countries but average less than 1 percent, are usually progressive, and typically are only assessed above a certain level of wealth.[45] The appeal of a wealth tax is obvious: at a time when both the share of capital in income and its role in driving inequality is rising, taxing wealth at a low rate could be an effective way to redistribute wealth endowments. It would also be a means of raising more tax revenue without directly reducing the incentives to work and innovate.

Unfortunately, wealth taxes are rare because they are notoriously difficult to implement. First, a broad domestic wealth tax is likely to be ineffective because people will move their mobile wealth into global tax havens. To be most effective, a broad wealth tax would have to be a global wealth tax, which would require a degree of coordination and cooperation amongst countries that currently does not exist. Second, data on personal wealth are difficult to obtain and inherently patchy. Accounting standards for valuing wealth are poor, and the value of many assets—such as art, collectables, and risky financial assets— is difficult to assess. Third, in order to pay the tax, people would be forced to regularly liquidate their assets, which could destabilize certain markets and would be very costly for people who have more of their wealth in illiquid assets, such as land or a business. And finally, there is strong evidence that people who are subject to wealth taxes cheat on them, in large part because wealth is easier to hide than income.

As a result, while wealth taxes seem to be an obvious part of the fiscal solution to both wealth and income inequality, as a practical matter in many countries they do not significantly reduce inequality and nor do they produce a great deal of tax revenue. That said, a wealth tax system modeled after Sweden could be implemented in places such as the US. In Sweden, households must list all of their assets (houses, financial assets, valuables) along with their incomes every year. Households are allowed to exclude all pensions, household goods, a standard deduction for automobiles and for a personal residence, and a standard deduction of roughly \$75,000 for singles and \$120,000 for married couples. Households would then have to pay a tax rate that escalates from 0.4 percent each year on their wealth over and above their threshold, but which ranges up to 2.2 percent each year for the richest households.[46] However, tax avoidance and tax evasion are pervasive in such a system without better means to internationally monitor wealth flows. Based on wealth data that leaked from hacked Swiss and Panama offshore tax haven accounts and that were released to the press, we know that not only are the wealthiest Swedes richer than what they report to Swedish tax authorities, but the cheating gets worse as the wealth gets larger. The wealthiest 1 percent of Swedes underpaid their taxes by 10 percent, while the wealthiest 0.01 percent underpaid their wealth tax by an incredible 30 percent.[47]

One radical form of a wealth tax that holds the potential to more accurately access wealth and, as a result, redistribute wealth much more effectively and efficiently has been proposed by Eric Posner and Glen Weyl. They refer to their tax as a COST tax on wealth, COST being short for "common ownership self-assessed tax".[48] Under a COST tax, every person would have to publicly declare the value of all of the assets that they own and pay an annual tax on this wealth. But here is the difference: once the value of an asset is publicly declared, anyone would have the right to buy it at that price. This system has a number of advantages. First, it eliminates the incentive to under-declare the value of your assets. For example, if you try to keep your wealth tax low by claiming that your house is only worth \$200,000 when it is worth much more than that, you are also opening yourself up to the danger that someone could then purchase it from you for that cheaper price. As a result, wealth assessments are likely to be much more accurate under a COST system.

In addition, COST systems increase the possibility that economic assets will be put to their most productive uses. For example, if someone sees a piece of land that they could use much more profitably than the current owner—and, as a result, values the land much more highly—they could quickly purchase this land at the current owner's assessed value. The monopolization of large amounts of land or other valuable assets by a small number of people would no longer be possible. Not only would this increase efficiency, but it would also eliminate the long, costly *eminent domain* legal battles that are common in most large public investment projects.

Finally, COST systems would raise a huge amount of tax revenue, most of which would be paid for by the wealthy. This revenue could then be used to finance public goods or distributed as a "social dividend" that could radically change the nature of wealth and income inequality. If a 7 percent a year COST tax was imposed in the US, it would redistribute one-third of the returns to capital from the rich to everyone else. This would translate into an annual subsidy for the median family (in terms of income) of about \$20,000 a year.[49]

Of course, the disadvantage of a COST system is that it radically changes the nature of private property. People would now be renting their assets by paying their wealth tax, and anyone could come along and purchase the assets they are renting at any time. While it has the potential to dramatically restructure wealth and income inequality, it also changes our relationship with property, which would be a difficult thing for many people to accept.

Land and Property Taxes

One form of a wealth tax that has long been a part of most tax systems is a tax on the value of land. Land taxes meet Smith's four maxims of taxation. They are efficient: taxing land won't reduce its supply. Because of this, the conservative Milton Friedman referred to a tax on unimproved land as "the least bad tax".[50] Taxing land is certain and convenient because it is fixed and can't be moved, it is hard to hide, and it is relatively easy to value. Finally, taxing land is fair because, in the words of Thomas Paine, everyone should have access to "the fruits of the earth".[51] As a result of the attractiveness of taxing land, property taxes (which include both land and structures) are common in most countries.

Some economists have taken this a step further and have argued that the ownership of land is a pernicious form of private property because it leads to the monopolization of important assets that have public benefits for everyone. The eminent economist Léon Walras argued that "Declaring individual land ownership ... means ... thwarting the beneficial effects of free competition by preventing the land from being used as is most advantageous for society."[52] Instead, Walras believed that land should be owned by the state and that the rents from land should be distributed to the public as a "social dividend"—in other words, similar to the COST tax on wealth we just discussed. This public ownership of land would be similar to what currently exists in China, where the government owns all land and upwards of 40 percent of all tax revenue comes from real estate leasing. Because the government retains ownership of the land, it can more freely distribute this land in ways that, presumably, will be most productive for Chinese society. Of course, because this land is distributed not through markets but via the Communist Party, corruption is rampant and the efficiency of land distribution in China is very low.[53]

Taxing real estate more heavily and progressively would be an effective way to deal with one important source of growing inequality in many countries, which is the boom in urban real estate prices (and the corresponding lack of growth in rural real estate prices). Housing prices have soared in many cities, with half of all urban land value in the US now located in only five cities. For example, in San Francisco between 1996 and 2016, median income doubled but the average house price went up by 3.6 times—80 percent of this rise was due to an increase in the price of land alone.[54] However, in the face of these booming land prices, property tax collections in most areas have remained flat, meaning that these huge land wealth windfalls are not being taxed.[55] Clearly, increased land and property taxes—including a national property tax—that are more comprehensive and progressive than current systems could be an important component of any serious policy reform to reduce inequality through fiscal policy. However, raising property taxes is difficult to sell politically, as property-owners make up a significant portion of those who vote, and houses are a significant fraction of the wealth of many middle-income families.

Wage Subsidy Programs

The fundamental problem with raising wages by mandating a minimum wage is that minimum wage laws essentially serve as a tax on firms that hire low-wage workers. A preferable alternative to minimum wage laws that more reliably helps the working poor and more clearly reduces inequality is for society as a whole (not just firms) to subsidize the wages of poorer workers. Wage subsidy programs aim to raise wages by shifting up the demand for labor through a government subsidy, as opposed to reducing the quantity demanded of labor by mandating that firms must pay higher wages.

An example of an effective wage subsidy program for the working poor in the US is the earned income tax credit (EITC). Under the EITC program, low-income families can earn tax credits—not just tax deductions—if they are employed but their income falls below a certain threshold based on the size of their family. Tax credits allow families that qualify for the EITC and owe zero taxes to still receive a tax refund from the government to support their income.

EITC programs have two distinct advantages over minimum wage laws. First, the EITC does not tax firms for hiring low-wage workers, so it is much less likely to create unemployment. Second, EITC focuses on low-income families with children, and not just low-wage workers. This is an advantage because many low-wage earners may actually be part of families from higher incomes—such as teenagers living at home or dual-income families in which one spouse is a high earner.

Unlike minimum wage laws, strong empirical evidence from multiple studies suggests that the EITC in the US actually increases employment (because you have to work to qualify for it) while reducing the number of families living below the poverty line by almost 10 percent. In addition, EITC benefits have been linked to increases in family health and educational attainment.[56] Studies also indicate that in conjunction with child tax credits, the EITC has reduced the Gini coefficient by almost 1 percent in the US.[57] As a result, it can be argued that the EITC program is one of the most effective methods of reducing inequality in the US by raising the incomes of the working poor. It has been so successful that many supporters have argued that the EITC should be expanded to include many in the middle-class, or maybe everyone in the entire population. This is the point of guaranteed universal basic income programs, which we will talk about later in this chapter.

EITC programs do have one shortcoming: by requiring recipients to work to qualify for benefits, the EITC increases the supply of labor, which puts some downward pressure on wages. In other words, workers do not get to keep all of the benefits of an EITC program because employers gain some of the benefits in the form of paying lower wages. By one estimate, workers only receive about 73 cents of every dollar spent on EITC.[58]

One alternative to the EITC is a negative income tax, championed by conservative stalwart Milton Friedman and pushed by Richard Nixon in the 1970s. Under a negative income tax, every family is guaranteed a minimum income, whether the adults work or not. Families that fall below this income receive a tax credit that gets them to this income, but which phases out as their income rises. In other words, benefits are "means-tested". The problem with means-testing is that the negative income tax actually becomes a tax on work because your benefits go down as you work more and your income rises. In fact, both the EITC and the negative income tax are means-tested programs, but only the EITC requires people to work and it phases out much more slowly. As a result, a negative income tax will actually create less employment than the EITC. However, because the supply of labor rises by less under a negative income tax, wages also fall by less, meaning that workers that do work get to keep more of the benefits of the program. In other words, to the extent that the worry is more about raising incomes and less about unemployment, the negative income tax is preferable. To the extent that unemployment is the primary worry, the EITC is the better option.

Social Spending and Public Investment

The US Supreme Court justice Oliver Wendell Holmes, Jr. said: "I like to pay taxes. With them, I buy civilization."[59] One way of using fiscal policy to facilitate more equality is to spend more on the public goods that benefit everyone, rich and poor alike. This includes spending on education, public infrastructure, basic research and development, public health, environmental protection, public information services, fair and accessible legal systems, etc. Because these public goods benefit everyone, however, they also suffer from the problem that people can free-ride off these goods, meaning too few of them will be provided by the free market unless they are provided (or subsidized) by the government. In an unequal world, the rich will be able to provide as many public goods for themselves as they want. As a result, it will be the poor that suffer the most when public investment is underfunded by governments.

Social spending programs such as welfare, healthcare spending, and retirement programs are income support programs, but they are also forms of public investment. In many ways, the most damaging aspect of poverty is not the missed consumption, but the hidden consequences of dealing with risk and variability in incomes. The poor tend to have extremely volatile incomes, and these ups and downs often prevent them from making the investments in their health, their education, and their retirement planning that would greatly improve their quality of life. This is the reason why, according to Anthony Atkinson and François Bourguignon, quoting the authors of a chapter in their edited volume, "No advanced economy achieved a low level of inequality ... with a low level of social spending, regardless of how well that country performed on other dimensions that matter for poverty, notably employment."[60]

Because of the federal nature of the US fiscal system, many US states do a particularly bad job of providing their citizens a safety net in the event of a negative life event. Some states, such as Oregon, offer a social safety net that is large enough to offset roughly half of the cost of a large negative shock to a family's income, such as job loss or a health crisis. But such generous states are the exception. Most states offer a safety net capable of offsetting only 5–10 percent of a negative shock to a family's income.[61]

The fact is that public investment across many developed countries has fallen to historic lows. In the US, federal government non-defense public investment (which excludes social insurance programs such as retirement, health, unemployment, and welfare benefits) reached its peak at only 1 percent of GDP in the 1960s, but has fallen to an astonishingly low 0.06 percent of GDP today, lower than at any time since World War II.[62] In other words, the US federal government is no longer choosing to make investments for tomorrow and has become solely focused on today.

Universal Basic Incomes

The idea behind a universal basic income (UBI) is that every adult and child should be provided with a uniform income by the government every year above what they earn through their work or wealth. With this basic income, every person would be guaranteed a minimum standard of living.

The idea of a UBI has a long history. The American political philosopher Thomas Paine, in his 1796 book *Agrarian Justice*, argued that everyone should be given a lump sum of money every year by the government, not just provided with certain goods or services. He argued for the creation of:

> a national fund, out of which there shall be paid to every person, when arrived at the age of twenty-one years, the sum of fifteen pounds sterling, as a compensation in part, for the loss of his or her inheritance, by the introduction of the system of landed

property. And also, the sum of ten pounds per annum, during life, to every person now living, of the age of fifty years, and to all others as they shall arrive at that age.[63]

Paine based his argument on the Christian assumption that the earth is the common endowment of all of mankind and the "fruits of the earth" should be shared. While the introduction of private property was necessary to raise overall prosperity, Paine believed it is also inherently unfair. "It is not charity but a right, not bounty but justice, that I am pleading for."[64]

Paine's arguments influenced many, including the libertarian John Stuart Mill, who wrote: "I conceive it to be highly desirable that the certainty of subsistence should be held out by law to the destitute able-bodied, rather than that their relief should depend on voluntary charity."[65] Mill likewise believed that the UBI should be granted to every adult, rich and poor alike, because a universal benefit was the fairest means of government assistance. By making it unconditional, Mill also thought that a UBI enhanced overall freedom of choice by allowing everyone the most flexibility to follow their own distinct desires, giving people the greatest chance to fully develop as human beings and achieve happiness. In Mill's opinion, a UBI was in the best interest of the poor and the rich alike. While it would protect the poor from poverty, it would also help protect the rich from populist rage.

Others have argued for a UBI as a way to encourage people to consider a wider range of unpaid jobs as a career, such as raising children, volunteering, and community organizing. To the extent that these jobs are crucial to our society but undercompensated, a UBI is a way of investing in valuable social capital that is currently underfunded. From an economic point of view, a UBI has distinct advantages over traditional social safety net systems such as food stamps or welfare that provide specific services only for specific individuals. First, a UBI is less patronizing because it is obligation free. UBI programs give people greater flexibility to spend their money and their time how they like. The government cannot dictate whether people have to work a job to receive benefits or what goods and services can be bought with these benefits. According to the Libertarian Matt Zwolinski:

> A basic income gives people an option—to exit the labor market, to relocate to a more competitive market, to invest in training, to take an entrepreneurial risk, and so on. And the existence of that option allows them to escape subjection to the will of others. It enables them to say "no" to proposals that only extreme desperation would ever drive them to accept. It allows them to govern their lives according to their own plans, their own goals, and their own desires. It enables them to be free.[66]

Second, a UBI would likely replace a large part of social safety net programs such as welfare, food, and housing assistance. As a result, it would not require the large government bureaucracy that is currently needed to make sure that money is spent in mandated ways. Instead, a UBI is a simple cash transfer system that would be much cheaper to implement.

Third, social safety nets that provide free education, healthcare, transportation, and food are essentially setting the price of these services at zero. This encourages their overuse—what is commonly referred to as "the tragedy of the commons". As a result of this overuse, the value of the services provided declines for everyone. But by raising incomes and putting cash into people's hands, a UBI stimulates demand and allows markets to price these goods appropriately, boosting their quantity supplied.

Finally, a UBI is not means-tested, so it makes everyone richer. This not only makes it more attractive politically, but it doesn't disincentivize the working poor from working. The same cannot be said for minimum wage laws. This also cannot be said for means-tested programs such as the EITC or the negative income tax, where benefits fall as income rises, essentially serving as a tax on earning more income for those at lower income levels.

Of course, there are objections to the UBI. The most common is that it rewards idleness. Of course, this is an objection that could also be made about accumulated wealth and the income earned off capital. Proponents of the UBI argue that few people would choose to be truly idle but instead would spend their time on valuable but unpaid activities such as their personal education, childcare, household production, the arts, or volunteering.

The second common objection raised about the UBI is related to the first, and it is that giving people income is not fair because it allows some people to live off the labor of others. As we talked about throughout this book— particularly in Chapter 3—fair is a concept that means different things to different people. Under Robert Nozick's "fruits of your own labor" conception of fairness, a guaranteed income for all is not fair because it is not earned. On the other hand, under John Rawls' difference principle, a UBI program can be fair if it works to the greatest benefit of the worst-off by favoring the disadvantaged. Many other liberals argue that the UBI is fair because we live in a world where endowments such as social capital, knowledge, organization, and institutions are jointly owned by the whole of society, so why shouldn't the whole of society earn a dividend from these endowments? And many libertarians believe that the UBI is fair because it enhances freedom of choice.

Another concern with the UBI is that it might not actually reduce absolute inequality because it would raise incomes for both the poor and the rich by the same amount (although it would reduce relative inequality, to some extent). To significantly redistribute income, the UBI would have to be financed with progressive taxation, which may not necessarily happen. In fact, some critics have argued that a UBI that is not globally available could actually increase inequality in the countries that adopt it by making them a more attractive destination for poorer migrants while at the same time requiring higher taxes that will trigger job and capital flight.

One final challenge with the UBI is the extent to which it would expand the role of government in the economy. According to the research of Philippe Van Parijs and Yannick Vanderborght, to be "basic" a UBI program would have to provide individuals with a level of income of 25 percent of per capita GDP.[67] In the US, this would be an income of $15,000 a person, which is roughly where the US poverty line is for a single adult. While a UBI would replace a great deal of the existing social safety net in many countries, because the UBI is universal and is given to every adult, it would require substantially higher tax revenues in most countries to fund it.

Many localities have experimented with guaranteed basic incomes, such as Ontario, Canada and several Dutch cities. Finland engaged in a two-year experiment in which 2,000 unemployed workers were given an unconditional $560 euros per month. However, in none of these experiments were the incomes truly universal because they were not given to every member of society. Surveys suggest that political support for the idea of universal basic incomes exists in Canada and many European countries. However, in the US, one survey suggests that 82 percent of Americans oppose the idea.[68] All of this said, the fact that UBI has many features that appeal to those on both the right and the left of the political spectrum makes it an interesting component of any fiscal policy reform program aimed at reducing inequality.

Guaranteed Employment/Conditional Cash Transfers

Many people simply cannot accept a government program that would allow an income grant to be given without also requiring recipients to work. For those who hold this view, joblessness itself is a problem, not just a lack of income. Proponents of guaranteed employment programs believe that not having a job impacts people's innate sense of worth and happiness (remember Plato's conception of *thymos*), and having large groups of permanently jobless can lead to crime and social dysfunction. In the words of the sociologist William Julius Wilson: "The consequences of high neighborhood joblessness are more devastating than those of high neighborhood poverty."[69]

Government "workfare" programs guarantee employment for all adults in return for receiving government benefits. While appealing to the "fruits of your labor" proponents, such enforced work programs have concerning implications for individual freedom. It is difficult not to think about the abuses that went on in Dickensian British poorhouses during an era when receiving government benefits was strictly tied to work. Also, government workfare programs require that the government provide jobs, not the market. They require a new government bureaucracy that has to be able to find suitable employment for every able-bodied adult that is not working. This is particularly challenging because most jobless workers at any point in time are lower-skilled, or have a very narrow set of skills that would make it difficult to match every worker with a job that complements their abilities. As a result, many workfare jobs closely resemble community service jobs assigned as a punishment to criminal offenders—not the message any society wants to send to law-abiding citizens who are trying to earn an income. The final problem with adopting government workfare is that new programs typically require the poor to do more for the same amount of benefits (or less) than they were already earning. In other words, they are primarily used as a way of punishing the poor. By itself, work-fare is not a means of reducing inequality.

However, this does not mean that conditional benefit programs cannot have important impacts on inequality. Conditional cash transfer programs such as the Bolsa Família program in Brazil (which covers one-fourth of Brazilians), Progresa in Mexico, or Di Bao in China pay families on the conditions that their children attend school and stay up-to-date with immunizations and well-ness health programs. These programs have been shown to improve schooling and health outcomes, and in both Brazil and Mexico these programs have reduced their Gini coefficients by 1 point.[70]

Universal Basic Assets

While a UBI addresses income inequality, it does not address the root cause of inequality, which is unequal endowments in education, wealth, and social capital. Having some form of universal basic assets (UBA) directly addresses wealth and endowment inequality. Ownership of assets—such as stocks, land, education, and social networks—gives people the leverage to generate an income and create more wealth through the benefits of compounding. If you inherit financial capital, you can invest the money in the stock market, buy a home, or pay for an education, thus leveraging your inheritance into an increased ability to generate more wealth and a higher income in the future. In other words, the old adage does hold: it takes money to make money. A UBA program aims to provide all citizens with these same advantages.

How would a UBA program work? In many ways, it works similar to a sovereign wealth fund. Many countries have sovereign wealth funds in which accumulated public wealth is held in financial assets—such as stocks, bonds, and real estate—which are managed in a manner similar to a university endowment or any other private wealth fund. For example, the Alaska Fund was built from royalties from the state's large oil industry and is now valued at 113 percent of the state's GDP. Norway's sovereign wealth fund, also built on oil revenue, controls nearly 60 percent of the country's wealth, or more than $160,000 per person. In theory, any government could purchase a share of the country's assets on behalf of the population—possibly by taxing existing wealth or inheritances—to create a social wealth fund that serves as an inheritance for everyone.

Once a UBA fund is in place, citizens could receive their share of the earnings every year as a "universal citizenship dividend". In Alaska in 2017, this was about $1,100 a person. Or, the revenues could be reinvested to increase the capital in the fund, as in Norway. While a UBA program is similar to a UBI program in that it can be used to generate a guaranteed income, an important difference is that people could also use their share of the fund as collateral to get a loan to buy a house, pay for an education, or take care of an important health expense. In other words, it would be a form of wealth insurance that currently does not exist for many people, including about half of the US population who have zero net wealth. As a result, UBAs are a way to help the poor make investments in their future that a UBI alone may not be able to help them make.

One form of a UBA program proposed by economists Darrick Hamilton and William Darity is "baby bonds", which would serve as a trust fund for every child born in the US.[71] The federal government would contribute to these accounts, contributing more to the accounts of children from poorer families, until the child reaches 18 years old, when they would take possession of the account. These economists view baby bonds as a way to explicitly deal with the racial wealth gap—the average white family has 20 times the wealth of the average black family—but in a non-discriminatory way.

Of course, there are potential complications with establishing a UBA. The most obvious is how to pay for it in the first place, particularly given the difficulties of taxing wealth that we talked about earlier. Hamilton and Darity's baby bonds proposal would cost about $82 billion a year, and not phase in for 18 years (until children born today reach adulthood). This is a large amount of money in terms of absolute dollars, but only a little over 2 percent of total federal government spending today.

Approving any significant new spending to support private wealth accumulation seems challenging given that governments have had an increasingly difficult time maintaining their existing levels of public wealth. While net private wealth has skyrocketed—from 200–350 percent of national income in most rich countries in 1970 to 400–700 percent today—net public wealth (public assets minus public debts) has declined in nearly every country except Norway since the 1980s. In China and Russia, public wealth has declined from 65 percent to 25 percent of national wealth. In the face of rising public debt, net public wealth has even become negative in recent years in the US and UK, and is only slightly positive in Japan, Germany, and France. The only exceptions to the general decline in public wealth are oil-rich countries with large sovereign wealth funds, such as Norway.[72]

A second problem with a UBA is with managing its funds: Who will do it? Will there be conflicts of interest? Will such a large fund have inordinate power in financial markets? Will the government be a passive or active investor? Will it change the behavior of firms to be owned by the government? Would this turn workers into owners, and counterintuitively give companies more power in the political process by making the management of private capital a primary responsibility of the government (and further weaken the power of labor in the process)? These practical questions related to control, power, and influence are particularly troublesome in democracies where capital has already seen its influence rise substantially.

IN CONCLUSION

In this chapter, we have briefly reviewed a number of policies that could potentially reduce income and wealth inequality. Some of these are structural reform policies aimed at fundamentally changing the organization of markets and of inequality in market income. The argument for focusing on structural reform instead of fiscal policy transfers is that structural reform can, in theory, reduce the rent-seeking behaviors and unequal endowments that are the root causes of inequality. Structural reform policies can correct for economic inequality at its source.

Other reform policies involve changing government fiscal policy and attempting to reduce the inequality of disposable income (after government taxes and transfers are taken into account). The argument for using fiscal policy to correct for inequality is that if governments get too involved in manipulating markets, they will reduce employment, productivity, and growth. Using fiscal policy to correct for market inequality treats the symptoms of the disease of inequality without putting the economy at risk of more invasive treatments.

It would be a reasonable conclusion to draw from this chapter that there is little that can be done to significantly generate more egalitarian outcomes in this age of rising inequality. All of the reforms we talked about in this chapter—increasing the power of organized labor, imposing minimum wage laws, taxing wealth, creating a universal basic income, etc.—have significant risks and costs that make it very unlikely that any single program can be the cure-all for inequality. The exact policy mix needed to create more egalitarian societies is likely to be multi-dimensional and combine many of the ideas discussed here. The policy mix is also likely to be very different in diverse countries, reflecting different institutions, different politics, and different histories and cultural attitudes about economic inequality.

However, it is possible to create more equitable societies. Looking across the globe, we see two broad models for reducing economic inequality that have been shown to be effective. The first model could be called the Asian model and has been adopted by countries such as South Korea, Japan, and Taiwan. These countries have relatively small governments and use little fiscal policy in the form of tax and transfer programs to redistribute income. Instead, these countries focus on structural reforms aimed at reducing rents and redistributing endowments over the long run so that market incomes remain relatively equal. These countries have built strictly egalitarian and meritocratic educational systems. Organized labor plays a big role in businesses and, in fact, workers are part owners of most corporations. Finally, wealth and inheritance is taxed at a very high rate, reducing the intergenerational inequality of wealth.

The second model is the European model, followed in Western Europe and Canada. In these countries, wealth, education, and other endowments are quite unequal, making market income very unequal. However, governments actively redistribute income through a complicated series of progressive income taxes and social welfare and spending policies. While not perfect, this "after the fact" approach to dealing with inequality does address many of the social and economic costs of inequality, even if it does not address its fundamental sources. And the end result is less inequality: while the US and Europe had similar levels of inequality in 1980, today the top 1 percent in the US gets twice the share of national income as it does in Europe, where more extensive fiscal redistribution policies have moved many families into the middle-class that would not be there in the US.[73]

Given today's rising inequality in income and wealth in Western democracies, an important question needs to be answered: Why don't the voters in these democracies vote for politicians who will adopt redistribution and structural reform policies that will reduce inequality? The answer to this question is not a simple one, but is linked to the fact that Western democracies are governed by political parties, which are really multi-dimensional coalitions. The growing political polarization in modern democracies cuts across class, making it difficult for political parties on both the right and the left to take a strong stand on adopting more egalitarian policies for fear of alienating some of the members of its coalitions. The stagnant poor and middle-class are divided between those who desire more redistribution (and support left-leaning parties) and those who feel a growing sense of nativism that blames immigrants, not the rich, for their declining relative fortunes (and support right-leaning parties). The rich and elites are divided between those with higher levels of education and white-collar jobs who worry about the social impact of growing inequality (and support left-leaning parties), and those rich who see their economic success as a just reward that properly incentivizes economic success (and support right-leaning parties). Even those who view economic inequality as a major issue are divided between those who see domestic inequality as the biggest worry and blame globalization for squeezing the poor and the middle-class of rich countries, and those who see reducing global poverty as the key goal and support more international trade as the best way to help these poor. As a result of all of this political division, Thomas Piketty has found that while richer voters in Western democracies (the US, UK, and France) used to be more likely to vote for right-leaning parties and against income redistribution policies 30 years ago, today income has little predictive power in determining voting behavior (although in regards to wealth, it remains the fact that wealthier voters are more likely to vote for the political right). In fact, today it is education and not income or wealth that is the strongest predictor of voting behavior, with more highly educated voters more likely to vote for the political left and less-educated voters for the political right.[74] In other words, class appears to be less closely defined by income than by education in Western democracies, and this has impacted people's voting behavior and preferences for redistribution policies in ways that still seem to be in flux and are not yet well understood. In the meantime, it is very difficult for governing coalitions to build any consensus around taking action to significantly address today's rising levels of economic inequality.

For the countries that have adopted more egalitarian economic policies, however, there is one characteristic that they all share. In each of these more egalitarian countries, there is a fundamental and widely held belief that there exists a social compact between citizens, and when some people have dramatically more than other people, this social compact is jeopardized. There is a widely held belief that inequality threatens social order, it threatens institutions, it threatens economic productivity, it threatens happiness, and it threatens the basic quality of life. When a country's citizens generally share this belief, it creates the political will to influence political systems which, in turn, changes economic policies. This appears to be the most fundamental difference between equal and unequal countries: Do their citizens care enough, or don't they?

NOTES

1. Norton and Ariely (2011).
2. Lakner (2017).
3. Derenoncourt and Montialoux (2019).
4. Dube et al. (2010).
5. See Meer and West (2016), Neumark and Wascher (2007), and Clemens and Wither (2014).
6. *The Economist* (2018f).
7. Taplin (2017).
8. *The Economist* (2018c).
9. Azar et al. (2018).
10. Naidu et al. (2018).
11. Checchi and Garcia-Penalosa (2008).
12. Bertrand and Mullainathan (2001).

13. Frick and Lehmann (2005).
14. Goldberg and Pavcnik (2016).
15. Garrett (2017).
16. Baker (2016).
17. Pavcnik (2017).
18. Autor et al. (2014).
19. Baldwin (2016).
20. Corak (2013).
21. Glazerman et al. (2013).
22. Corak (2013).
23. Ibid.
24. Goldrick-Rab (2016).
25. Putnam (2000).
26. *Monty Python* (1970).
27. IMF (2017), Ostry et al. (2014), and Lindert (2009).
28. Saez et al. (2012) and McClelland and Mok (2012).
29. Saez et al. (2012).
30. Hoyes and Patel (2015).
31. Muñoz (2019).
32. Thaler (1985).
33. Ostry et al. (2014).
34. Chauvel (2013).
35. IMF (2017).
36. Alvaredo et al. (2013).
37. Pollack and Thiess (2011).
38. Scheidel (2017).
39. Causa and Hermansen (2017).
40. *The Economist* (2018d).
41. Technically, an inheritance tax is paid by the recipient based on their personal wealth, while an estate tax is paid on the total value of the transfer. The US actually imposes an estate tax.
42. Americans for Tax Fairness (2018).
43. Palomino et al. (2019).
44. Wolff (2017).
45. Ibid.
46. Ibid.
47. Alstadaester et al. (2018).
48. Posner and Weyl (2018).
49. Ibid.
50. Cited in Tideman (1994).
51. Paine (1797).
52. Walras (2010, p. 148).
53. For a discussion of land distribution in China, see Economy (2018).
54. *The Economist* (2018e).
55. Albouy et al. (2018).
56. See Hoyes and Patel (2015) and Nichols and Rothstein (2015).
57. Hungerford (2010).
58. Rothstein (2010).
59. Holmes (1927).
60. Atkinson and Bourguignon (2014, p. lvi).

61. Fleck and Simpson-Bell (2019).
62. Center for American Progress (2015).
63. Paine (1797).
64. Ibid.
65. Mill (1848).
66. Zwolinski (2013).
67. Van Parijs and Vanderborght (2017).
68. Ibid. and Rasmussen Reports (2011).
69. Wilson (1996, p. xiii).
70. Soares et al. (2007).
71. Hamilton and Darity (2010).
72. Alvaredo et al. (2018a).
73. Blanchet et al. (2019) and Derndorfer and Kranzinger (2018).
74. Piketty (2018).

8. What is the future of economic inequality?

There is a long history of bad predictions in economics, so whenever economists look towards the future, we do it with a great deal of trepidation. One could be excused for thinking that the Chinese philosopher Lao Tzu was talking about economists when he said: "Those who have knowledge, don't predict. Those who predict, don't have knowledge." Forecasting in economics is particularly treacherous because economies evolve over time. As a result, while it is easy to make the assumption that past trends will continue into the future, unexpected shocks and permanent changes to the economy are not just possible, but probable. As a result, economists tend to miss turning points and dramatic structural changes. In addition, economists often tend to focus on a small number of factors in their models in order to make them more tractable in the face of complexity. But when it comes to forecasting something like economic inequality that has causes that are multi-dimensional, any single model will almost certainly miss something important. For these reasons, it has been said—rightly, I am afraid—that an economist is someone who can only tell you why something happened *after* it has happened.

Having admitted this, it is also better to look forward with uncertainty (and humility) than to fail to look forward at all. There is real value in looking out the front window when you are driving a car, even if it is foggy and there could be unexpected turns in the road. For that same reason, it is important to try and discern the most likely path of inequality in the future, even if that path is sure to be different from what we expected. That is what we are going to do in this chapter, while, at the same time, looking forward to the factors that are hardest to predict and that are the most likely to play a role in making our forecasts of future inequality wrong.

WHERE ARE WE NOW AND WHAT ARE THE TRENDS IN INEQUALITY?

Before we look forward, let's make sure that we understand where we are right now. In this book, I've argued that understanding inequality is key to understanding how economics actually works. In the real world, it is not just our *absolute* standing that matters in shaping our behavior, but it is our *relative* status that is the primary influence on our decision-making, how we act, and how we feel about ourselves. Inequality is the outcome of economic actions, but also fundamentally influences economic decisions because of our psychology, the importance of the sharing of ideas in innovation, and the importance of social status in our happiness. Decades of research in economics, politics, psychology, sociology, and neuroscience have established a link between inequality and important economic phenomena such as the power of networks in generating new ideas; the significance of social norms and status in decision-making and risk-taking; the crucial roles of social capital and trust; the market failures created by information externalities; the importance of coordination failure and historical path dependence; the impact of financial market failures and macroeconomic instability; the political economy of democratic capitalism; and the primacy of economic institutions.

Few of these phenomena show up in Classical economic theory, where only absolute matters and individuals themselves largely determine their own productivity. When markets work perfectly and externalities are ignored, then everything is already perfect and any policies adopted to enhance equity will also harm efficiency. This strict Classical tradeoff between efficiency and equity is the creed of those who believe that any attempt to mitigate inequality is dangerous and that the sole focus of economics should be on increasing the size of the pie, not on how it is sliced.

However, what we have learned during this new era of inequality is that Classical thinking is at best simplistic, and at worst willfully ignorant. New thinking and a vast array of interdisciplinary research is showing us that not only is productivity a social phenomenon, not an individual one, but even our individual happiness is a function of how we view our place in society. Until we understand the vast and complicated ways in which we are interconnected, we cannot understand why inequality is so costly to efficiency, to our society, and to our individual mental and physical health. When we do begin to understand these webs of connections, we see that there can be virtuous circles (or vicious cycles) that exist between efficiency and equity. Greater equity produces positive externalities that leak and match in ways that enhance everyone's well-being, and these positive externalities are maximized when families and social networks are strong, barriers to inclusion are low, educational achievement is high, and income and social mobility exists. As economists begin to understand the power of these connections, inequality has finally risen above its traditional spot as a periphery issue in economics. Inequality should now be a fundamental aspect of our economic theories and also of our public policy discussions if we aim to improve the quality of life for everyone, rich and poor alike.

This is why the current trends in domestic inequality across most countries are so disturbing. In our era of rising inequality, changes in our economics—

such as the growing importance of education-intensive labor, intangible capital, the role of globalization, and the creation of economic superstars and winner-takes-all markets—have not only changed the ways that we organize ourselves in our work, but also the ways that we organize our families, our broader society, and our politics. All of these factors are contributing to the growing gap between the rich and the poor. More importantly, they are also contributing to worsening public health, greater social conflict, growing polit-ical polarization, more stress, riskier behavior, and a general feeling of unhap-piness and discontent that permeates much of our society and our discourse. While a small number of rich have the safety net of their social networks and their net wealth, many of the rest of us feel like we have been disrespected, left behind, isolated, and forgotten.

How much has within-country inequality increased? As we discussed in Chapter 2, most countries have seen their income Gini coefficients rise by more than 20 percent from their lows in the 1970s. The countries that have seen the fastest increases in inequality are either the fastest-growing countries (China and India), Anglo-Saxon countries (US, UK, Canada, and Australia), or countries that have become more authoritarian (Russia, Egypt).

The biggest changes in inequality can be seen in the unprecedented rise of the top 10 percent, top 5 percent, top 1 percent, top 0.1 percent, and top 0.01 percent, with each of these privileged groups rising significantly faster than the group right below it. The share of total income going to the top 10 percent has increased in every region of the world since 1980. In the US between 1979 and 2007, 60 percent of all the gains in market income went to the top 1 percent, while only 9 percent went to the bottom 90 percent. Of this top 1 percent, it is the top 0.1 percent and top 0.01 percent who have done the best: the top 0.1 percent raised its share of total income by four times what it was in 1970, and the top 0.01 percent raised its share of total income by six times.

The rise of those at the top has coincided with the relative decline of the bottom 50 percent. The percentage of the population in the middle-class has been falling in every major developed democracy since 1980. In the US, the top 1 percent now earns more than 27 percent of total income, while the bottom 50 percent has seen its share of total income fall from 21 percent to only 12 percent.

When we look at wealth, we see even greater disparity. In 2018, it took only the 28 richest people in the world to accumulate a total amount of wealth equal to the bottom half of the world's population. The 20 wealthiest Americans on the Forbes 400 list own more than the bottom half of the US population, while the average American household only has enough wealth to sustain its normal spending for less than a week. All together, the Forbes 400 members have as much wealth as all African Americans plus one-third of the American Latino population combined. The share of wealth going to the top 1 percent has risen in all countries since the mid-1980s, and has roughly doubled in the US, China, and Russia.

All of these facts and figures can seem overwhelming, and also depressing. Will it get worse in the future? Could inequality eventually reach levels not seen since pre-industrial times, back when slavery and serfdom were common? Or has inequality simply regressed to its mean, which is closer to the inequality levels of the 1930s than the 1970s?

There have been few comprehensive forecasts of future changes in inequality within specific countries. In one forecast that focuses specifically on the US, Mark Zandi estimates that inequality in the US has peaked and will remain steady.[1] There are factors that will continue to drive US inequality higher, such as an aging US population that reduces the labor force participation rate, as well as automation that reduces employment in some sectors. However, Zandi estimates that these factors will be offset by a decline in two other trends that have played an important role in rising inequality. The first of these is that the decline in manufacturing wages relative to wages in services jobs should slow as many manufacturing jobs that were vulnerable to globalization have already left the US. In addition, Zandi forecasts that rising global incomes should increase US exports and end the trend of rising US trade deficits. However, this forecast is highly dependent upon the income growth forecast in the US, and future recessions—which, as we have talked about, may be more likely in the face of growing inequality and higher debt levels in the US—put wide confidence intervals around such forecasts.

Even if income inequality within countries like the US remains stagnant, wealth inequality is very likely to increase. Another group of economists made "business as usual" assumptions to forecast the share of wealth going to the top 1 percent, the top 0.1 percent, and the top 0.01 percent in the US, Europe, and China.[2] They predict that the richest 1 percent (greater than $1.3 million in wealth), the richest 0.1 percent (greater than $5.9 million in wealth), and the richest 0.01 percent (greater than $29.3 million in wealth) in these three areas will increase their share of total wealth by 1 percent every five years, meaning that almost all future changes in wealth inequality would be driven by the gains of those at the tip-top of the wealth distribution. Figure 8.1 shows what this looks like if projected out to the year 2050. The top 0.1 percent wealthiest would catch up the wealth share of the upper-middle-class, which is defined as the 40 percent of the population above the median but below the top 10 percent. This means that while today the wealthiest top 0.1 percent is about 200 times wealthier than the upper-middle-class, by 2050 they would be 400 times richer than the upper-middle-class. When viewed within the context of the dangers that rising inequality poses to our economy, our society, our politics, and our personal happiness, such "status quo" forecasts regarding wealth lead to some very sobering predictions about the future.

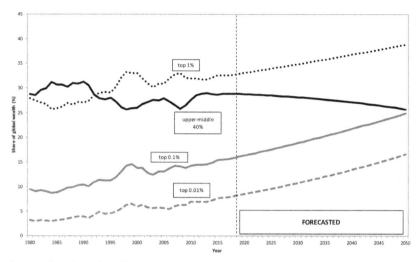

Source: Alvaredo et al. (2018a).

Figure 8.1   Wealth inequality in the US, Europe, and China

On the brighter side, in regards to global inequality, the decline in between-country inequality will most likely continue to lead to an overall decline in global inequality. This is despite the fact that as more countries become richer, global growth will begin to slow because of diminishing marginal returns. The economists Tomas Hellebrandt and Paulo Mauro estimate that the global Gini will decrease by 0.04 points by 2035. This decline occurs because the projected fall in between-country inequality will reduce the global Gini by 0.1 points, which is large enough to overcome the impact of the expected rise in within-country inequality that drives the global Gini higher by 0.06 points.[3] Figure 8.2 presents the global distribution of income in 2003, 2013, and the predicted distribution in 2035. We can see that the world's distribution of income will become considerably more equitable according to these projections. This predicted decline in global income inequality is driven by two factors. The first is the continuing fall in population growth in many poorer countries, particularly in sub-Saharan Africa. The second factor contributing to the overall decline in global inequality is the continuation of strong global growth, particularly in India, and in Indonesia, Bangladesh, Thailand, and Vietnam. In fact, global median income doubled between 1980 and 2015 and is forecasted to rise to $4,000 by 2035 and more than $7,000 a person by 2050. Interestingly, growth in China will soon begin to add to global inequality because China will have risen above global average income and has already

reduced a great deal of poverty. However, while global inequality is very likely
to decline for at least the next 20 years, according to the forecasted global Gini
coefficient of .61 in 2035 (higher than the most unequal of countries) we will
be nowhere near an egalitarian utopia.

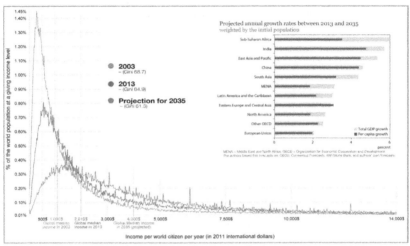

Source: Roser (2018), used with permission, data from Hellenbrandt and Mauro (2015).

Figure 8.2   *The global income distribution in 2003, 2013, and projected*
                 for 2035

However, while the global Gini coefficient is likely to fall, this will mask
increasing income disparities among many subgroups within the global income
distribution. The share of income going to the top 1 percent is still predicted
to rise from 21 percent today to more than 24 percent, while the income share
of the bottom 50 percent is still expected to fall slightly.[4] While the reduction
in between-country inequality is expected to dominate, changes in domestic
inequality will be crucially important in determining exactly how the top 10
percent performs relative to the bottom 50 percent within every country. In
countries that follow the path of US-style inequality, the gains in the incomes
of the rich are most likely to come at the expense of relative declines of the
bottom 50 percent. For countries that exhibit more European-style inequality,
the bottom 50 percent could see gains in income relative to the top 1 percent.

Likewise, gains in the *absolute* income of the bottom 50 percent are highly
sensitive to changes in domestic income distributions. Therefore, the average
income of the global bottom 50 percent would be twice as high if future changes
in within-country inequality follow the path of European-style inequality as

opposed to following the path of US-style inequality. In other words, income inequality matters not just for relative income, but also for absolute levels of income and the eradication of poverty. If instead of rising, the Gini coefficient would fall by 1 percent a year instead, an additional 120 million people could be risen out of global poverty by the year 2030—an impact greater than an (unlikely) 2 percent increase in global economic growth rates.[5] On the other hand, growth alone will not guarantee reductions in global poverty if too large a share of the gains goes to the top 10 percent.

WHAT FACTORS WILL INFLUENCE THE FUTURE OF ECONOMIC INEQUALITY?

When talking about something as complex and varied as the causes of economic inequality, speculating about what factors will play the biggest role in future changes in inequality feels as perilous as speculating about what the weather will be on May 20, 2055. As the baseball player Yogi Berra said, "The future ain't what it used to be." While we have learned about the factors that have driven inequality higher and lower in the past, to assume that these same factors will be just as important in the future could be as mistaken as investing in horse carriages 100 years ago. New innovations and structural changes to the economy are likely to set off chains of events that could create a future that could never be imagined today.

However, in the words of Mark Twain, while history doesn't repeat itself, it often rhymes. There are good reasons to think that we do understand a great deal about the drivers of future economic inequality. Experience tells us that three primary factors will play the crucial roles in determining the income and wealth ladders of the future, and who stands on each rung. Let's take a brief and speculative look at each of these three factors.

Technological Innovation

Skills-based technological change has been one of the most important forces driving this current era of rising inequality, and it seems quite likely that technological innovation will drive future changes in the distribution of income and wealth as well, although the direction of these changes is uncertain.

Technology has the potential to reduce inequality. Historically, we have seen innovations in technology that have increased the returns to less-skilled workers: innovations such the steam engine, public sanitation, electrical engineering, and the internal combustion engine. These innovations improved the productivity of almost all workers and raised standards of living across the board without creating greater income gaps between workers.

Unfortunately, there doesn't seem to be any evidence of new broad-based, productivity-enhancing innovations on the immediate horizon. Instead, the current trend continues to be one of automation that eliminates mid-skilled jobs—jobs in manufacturing, office/clerical, and sales. Those mid-skilled workers that have not been able to move into higher-skilled jobs—professional, technical, and management—are being forced to move into lower-skilled jobs that have not yet been automated. These lower-skilled and lower-paying jobs tend to be personal-service jobs such as healthcare, hospitality, security services, and janitorial services.[6] In other words, as mid-skilled jobs gradually disappear, those workers that can't move up are moving down.

The labor economist David Autor looked at new job classifications in US census data to identify the new jobs of the future, and the jobs of the future appear to fall into one of three categories.[7] First, there are "frontier jobs", meaning high-tech jobs that focus on innovation and ideas, such as computer programing, data analytics, and artificial intelligence analysis. Frontier jobs are more urban, more likely to be filled by men, and also higher-paying than average. But the second category is equally important: "wealth workers". These are jobs that require less education and are linked to the rising incomes of those at the top of the income distribution. This would include jobs such as oyster preparers (I'm not making this up), personal trainers, and sommeliers. These jobs are also more urban, more likely to be filled by women, but only pay average wages because the workers who have the skills to fill these are not in short supply. The third and final category is "last mile jobs". This includes jobs that have already been automated to a large extent, but have personal-service components that need to be conducted by people (although often virtually, and not in person). This includes delivery and customer services, technicians, and sales people. These jobs are low paying, less likely to be in urban areas, and very likely to be replaced in the future as automation continues to advance.

These current trends point towards a growing wage gap between those with and without a college education, and a continuing rise in economic inequality. The future appears golden for groups that are already economically privileged: highly educated, urban, and young workers. It appears to be a lot less promising for those without a college education, those who are older and less able to retrain, and those unwilling to migrate to urban areas. In Autor's words, "It is not clear that the US is still a 'land of opportunity' for non-college adults."[8]

Could there be future innovations that will increase the returns to mid- and lower-skilled workers, and make many workers more productive, as opposed to unnecessary? In other words, could the work of the future reflect more of the overall distribution of people's natural skills and attributes, and not be so focused on only those workers who can obtain a college education? The answer is: possibly. As high-skilled labor gets more expensive, there are economic incentives to develop technologies that can be conducted using low-skilled labor. While it is difficult to say exactly what these future technologies might be, they might be found in 3D printing and digital production, which allow more forms of manufacturing to take place not just where wages are the lowest, but anywhere that people live and consume. This could reduce wage gaps between people and places that could also reduce overall inequality. Broad-based productivity-enhancing technologies might also be found in future advances in biomedical engineering, which offer everyone the chance to live longer, live healthier, and become more productive.

On the other hand, it is also possible that the trend towards automation could pick up pace. In the future, robotics with dexterity and vision, self-driving vehicles, and artificial intelligence could change or eliminate a wide range of jobs that don't seem like they could be possibly replaced by a machine today. In Chapter 5, we talked about the ways that robotic automation is placing, and will continue to place, increasing pressure on jobs that are neither creative, nor variable, nor highly cognitive. The number of industrial robots is expected to quadruple from their current levels, and have decreased employment and wages by amounts that far exceed that of globalization.[9] Looking farther into the future, some studies have concluded that half of all jobs could be replaced by existing automation technology, and almost all jobs will be significantly disaggregated and re-bundled into tasks that machines can do and can't do.[10]

Probably the foreseeable technology with the potential to have the biggest impact on inequality is artificial intelligence (AI). One definition of human intuition and creativity is simply "pattern recognition". This is exactly what artificial intelligence is based upon—the idea that with enough information, judgment is unnecessary. As a result, AI threatens to replace almost any human in any job, even jobs that are inherently creative and unique. Consider one example of the potential power of AI, which is playing chess. Stockfish 8, which was the world computer chess champion in 2016, was beaten by Google's AlphaZero chess computer in 2017. Stockfish 8 is not based on AI but instead based on sheer calculation power—it calculated 70 million moves a second by analyzing an extensive history of human-played chess to calculate every move it made. AlphaZero, on the other hand, is much less computationally proficient and only makes 80,000 calculations a minute. It also knew nothing about chess before it entered the competition—it learned chess through machine learning, or playing against itself for only four hours. By all accounts, it played creatively—more creatively than any human—but without human help.[11] If machines can learn to play chess in four hours, they can potentially do anything: compose music, design buildings, and maybe—perish the thought—even write books about economic inequality.

Today, it appears that most of the gains from innovation in ICT are going to two groups that are not mutually exclusive: the highly educated and the wealthy owners of capital. Increasingly, the top 1 percent not only own most of the world's wealth but also the most access to idea networks, intangible capital, information, data, creativity, and political power. Could AI eliminate the economic power of a good chunk of the world's population and create an affluent class that has access to AI and capital, and a permanent underclass that doesn't? At the danger of sounding alarmist, the historian and philosopher Yuval Noah Harari worries about a future in which the human race goes through a process of speciation in which we gradually evolve into different biological castes, with some elites forming permanent ruling oligarchies and the rest becoming a permanent poverty class.[12]

The fundamental question here is whether future technologies like AI look more like technologies of the past, or whether this is something fundamentally new. In the past, technological innovation has not led to the elimination of jobs overall, but the destruction of some jobs and the creation of other jobs in even greater number, despite fears to the contrary. As we have seen, Queen Elizabeth I banning knitting machines in 1589 and the Luddites smashing sewing machines in 1793, in both cases were based on the fear that new technologies that increased the productivity of workers would also steal their jobs. The problem with Luddite thinking is that they assumed that labor-saving machinery would be used to produce the same amount of output, just using less labor. Instead, what we have observed throughout history is that labor-saving capital and technology is used to produce *more* of these goods, and many other new goods, using *more* labor overall. In other words, technology and capital have not been used to replace jobs, but to generate more and different jobs devoted to meeting our unlimited desires for new forms of consumption. Of course, the transition from old jobs to new jobs in different industries is often costly to certain individuals. This is the reason for the short-sighted resistance to new methods of production that has existed throughout history, from the Luddites nearly 200 years ago to possibly those people today who fear that robots will leave us all unemployed in the future.

However, if the vast majority of the future benefits from technology go to a smaller and smaller group of people, will it create enough overall demand to fuel the job creation needed to replace the jobs lost? And will the jobs created be at such low wages that the gap between the haves and the have-nots gets even wider over time? If this is the case, a vicious cycle between technology and inequality could lead to a future of work that is potentially very different from the nature of work today—different from a future we can really even imagine. We have all grown up in a world where most people earn a living— and develop an important sense of self-worth—by selling their labor. What if this ceases to be true? What if only a small number of people are needed to produce almost everything we consume, which in the future would be the luxuries of the rich and the stagnant living standards of everyone else? How do we provide not only sufficient income that can sustain improved standards of living for everyone, but also a sense of purpose and esteem for every individual?

Changes in Globalization

Globalization has played an important role in reducing global inequality, but at the same time it has also contributed to growing within-country inequality in developed countries. The economic impacts of modern global supply chains are much messier than when international trade could be thought of in terms of simple national comparative advantage across final products. There is good reason to believe that the race between technology and education will increasingly go global, that future advances in productivity will be increasingly driven by intensive specialization at every stage of the production process, and that any inequality in skills between people will be amplified into even more domestic inequality in the future.

However, while the increasing development of global supply chains and global information networks seems inexorable, there are reasons to think that the next wave of globalization could look much different than the last. In fact, we might already be in it. The growth of globalization has slowed since the Global Financial Crisis of 2008, and international trade has actually fallen from 61 percent of world GDP before the crisis to 58 percent today. For a variety of reasons, we might have moved from an era of globalization to an era of, in the words of trend-watcher Adjiedj Bakas, "slowbilization".[13]

Future globalization could be upended by future innovation. Developing technologies such as 3D printing and digital production create the real possibility that mass production in factories could disappear. Instead of organizing manufacturing based on the location of physical capital and economies of scale, future manufacturing may take place locally on a piecemeal basis, as needed, and in less labor-intensive ways. This kind of localized, miniaturized manufacturing poses a significant threat to developing countries that have followed a strategy of investing in labor-intensive industries and taking advantage of global supply chains. Big parts of global supply chains might become obsolete when anything can be produced anywhere at any time.[14]

Another factor influencing the future of globalization is that international trade is not only an economic but also a political process: it is dependent upon open trade policies that reduce barriers on goods and services as they move across borders. But growing discontent with international trade in developed countries, coupled with a rise in populism and nationalism across the globe, is leading to changes in trade policy that could put an end to today's era of globalization. This has happened before. Our current age of globalization is actually the second age of globalization. The first took place in the late 1800s and peaked in the early 1900s, coming to an end because of wars (World War

I and II), a global economic slowdown (the Great Depression), and a rise in populism and protectionist policies. While there do not appear to be any global wars on the horizon, it is possible that growing economic nationalism and future trade wars between countries could break enough links in global supply chains to knock the global economy back to a state that looks more like the closed economies of the 1960s. While this might reduce relative income inequality, this would also portend a return to the productivity and absolute income levels of the 1960s, which are less than one-third of what they are today in many developed countries.

The global economic impacts of climate change also have potentially important implications for future global inequality. Rising carbon levels are leading to higher global temperatures, rising sea levels, and more extreme weather events. According to most international organizations and many leading economists, climate change threatens to increase both within-country and between-country inequality because the poor will disproportionally suffer from the impacts of climate change for three reasons. First, the poor are more exposed to climate change because they are more likely to live in areas impacted by rising sea levels, mudslides, drought, and water scarcity. Second, the poor are more susceptible to the adverse effects of climate change because they lack access to disaster relief, healthcare, political and social connections, or physical capital needed to protect them from disasters. And finally, the poor are less able to recover from climate-related disasters without access to the safety net of wealth and social connections.[15] There is empirical evidence that past natural disasters have worsened wealth inequality in the US, which, in turn, contributes to future income inequality.[16]

As the historian Walter Scheidel has documented (see Chapter 5), the only factors that have significantly reduced inequality in the long run are catastrophic events that have also significantly reduced standards of living and created massive amounts of human misery, such as wars, state failures, and pandemics. The historical summary of the rise and fall of economic inequality is one of growth versus disaster. Climate change threatens to be the first human disaster that could contribute to greater inequality and lower standards of living at the same time. Hence, the call from the vast majority of economists to do something about rising carbon levels.[17] This includes the almost unanimous support of economists for a tax on carbon emissions.[18]

Changes in Public Policy

While it will certainly be true that external events will occur that will change the future of inequality in ways that we can't control, it also remains true that each of us as citizens have the tools to work together to change the level of inequality within our own countries. Inequality is not immutable; we do have the power to shape future inequality, but it will require a concerted effort to educate the public and change our political discussions so that inequality becomes a core issue in our policymaking, not a secondary issue as it has often been treated.

Which changes in public policies are most likely to effectively deal with inequality? In Chapter 7, we talked about a number of public policies that could create greater egalitarianism. In terms of domestic inequality, creating more equality means adopting structural reform policies that change the workings of markets (such as changes in labor laws, creating more market competition, and improving education) and adopting fiscal policies that transfer resources from the richer to the poorer citizens (such as increasing the progressiveness of taxation and providing universal guaranteed incomes).

Structural reform policies that redistribute endowments and change the workings of markets are the most politically difficult to adopt, particularly in countries like the US that profess a commitment to the efficiency of market outcomes. The most plausible structural reform policies that could be enacted come in one of four forms. The first would be improvements in education for the poor. It is clear that education needs a helping hand because it is currently losing the race with technology. As evidenced by the growing education wage gap, the rate at which workers are being appropriately educated is not keeping up with the rate that educated workers are demanded in the marketplace. In the US, there is no evidence that public schools magnify the endowment gaps that children are born with, but public schools do not reduce it either. This has to change. Schools have to concentrate more resources on young people who are disadvantaged—they currently do the opposite of this in the US. Educational systems have to make sure that all students have an opportunity to be exposed to the best teachers, and that these teachers are paid (and respected) according to the valuable, highly skilled workers they are. While the rate of educational achievement among those at the top of the income distribution has skyrocketed, for those children on the lower rungs of the income ladder, college is the exception, not the rule. This is in part because the poor have unequal access to quality primary and secondary education, but also because higher education has gotten more expensive. To change this, more financial aid must be made available for students attending colleges and universities.

A second important structural reform would be for governments to find ways to provide resources that help poor parents to parent more like rich parents. This includes policies to address a wide range of unequal parenting endowments; for example, support for universal pre-school, more generous parental leave policies, and greater support for early childhood home visiting programs that provide health checkups, parenting advice, breastfeeding support, and guidance for dealing with government bureaucracy.

Third, as discussed in Chapter 6, an effective structural reform to reduce inequality would be for governments to encourage more migration. This includes encouraging more domestic migration so that workers can move to areas where they are most productive. This could be achieved by providing more support to workers to move to urban areas where wages are higher because of the increased availability of idea networks where a worker's skills will better leak and match. Support for domestic migration should also come in the form of investments in public capital that make cities more liveable and that create environments that pull people to live there and not push them away. This includes investing in better public schools, higher-density affordable housing, and more public spaces. Workers could also be supported to move through tax incentives and subsidized job retraining programs.

Cross-country immigration is a more challenging proposition in this era of growing nativism. In terms of sheer economics, as long as "where?" remains the biggest question in global inequality—meaning that the citizenship premium still holds—then allowing more people to move to places where institutions allow them to be most productive will also lead to increases in global incomes on a massive scale and reduce global inequality. There is no single economic policy that has greater potential for reducing global inequality and improving global human welfare than adopting freer and more open migration. It is true that workers in richer recipient countries—most likely lower-skilled workers in these richer countries—will face increased competition from immigrants and could see their wages decrease, increasing domestic inequality. However, this outcome is not guaranteed, as new immigrants also create new leaks and matches that have the potential to raise the wages of all current residents. The key to ensuring that everybody wins from migration is to create free and socially mobile environments for immigrants where they can easily integrate themselves into society and into the social information networks of the countries they move to. The more that immigrants are discriminated against or blocked from taking advantage of the productive institutions that their new country offers, the more likely it is that immigration will worsen domestic inequality. Of course, as mentioned before, growing nationalism and populism in many countries makes increasing the level of cross-country immigration in many countries unlikely, at least in the near future.

A more radical solution for increasing the amount of migration would be to auction off visas and use the proceeds to finance public investments or a social dividend that would allow more people to directly benefit from migration. In fact, the highly successful H1-B visa program in the US—which allows individual US firms to sponsor skilled migrant workers—could be extended not just to firms but to individual US citizens who would be willing to sponsor and mentor migrants for a share of the increased income they earn once they are able to work in the US.[19]

The fourth and final structural reform involves reducing economic rents. It is clear that market power is rising across most industries, increasing economic rents and economic inequality as a result. Growing power and skyrocketing wealth allow elites to use their outsized influence to not only leverage their rents today, but also to ensure that their power persists into the future through their influence on politics. Antitrust and competition policies must be enforced—in ways talked about in Chapter 7—so that markets become as efficient as those who don't worry about inequality think that they already are. Also, encouraging collective bargaining appears to be necessary to allow the power of organized labor to compete with the growing power of monopolists. Finally, restrictions on money and other political reforms are needed so that it is not so easy for elites to gain access to political power, or to use their money like a megaphone to shout above everyone else. In other words, democratic republics need to consider every option that will allow them to move closer to the "one person, one vote" ideal.

The structural reform policies just discussed aim to change market income. On the other hand, fiscal redistribution policies aim to reallocate market income after it has been earned. Because it is based on outcomes, government redistribution policies are easier to understand. Because it has been the most common tool in achieving greater inequality in Western countries, government redistribution policies are also the most realistic approach to changing inequality in the near-term.

The fight over income and wealth redistribution through the use of taxation and transfer payments is eternally ongoing within countries. Beginning in the early 1980s, the politics of taxation turned more conservative and top tax rates fell across most countries. Today, these top tax rates remain low, and debates about dealing with inequality through adopting more progressive taxation have become increasingly polarized. On one extreme, you have free-market conservatives who prioritize personal freedom and who are terrorized by fears that taxes will harm efficiency; they are usually supported publicly and privately by wealthy elites. On the other hand, you have liberal populists who talk about adopting punitive income taxes on the wealthy and large wealth taxes that have much more chance of chasing wealth to offshore tax havens than they have to raise revenue and promote equality. While it might seem like a positive development that more people are talking about inequality, much of this public discourse has congealed into either hardened opposition to any changes in tax policy, or imposing the most penal tax rates without consideration of their full consequences.

The most effective means for promoting equity through fiscal policy is an approach that is somewhere in the middle between the two noisy extremes. First, reasonable levels of progressive taxation can be used to promote equality and efficiency. While it is difficult to identify a solid empirical relationship between higher taxes and lower growth, there is a strong empirical relationship between higher inequality and lower growth. More progressive taxation can be used to promote faster growth if it is done with an eye towards promoting equality and not just punishing those who have enjoyed economic success.

On the other hand, progressive taxation must occur in moderation. Adopting more progressive income taxes that don't punish the rich can be done because it has been done in the recent past in most developed countries. In regards to taxing wealth, in an increasingly global world, imposing a wealth tax that is large enough to significantly reduce wealth inequality should be done on a cooperative basis across countries, or else it will lead to a great deal of tax avoidance and wealth flight to tax havens. This is a tall order, and not easily done. However, it remains a fact that most wealth continues to inhabit safe havens, not tax havens. In other words, if moderate wealth taxes were widely adopted in richer countries, most wealth will stay where it already is because taxes are just one of the many factors that determine the returns to wealth. As a result, the most effective—but not necessarily the most likely—approach to significantly reducing income inequality would be for the countries that are the biggest wealth havens—primarily in North America, Europe, and East Asia—to better share financial information and adopt a shared, moderate global wealth tax, possibly along the lines of the Swedish wealth tax discussed in Chapter 7.

In regards to government transfer programs, there is at least as big of a gap between the policies of the political right and the political left as there is on taxes. However, there is one option that could bring them together—a guaranteed universal income that promotes higher standards of living for the poor, greater economic freedom, and less government bureaucracy. It is the one of the few fiscal policy ideas that have the potential to bridge the fissure in our polarized politics, while at the same time promoting reductions in poverty (if not a general decline in overall inequality).

Of course, it could be the case that none of these things happen. Or that some or all of these things happen. And almost certainly, some other things will happen to change future inequality that found no place in this book. The most important thing to keep in mind, however, is that if nothing is done to mitigate growing economic inequality, it is not a failure of economics or necessarily even of politics. It is a failure of us.

IN CONCLUSION: WHAT DO WE WANT OUR WORLD TO LOOK LIKE IN THE FUTURE?

In our increasingly globalized world, the worldwide ramifications of inequality define how we feel about our current age. As visualized in the global "Elephant Curve", it is the best of times for the world's median person, best of times for the global rich, and good times for many of the global poor. However, it also feels like the worst of times for those above the median person in the global income distribution—primarily the poor and middle-class and in richer countries—who feel threatened by the growing economic power of the rising global poor and discouraged by the global rich who have almost disappeared into the distance.

It's hard to make predictions, particularly about the future. While we can't say for sure what future inequality will look like, we can begin to come to grips with what it should look like. Are we maximizing the productivity of every individual in society, and our own aggregate productivity as well? Is it possible to create societies that are more equitable and more prosperous? If you answered no to these questions after a careful consideration of the research in this book, then, while I don't agree with you, I do commend your commitment to learning about a topic you were likely skeptical about to begin with. Now, maybe more than ever, we need people who are willing to challenge their own preconceptions and listen to those with different viewpoints.

On the other hand, for those who are convinced that we are not doing the best that we can do regarding our current levels of economic inequality, I agree. The argument that 40 years of growing inequality does not matter is based on three mistaken beliefs. The first is that many people believe that individual productivity is something that is easily measured. In reality, how much of our individual income any of us can legitimately claim to have earned is profoundly unknowable because so much of our productivity depends upon things out of our control. We know that what we produce is determined by networks, not by ourselves alone. In a multitude of ways, we make the others around us more productive when we make ourselves more productive, both now and in the future.

The second reason why inequality matters is that we know that perceptions of fairness and respect inherently matter, and, as a result, relative matters more than absolute. We are social animals, and when we feel like our work is not valued, not recognized, and not adequately compensated, we not only fail to work as hard and as creatively as we can, but we also begin to make riskier decisions, invest less in the future, and become less involved in creating the positive externalities for the people around us upon which our economic growth is founded.

Finally, inequality impacts our institutions, which influence our ability as a society to function effectively and productively. More unequal societies become less cooperative societies, and are more likely to suffer from political dysfunction, lower public health, worse educational outcomes, less intergenerational mobility, more rent-seeking, fewer public goods, more discrimination, conflicts such as crime and war, and greater macroeconomic and financial instability. The key to prosperity is to create leaks and matches, not cracks and clashes. Creating more equitable societies is an important part of this.

While there will never be agreement about what constitutes a fair society, there is solid evidence that we can create a more fair society that also expands the size of the pie for everyone to enjoy. Inequality is one measure of incentives: a world with zero inequality would also be a world where there is little incentive to work harder and get ahead. But the opposite extreme is a "winner-takes-all" economy, where a small group of elites reap all of the benefits, and the vast majority is left to struggle. The best outcome is obtaining a "growth-maximizing level of inequality". This is where a society is making the best use of its resources, the most important of which are the ideas and hard work of all of its citizens.

The exact level of growth-maximizing inequality is impossible to pinpoint. However, the weight of the evidence presented in this book tells us that we have more inequality than is good for us. Too many people have too few incentives to work hard given the relatively measly returns for unskilled labor in labor markets, or to make costly investments in education given how unlikely it is for most people to rise above the income levels that their family and the people around them have been stuck at for generations. In economic terms, these are wasted resources. In human terms, these are unfulfilled potential and unfulfilled lives.

Ebenezer Scrooge in Charles Dickens' *A Christmas Carol* asks: "Is this what must be, or what might be?" As I talked about in the preface of this book, economics is not a dismal science; instead it is one of the most consistently optimistic of sciences. Economics is the study of the possible. And economics tells us that reducing inequality is a possibility, but not a certainty. There are policies that we can adopt that will move us closer to what is better for all of us. But it requires a commitment to change within an increasingly polarized society where power is increasingly held by an alarmingly small group of people privileged by existing inequality.

We can change the future, but only by rejecting the notion that growing inequality is just the way that the world is, and extreme inequality has to be accepted like bad weather. Economic inequality is not deterministic, but instead shaped by the actions of each of us. Inequality creates vicious cycles and virtuous circles that can lead to cascading impacts to the betterment or the worsening of our societies, meaning that small changes in policy have the possibility of creating outsized effects.

Thomas Piketty captures the socio-political nature of inequality well in the following quote:

> One should be wary of any economic determinism in regard to inequalities of wealth and income. The history of the distribution of wealth has always been deeply

political, and it cannot be reduced to purely economic mechanisms … The history of inequality is shaped by the way economic, social, and political actors view what is just and what is not, as well as by the relative powers of those actors and the collective choices that result. It is the joint product of all relative actors combined … How this history plays out depends on how societies view inequalities and what kinds of policies and institutions they adopt to measure and transform them.[20]

In other words, economic policies that could impact economic inequality are just like inequality itself: change only comes about as the result of complicated synergies between people with different backgrounds and different levels of privilege, all interconnected in webs composed of externalities and ideas and social norms and psychology. Whether we like it or not, in ways that we already understand and in ways we are just beginning to understand, we are all in this together.

NOTES

1. Zandi (2017).
2. Alvaredo et al. (2018a).
3. Hellebrandt and Mauro (2015).
4. Alvaredo et al. (2018b).
5. Lakner et al. (2019).
6. Autor (2019).
7. Ibid.
8. Ibid.
9. Acemoglu and Restrepo (2016).
10. Manyika et al. (2017) and Brynjolfsson et al. (2018).
11. Harari (2018).
12. Ibid.
13. Bakas (2019).
14. Frey and Osborne (2016).
15. Islam and Winkel (2017).
16. Howell and Elliot (2017).
17. *Wall Street Journal* (2019).
18. Howard and Sylvan (2015).
19. See Posner and Weyl (2018) for a more detailed discussion of auctioning visas.
20. Piketty (2014, p. 20).

Bibliography

Acemoglu, D. and D. Autor (2011), 'Skills, tasks and technologies: implications for employment and earnings', in O. Ashenfelter and D. E. Card (eds), *Handbook of Labor Economics*, Amsterdam: Elsevier, pp. 1043–1171.

Acemoglu, D., S. Johnson, and J. Robinson (2001), 'The colonial origins of comparative development: an empirical investigation', *American Economic Review* 91 (5): 1369–1401.

Acemoglu, D., S. Naidu, P. Restrepo, and J. Robinson (2014), 'Democracy does cause growth', NBER Working Paper 20004, accessed April 14, 2018 at http://www.nber.org/papers/w20004.

Acemoglu, D. and P. Restrepo (2016), 'The race between machine and man: implications of technology for growth, factor shares and employment', NBER Working Paper 22252, accessed May 12, 2018 at https://bfi.uchicago.edu/sites/default/files/research/Man_Vs_Machine_October_16_2015.pdf.

Acemoglu, D. and J. Robinson (2012), *Why Nations Fail: The Origins of Power, Prosperity, and Poverty*, New York: Crown Publishing Group.

Adler, N., E. Epel, G. Castellazzo, and J. Ickovics (2000), 'Relationship of subjective and objective social status with psychological and physiological functioning: preliminary data in healthy white women', *Health Psychology* 19 (6): 586–592.

Agarwal, S., V. Mikhed, and B. Scholnick (2016), 'Does inequality cause financial distress? Evidence from lottery winners and neighboring bankruptcies', FRB of Philadelphia Working Paper 16-4, February 11, accessed April 14, 2017 at https://ssrn.com/abstract=2731562.

Ager, P., L. Boustan, and K. Eriksson (2019), 'The intergenerational effects of a large wealth shock: white southerners after the Civil War', NBER Working Paper 25700, accessed April 14, 2019 at https://www.nber.org/papers/w25700.

Akerlof, G. and J. Yellen (1990), 'The fair wage-effort hypothesis and unemployment', *Quarterly Journal of Economics* 105 (2): 255–283.

Albouy, D., G. Ehrlich, and M. Shin (2018), 'Metropolitan land values', *The Review of Economics and Statistics* 100 (3): 454–466.

Alstadaester, A., N. Johannesen, and G. Zucman (2018), 'Tax evasion and tax avoidance', Working Paper, accessed November 12, 2018 at http://gabriel-zucman.eu/files/AJZ2018b.pdf.

Altintas, E. (2015), 'Educational differences in fathers' time with children and two parent families: time diary evidence from the US', *Family Science* 6 (1): 293–301.

Alvaredo, F., A. Atkinson, T. Piketty, and E. Saez (2013), 'The top 1 percent in international and historical perspective', *Journal of Economic Perspectives* 27 (3): 3–20.

Alvaredo, F., L. Chancel, T. Piketty, E. Saez, and G. Zucman (2018a), 'World inequality report 2018', accessed February 8, 2018 at http://wir2018.wid.world/files/download/wir2018-full-report-english.pdf.

Alvaredo, F., L. Chancel, T. Piketty, E. Saez, and G. Zucman (2018b), 'The elephant curve of global inequality and growth', *AEA Papers and Proceedings* 108 (1): 103–108.

Americans for Tax Fairness (2018), 'Fact sheet: the estate (inheritance) tax', accessed November 12, 2018 at https://americansfortaxfairness.org/tax-fairness-briefing -booklet/fact-sheet-the-estate-inheritance-tax/.

Ansolabehere, S., J. de Figueiredo, and J. Snyder, Jr. (2003), 'Why is there so little money in US politics?', *Journal of Economic Perspectives* 17 (1): 105–130.

Arnold, J. (2008), 'Do tax structures affect aggregate economic growth? Empirical evidence from a panel of OECD countries', Organisation of Economic Co-operation and Development Working Paper 643, accessed March 24, 2018 at http://www .oecd.org/officialdocuments/publicdisplaydocumentpdf/?cote=ECO/WKP(2008)51 &docLanguage=En.

Arrow, K. (1972), 'Gifts and exchanges', *Philosophy and Public Affairs* 1 (4): 343–362.

Assouad, L., L. Chancel, and M. Morgan (2018), 'Extreme inequality: evidence from Brazil, India, the Middle East, and South Africa', *AEA Papers and Proceedings* 108 (1): 119–123.

Atkinson, A. (2015), *Inequality: What Can be Done?*, Cambridge, MA and London: Harvard University Press.

Atkinson, A. and F. Bourguignon (2014), 'Introduction: income distribution today', in A. Atkinson and F. Bourguignon (eds), *Handbook of Income Distribution*, Amsterdam: Elsevier, pp. 1–12.

Atkinson, A., J. Hasell, S. Morelli, and M. Roser (2017), 'The chartbook of economic inequality', accessed February 8, 2018 at https://www.chartbookofeconomicinequality .com/.

Atkinson, A. and C. Lakner (2017), 'Capital and labor: the factor income composition of top incomes in the United States, 1962–2006', World Bank Policy Research Working Paper 8268, December 12, accessed May 18, 2018 at https://papers.ssrn .com/sol3/papers.cfm?abstract_id=3086335.

Attanasio, O. and L. Pistaferri (2015), 'Consumption inequality', *Journal of Economic Perspectives* 30 (2): 3–28.

Autor, D. (2014), 'Education, and the rise of earnings inequality among the "Other 99 Percent"', *Science* 344 (6186): 843–851.

Autor, D. (2019), 'Work of the future, work of the past', speech given to the American Economic Association, January 4, accessed January 22, 2019 at https://economics .mit.edu/files/16560.

Autor, D., D. Dorn, G. Hanson, and J. Song (2014), 'Trade-adjustment: worker-level evidence', *Quarterly Journal of Economics* 129 (4): 1799–1860.

Azar, J., I. Marinescu, M. Steinbaum, and B. Taska (2018), 'Concentration in US labor markets: evidence from online vacancy data', NBER Working Paper 24395, accessed November 11, 2018 at https://www.nber.org/papers/w24395.

Bakas, A. (2019), 'Globalization and slowbilization', accessed January 27, 2019 at https://www.bakas.nl/kapitalisme-Slowbalisering-TrendLezing&lang=en.

Baker, D. (2016), 'Inequality as policy: selective trade protectionism favors higher earners', Institute for New Economic Thinking, October 27, accessed November 11, 2018 at https://www.ineteconomics.org/perspectives/blog/inequality-as-policy -selective-trade-protectionism-favors-higher-earners.

Bakija, J., A. Cole, and B. Heim (2012), 'Jobs and income growth of top earners and the causes of changing income inequality: evidence from US tax return data', Williams College unpublished manuscript, accessed April 10, 2018 at https://web.williams .edu/Economics/wp/BakijaColeHeimJobsIncomeGrowthTopEarners.pdf.

Bakker, B. and J. Felman (2014), 'The rich and the great recession', IMF Working Paper 14/225, December, accessed April 14, 2018 at https://www.imf.org/external/pubs/ft/wp/2014/wp14225.pdf.

Baldwin, R. (2016), *The Great Convergence: Information Technology and the New Globalization*, Cambridge, MA: Harvard University Press.

Barro, R. and J. Lee (2013), 'A new data set of educational attainment in the world, 1950–2010', *Journal of Development Economics* 104: 184–198.

Bartels, L. M. (2010), *Unequal Democracy: The Political Economy of the New Gilded Age*, Princeton, NJ: Princeton University Press.

Barth, E., A. Bryson, J. Davis, and R. Freeman (2016), 'It's where you work: increases in earnings dispersion across establishments and individuals in the US', *Journal of Labor Economics* 34 (2): S67–S97.

Baten, J. and C. Mumme (2013), 'Does inequality lead to civil wars? A global long-term study using anthropometric indicators (1816–1999)', *European Journal of Political Economy* 32 (C): 56–79.

Bebchuk, L., K. Cremers, and U. Peyer (2011), 'The CEO pay slice', *Journal of Financial Economics* 102 (1): 199–221.

Becker, G. (1971), *The Economics of Discrimination*, Chicago: University of Chicago Press.

Becker, G. and K. Murphy (2007), 'The upside of income inequality', American.com, accessed on September 9, 2019 at http://www.aei.org/publication/the-upside-of-income-inequality/.

Bell, L. and R. Freeman (2001), 'The incentive for working hard: explaining hours worked differences in the US and Germany', *Labour Economics* 8 (2): 181–202.

Benjamin, D., D. Cesarini, C. Chabris, E. Glaeser, D. Laibson, V. Guðnason, T. Harris, L. Launer, S. Purcell, A. Smith, M. Johannesson, J. Beauchamp, N. Christakis, C. Atwood, B. Hebert, J. Freese, R. Hauser, T. Hauser, P. Magnusson, A. Grankvist, C. Hultman, and O. Lichtenstein (2012), 'The promises and pitfalls of genoeconomics', *Annual Review of Economics* 4: 627–662.

Bentham, J. (1781), *An Introduction to the Principles of Morals and Legislation*, reprinted (1948), New York: Hafner Publishing.

Bernanke, B. (2007), 'The level and distribution of economic well-being', speech before the Greater Omaha Chamber of Commerce, Omaha, Nebraska, February 6, accessed March 24, 2018 at https://www.federalreserve.gov/newsevents/speech/bernanke20070206a.htm.

Bertrand, M., M. Bombardini, R. Fisman, and F. Trebbi (2018a), 'Tax-exempt lobbying: corporate philanthropy as a tool for political influence', accessed July 4, 2019 at https://papers.ssrn.com/sol3/papers.cfm?abstract_id=3095686.

Bertrand, M., M. Bombardini, R. Fisman, B. Hackinen, and F. Trebbi (2018b), 'Hall of mirrors: corporate philanthropy and strategic advocacy', accessed July 4, 2019 at https://economics.stanford.edu/sites/g/files/sbiybj9386/f/bbfht5dec2018.pdf.

Bertrand, M. and S. Mullainathan (2001), 'Are CEOs rewarded for luck? The ones without principals are', *Quarterly Journal of Economics* 116 (3): 901–932.

Bertrand, M. and S. Mullainathan (2004), 'Are Emily and Greg more employable than Lakisha and Jamal? A field experiment on labor market discrimination', *American Economic Review* 94 (4): 991–1013.

Besley, T. and M. Kudamatsu (2006), 'Health and democracy', *American Economic Review* 96 (2): 313–318.

Bessen, J. (2016), 'Information technology and learning on-the-job', Boston University School of Law, Law and Economics Research Paper 16-47, accessed May 18, 2018 at http://dx.doi.org/10.2139/ssrn.2867134.

Bettencourt, L., J. Lobo, D. Helbing, C. Kühnert, and G. West (2007), 'Growth, innovation, scaling, and the pace of life in cities', *Proceedings of the National Academy of Sciences* 104 (17): 7301–7306.

Beugelsdijk, S., H. De Groot, and A. Van Schaik (2004), 'Trust and economic growth: a robustness test', *Oxford Economic Papers* 56 (1): 118–134.

Bircan, C., T. Brück, and M. Vothknecht (2010), 'Violent conflict and inequality', IZA Discussion Paper 4990, accessed April 10, 2018 at https://ssrn.com/abstract= 1631125.

Bivens, J. and L. Mishel (2013), 'The pay of corporate executives and financial professionals as evidence of rents in top 1 percent incomes', *Journal of Economic Perspectives* 27 (3): 57–78.

Bivens, J. and L. Mishel (2015), 'Understanding the historic divergence between productivity and a typical worker's pay', Economic Policy Institute Briefing Paper 406, accessed January 6, 2019 at https://www.epi.org/publication/understanding -the-historic-divergence-between-productivity-and-a-typical-workers-pay-why-it -matters-and-why-its-real/.

Blair, I., C. Judd, and K. Chapleau (2004), 'The influence of Afrocentric facial features in criminal sentencing', *Psychological Sciences* 15 (10): 383–386.

Blanchet, T., L. Chancel, and A. Gethin (2019), 'How unequal is Europe? Evidence from distributional national accounts, 1980–2017', WID.com Working Paper 2019/06, accessed June 26, 2019 at https://wid.world/document/bcg2019-full-paper/

Blanchflower, D. and A. Oswald (2004), 'Well-being over time in Britain and the USA', *Journal of Public Economics* 88 (7–8): 1359–1386.

Board of Governors of the Federal Reserve System (1955), 'Minutes of the Federal Open Market Committee', August 2, accessed July 17, 2018 at https://fraser.stlouisfed .org/scribd/?item_id=22678&filepath=/docs/historical/FOMC/meetingdocuments/ fomcropa19550802.pdf.

Bonica, A., N. McCarty, K. Poole, and H. Rosenthal (2013), 'Why hasn't democracy slowed rising inequality?', *Journal of Economic Perspectives* 27 (3): 103–124.

Bonica, A. and H. Rosenthal (2015), 'The wealth elasticity of the political contributions by the Forbes 400', Working Paper, accessed April 14, 2018 at http://piketty.pse.ens .fr/files/BonicaRosenthal2015.pdf.

Bonnet, O., P. Bono, G. Chapelle, and E. Wasmer (2014), 'Capital is not back: a comment on Thomas Piketty's "Capital in the 21st Century"', accessed May 14, 2018 at https://voxeu.org/article/housing-capital-and-piketty-s-analysis.

Bosworth, B., G. Burtless, and K. Zhang (2016), 'Later retirement, inequality in old age, and the growing gap in longevity between rich and poor', *Economic Studies at Brookings*, accessed April 6, 2018 at https://www.brookings.edu/wp-content/ uploads/2016/02/BosworthBurtlessZhang_retirementinequalitylongevity_012815 .pdf.

Bourdreaux, D. and M. Perry (2013), 'The myth of a stagnant middle class', *Wall Street Journal*, January 23, accessed March 24, 2018 at https://www.wsj.com/articles/ SB10001424127887323468604578249723138161566.

Bourguignon, F. (2015), *The Globalization of Inequality*, Princeton, NJ: Princeton University Press.

Bowles, S. and H. Gintis (2002), 'The inheritance of inequality', *Journal of Economic Perspectives* 16 (3): 3–30.

British Medical Journal (1996), 'Editor's choice', April 20, accessed April 6, 2018 at https://www.bmj.com/content/312/7037/0.

Brown-Iannuzzi, J., K. Lundberg, A. Kay, and B. Payne (2015), 'Subjective status shapes political preferences', *Psychological Sciences* 26 (1): 15–26.

Brynjolfsson, E., S. Kim, and J. Oh (2013), 'User investment and firm value: case of internet firms', Proceedings of the 2013 Workshop on Information Systems and Economics, Milan, Italy, December.

Brynjolfsson, E. and A. McAffee (2014), *The Second Machine Age: Work, Progress, and Prosperity in a Time of Brilliant Technologies*, New York: W. W. Norton.

Brynjolfsson, E., T. Mitchell, and D. Rock (2018), 'What can machines learn and what does it mean for occupations and the economy?', *AEA Papers and Proceedings* 108 (May): 43–47.

Burtless, G. (2007), 'Globalization and income polarization in rich countries', *Brookings Issues in Economic Policy*, April 1, accessed May 18, 2018 at https://www.brookings.edu/research/globalization-and-income-polarization-in-rich-countries/.

Bussolo, M., I. Torre, and H. Winkler (2018), 'Does job polarization explain the rise in earnings inequality? Evidence from Europe', World Bank Policy Research Working Paper 8652, accessed June 26, 2019 at http://documents.worldbank.org/curated/en/822791543242066700/pdf/WPS8652.pdf.

Callan, M., N. Shead, and J. Olsen (2011), 'Personal relative deprivation, delay discounting, and gambling', *Journal of Personality and Social Psychology* 101 (5): 955–973.

Calomiris, C. W. and S. H. Haber (2014), *Fragile by Design: The Political Origins of Banking Crises*, Princeton, NJ: Princeton University Press.

Card, D., A. Mas, E. Moretti, and E. Saez (2012), 'Inequality at work: the effect of peer salaries on job satisfaction', *American Economic Review* 102 (6): 2981–3003.

Carnegie, A. (1889), 'Wealth', *North American Review* 149 (397): 682–699.

Case, A. and A. Deaton (2015), 'Rising morbidity and mortality in midlife among white non-Hispanic Americans in the 21st century', *Proceedings of the National Academy of Sciences* 112 (4): 15078–15083.

Causa, O. and M. Hermansen (2017), 'Income redistribution through taxes and transfers across OECD countries', OECD Economics Department Working Paper 1453, accessed June 26, 2019 at https://www.oecd-ilibrary.org/docserver/bc7569c6-en.pdf?expires=1561575259&id=id&accname=guest&checksum=2161FBA2347BB1CCA7FFA03699AE6FA8.

Center for American Progress (2015), 'Report of the Commission on Inclusive Prosperity', chaired by Lawrence Summers and Ed Balls, accessed November 12, 2018 at https://cdn.americanprogress.org/wp-content/uploads/2015/01/IPC-PDF-full.pdf.

Charles, K., E. Hurst, and A. Killewald (2013), 'Marital sorting and parental wealth', *Demography* 50 (1): 51–70.

Chauvel, L. (2013), 'Welfare regimes, cohorts, and the middle class', in J. C. Gornick and M. Jäntti (eds), *Income Inequality: Economic Disparities and the Middle Class in Affluent Countries*, Redwood City, CA: Stanford University Press, pp. 114–141.

Checchi, D. and C. Garcia-Penalosa (2008), 'Labour market institutions and income inequality', *Economic Policy* 23 (1): 601–649.

Chetty, R., D. Grusky, M. Hell, N. Hendren, R. Manduca, and J. Narang (2016), 'The fading American dream: trends in absolute income mobility since 1940', NBER Working Paper 22910, accessed April 7, 2018 at http://www.equality-of-opportunity.org/papers/abs_mobility_paper.pdf.

Chetty, R. and N. Hendren (2018), 'The impacts of neighborhoods on intergenerational mobility I: childhood exposure effects', *Quarterly Journal of Economics* 133 (3): 1107–1162.

Chetty, R., N. Hendren, M. Jones, and S. Porter (2018), 'Race and economic opportunity in the United States: an intergenerational perspective', NBER Working Paper 24441, accessed April 15, 2019 at https://www.nber.org/papers/w24441.

Chetty, R., N. Hendren, P. Kline, E. Saez, and N. Turner (2014a), 'Is the United States still a land of opportunity? Recent trends in intergenerational mobility', *American Economic Review* 104 (5): 141–147.

Chetty, R., N. Hendren, P. Kline, and E. Saez (2014b), 'Where is the land of opportunity? The geography of intergenerational mobility in the United States', Equality Project Working Paper, June, accessed April 28, 2018 at http://www.equality-of -opportunity.org/assets/documents/mobility_geo.pdf.

Christian, M. S. (2014), 'Human capital accounting in the United States: context, measurement, and application', in D. W. Jorgenson, J. S. Landefeld, and P. Schreyer (eds), *Measuring Economic Sustainability and Progress*, Chicago: University of Chicago Press, pp. 461–491.

Clark, A. and A. Oswald (1996), 'Satisfaction and comparison income', *Journal of Public Economics* 61 (3): 359–381.

Clark, G. (2014), *The Son Also Rises: Surnames and the History of Social Mobility*, Princeton, NJ: Princeton University Press.

Clemens, J. and M. Wither (2014), 'The minimum wage and the great recession: evidence of effects on the employment and income trajectories of low-skilled workers', NBER Working Paper 20724, accessed November 11, 2018 at https://www.nber .org/papers/w20724.pdf.

Clemens, M., C. Montenegro, and L. Pritchett (2009), 'The place premium: wage differences for identical workers across the US border', HKS Faculty Research Working Paper Series RWP09-004, accessed July 27, 2018 at https://dash.harvard .edu/bitstream/handle/1/4412631/Clemens%20Place%20Premium.pdf?sequence=1.

Cohn, A., E. Fehr, and L. Goette (2014a), 'Fairness and effort-evidence from a field experiment', *Management Science* 61 (8): 1777–1794.

Cohn, A., E. Fehr, B. Herrmann, and F. Schneider (2014b), 'Social comparison and effort provision: evidence from a field experiment', *Journal of the European Economic Association* 12 (4): 877–898.

Collier, P. (2007), *The Bottom Billion: Why the Poorest Countries are Failing and What Can Be Done About It*, Oxford: Oxford University Press.

Collier, P. and A. Hoeffler (2004), 'Greed and grievance in civil war', *Oxford Economic Papers* 56 (4): 563–595.

Collins, C. and J. Hoxie (2017), 'Billionaire bonanza: the Forbes 400 and the rest of us', report by the Institute of Policy Studies, accessed February 8, 2018 at https:// inequality.org/wp-content/uploads/2017/11/BILLIONAIRE-BONANZA-2017 -Embargoed.pdf.

Comin, D., W. Easterly, and E. Gong (2010), 'Was the wealth of nations determined in 1000 BC?', *American Economic Journal: Macroeconomics* 2 (2010): 65–97.

Congressional Budget Office (2011), 'Trends in the distribution of household income between 1979 and 2007', October 25, accessed May 7, 2018 at https://www.cbo.gov/ publication/42729.

Conley, D., E. Rauscher, C. Dawes, P. Magnusson, and M. Siegal (2012), 'Heritability and the equal environments assumption: evidence from multiple samples of misclassified twins', *Behavioral Genetics* 43 (5): 415–426.

Conti, G. and J. Heckman (2012), 'The economics of child well-being', NBER Working Paper 18466, accessed May 12, 2018 at http://www.nber.org/papers/w18466.pdf.

Corak, M. (2013), 'Income inequality, equality of opportunity, and intergenerational mobility', *Journal of Economic Perspectives* 27 (3): 79–102.

Corak, M. (2016), 'Inequality from generation to generation: the United States in comparison', IZA Discussion Paper 9929, accessed February 9, 2018 at http://ftp.iza.org/dp9929.pdf.

Corrado, C. and C. Hulten (2010), 'How do you measure a "technological revolution"?', *American Economic Review* 100 (2): 99–104.

Coyle, D. (1998), *The Weightless World: Strategies for Managing the Digital Economy*, Cambridge, MA: MIT Press.

Credit Suisse Research Institute (2017), 'Global wealth report', accessed February 8, 2018 at http://publications.credit-suisse.com/tasks/render/file/index.cfm?fileid=12DFFD63-07D1-EC63-A3D5F67356880EF3.

Cullen, M., C. Cummins, and V. Fuchs (2012), 'Geographic and racial variation in premature mortality in the US: analyzing the disparities', *PLoS ONE*, April 17, accessed April 6, 2018 at https://journals.plos.org/plosone/article?id=10.1371/journal.pone.0032930.

Deaton, A. (2013), *The Great Escape: Health, Wealth, and the Origins of Inequality*, Princeton, NJ: Princeton University Press.

DeCelles, K. and M. Norton (2016), 'Physical and situational inequality on airplanes predicts air rage', *Proceedings of the National Academy of Sciences* 113 (20): 5588–5591.

Deininger, K. and L. Squire (1998), 'New ways of looking at old issues: inequality and growth', *Journal of Development Economics* 57 (2): 259–287.

DePaoli, J., F. Jonanna, E. Ingram, M. Maushard, J. Bridgeland, and R. Balfanz (2015), '2015 building a grad nation report', Alliance for Excellent Education, America's Promise Alliance, Civic Enterprise, accessed May 20, 2018 at http://gradnation.americaspromise.org/sites/default/files/d8/18006_CE_BGN_Full_vFNL.pdf.

Derenoncourt, E. (2016), 'Testing for persistent slaveholder dynastic advantage, 1860–1940', unpublished manuscript.

Derenoncourt, E. and C. Montialoux (2019), 'Minimum wages and racial inequality', Working Paper, accessed June 26, 2019 at http://www.ecineq.org/ecineq_paris19/papers_EcineqPSE/paper_448.pdf.

Derndorfer, J. and S. Kranzinger (2018), 'The decline of the middle class: new evidence for Europe', Working Paper, accessed June 26, 2019 at http://www.ecineq.org/ecineq_paris19/papers_EcineqPSE/paper_64.pdf.

de Soto, H. (2000), *The Mystery of Capital: Why Capitalism Triumphs in the West and Fails Everywhere Else*, New York: Basic Books.

de Tocqueville, A. (1835), *Democracy in America*, London: Saunders and Otley.

Diamond, J. (1997), *Guns, Germs, and Steel: The Fates of Human Societies*, New York: W. W. Norton.

Diamond, P. and E. Saez (2011), 'The case for a progressive tax: from basic research to policy implications', *Journal of Economic Perspectives* 25 (4): 165–190.

Doepke, M. and M. Tertilt (2016), 'Does female empowerment promote economic development?', Working Paper, University of Chicago, accessed January 21, 2019 at https://economics.uchicago.edu/sites/economics.uchicago.edu/files/uploads/PDF/Tertilt_Female_Empowerment.pdf.

Dolan, K. (2017), 'Forbes 2017 billionaires list: meet the richest people on the planet', accessed February 8, 2018 at https://www.forbes.com/sites/kerryadolan/2017/03/20/forbes-2017-billionaires-list-meet-the-richest-people-on-the-planet/#3fc76e4762ff.

Drutman, L. (2015), *The Business of America is Lobbying: How Corporations Became Politicized and Politics Became More Corporate*, Oxford: Oxford University Press.

Dube, A., T. Lester, and M. Reich (2010), 'Minimum wage effects across state borders: estimates using contiguous counties', *Review of Economics and Statistics* 92 (4): 945–964.

Dupont, B. and J. Rosenbloom (2016), 'The impact of the civil war on southern wealth mobility', NBER Working Paper w22184, April, accessed May 12, 2018 at http://www.nber.org/papers/w22184.

Easterlin, R., L. McVey, M. Switek, O. Sawangfa, and J. Zweig (2010), 'The happiness–income paradox revisited', *Proceedings of the National Academy of Sciences* 107 (52): 22463–22468.

Eberhardt, J., P. Davies, V. Purdie-Vaughs, and S. Johnson (2006), 'Looking death-worthy: perceived stereotypicality of black defendants predicts capital-sentencing outcomes', *Psychological Sciences* 17 (5): 674–679.

The Economist (2017a), 'Globalization has marginalized many regions in the rich world', October 12, accessed February 9, 2018 at https://www.economist.com/news/briefing/21730406-what-can-be-done-help-them-globalisation-has-marginalised-many-regions-rich-world.

The Economist (2017b), 'The case for taxing death', November 23, accessed May 15, 2018 at https://www.economist.com/leaders/2017/11/23/a-hated-tax-but-a-fair-one.

The Economist (2018a), 'Plunging response rates to household surveys worry policy-makers', May 24, accessed June 3, 2018 at https://www.economist.com/international/2018/05/26/plunging-response-rates-to-household-surveys-worry-policymakers.

The Economist (2018b), 'Hitting pay dirt', May 26, accessed June 3, 2018 at https://www.economist.com/business/2018/05/26/american-firms-reveal-the-gulf-between-bosses-and-workers-pay.

The Economist (2018c), 'The techlash against Amazon, Facebook and Google—and what they can do', January 20, accessed November 11, 2018 at https://www.economist.com/briefing/2018/01/20/the-techlash-against-amazon-facebook-and-google-and-what-they-can-do.

The Economist (2018d), 'Stuck in the past: overhaul tax for the 21st century', August 9, accessed November 12, 2018 at https://www.economist.com/leaders/2018/08/09/overhaul-tax-for-the-21st-century.

The Economist (2018e), 'On firmer ground: the time may be right for a land-value tax', August 9, accessed November 12, 2018 at https://www.economist.com/briefing/2018/08/09/the-time-may-be-right-for-land-value-taxes.

The Economist (2018f), 'Across the West powerful firms are becoming even more powerful', November 17, accessed November 20, 2018 at https://www.economist.com/special-report/2018/11/15/across-the-west-powerful-firms-are-becoming-even-more-powerful.

Economy, E. (2018), *The Third Revolution: Xi Jinping and the New Chinese State*, Oxford: Oxford University Press.

Edenbrandt, A. (2010), 'Does democracy promote education?', University of Copenhagen Working Paper, January 5, accessed April 14, 2018 at http://lup.lub.lu.se/luur/download?func=downloadFile&recordOId=1544971&fileOId=1647148.

Edlund, L. and W. Kopczuk (2009), 'Women, wealth, and mobility', *American Economic Review* 99 (1): 146–178.

Elsby, M., B. Hobijn, and A. Sahin (2013), 'The decline of the US labor share', *Brookings Papers on Economic Activity* 44 (2): 1–63.

Emerson, R. W. (1860), *The Conduct of Life*, Boston: Tickner and Fields.

Epp, D. and E. Bourghetto (2018), 'Economic inequality and legislative agendas in Europe', Working Paper, accessed July 28, 2018 at https://enricoborghetto.netlify .com/working_paper/EuroInequality.pdf.

Faulkner, W. (1951), *Requiem for a Nun*, New York: Random House.

Fearon, J. and D. Laitin (2003), 'Ethnicity, insurgency, and civil war', *American Political Science Review* 97 (1): 75–90.

Feldstein, M. (1998), 'Income inequality and poverty', NBER Working Paper 6770, accessed February 20, 2019 at https://www.nber.org/papers/w6770.pdf.

Ferguson, N. (2009), *The Ascent of Money: A Financial History of the World*, New York: Penguin Books.

Ferrer-i-Carbonell, A. and X. Ramos (2013), 'Inequality and happiness', Working Paper, accessed April 6, 2018 at http://digital.csic.es/bitstream/10261/111371/4/ Post_Print_Ferrer-i-Carbonell%26Ramos.pdf.

Fischbacher, U., S. Gachter, and E. Fehr (2001), 'Are people conditionally cooperative? Evidence from a public goods experiment', *Economics Letters* 71 (3): 397–404.

Fix, M. and R. Struyk (1993), *Clear and Convincing Evidence: Measurement of Discrimination in America*, Washington, DC: Urban Institute Press.

Fleck, J. and C. Simpson-Bell (2019), 'Public insurance in heterogeneous fiscal federations: evidence from American households', Working Paper, accessed June 26, 2019 at http://www.ecineq.org/ecineq_paris19/papers_EcineqPSE/paper_139.pdf.

Fliessbach, K., C. Phillipps, P. Trautner, M. Schnabel, C. Elger, A. Falk, and B. Weber (2012), 'Neural responses to advantageous and disadvantageous inequity', *Frontiers in Human Neuroscience* 35 (1): 1–9.

Fortune (2018), 'Bitcoin investors aren't paying their cryptocurrency taxes', February 13, accessed May 15, 2018 at http://fortune.com/2018/02/13/bitcoin-cryptocurrency -tax-taxes/.

Fournier, J. and Å. Johansson (2016), 'The effect of the size and the mix of public spending on growth and inequality', OECD Department of Economics Working Paper 1344, November 25, accessed April 14, 2018 at http://www.oecd.org/eco/ public-finance/The-effect-of-the-size-and-the-mix-of-public-spending-on-growth -and-inequality-working-paper.pdf.

Frank, R. (2007), *Falling Behind: How Rising Inequality Harms the Middle Class*, Berkeley, CA: University of California Press.

Frank, R. and P. Cook (1995), *The Winner-Take-All Society: Why the Few at the Top Get So Much More than the Rest of Us*, New York: Penguin Books.

Frankfurt, H. (2015), *On Inequality*, Princeton, NJ: Princeton University Press.

Freund, C. and S. Oliver (2014), 'The missing women in the inequality discussion', accessed January 11, 2018 at https://piie.com/blogs/realtime-economic-issues -watch/missing-women-inequality-discussion.

Frey, C. and M. Osborne (2016), 'Technology at work v2.0: the future is not what it used to be', accessed January 26, 2019 at https://www.oxfordmartin.ox.ac.uk/ downloads/reports/Citi_GPS_Technology_Work_2.pdf.

Frick, B. and E. Lehmann (2005), 'Corporate governance in Germany: ownership, codetermination and firm performance in a stakeholder economy', in H. Gospel and A. Pendleton (eds), *Corporate Governance and Labour Management: An International Comparison*, Oxford: Oxford University Press, pp. 122–145.

Friedman, J. and W. Kraus (2011), *Engineering the Financial Crisis: Systemic Risk and the Failure of Regulation*, Philadelphia, PA: University of Pennsylvania Press.

Friedman, M. (1980), *Free to Choose*, New York: Harcourt, Brace, & Company.

Friedman, T. (2000), 'Foreign affairs; parsing the protests', *New York Times*, April 14, accessed July 17, 2018 at http://www.nytimes.com/2000/04/14/opinion/foreign-affairs-parsing-the-protests.html.

Friedman, T. (2001), 'Foreign affairs: protesting for whom', *New York Times*, April 25, accessed September 9, 2019 at https://www.nytimes.com/2000/04/14/opinion/foreign-affairs-parsing-the-protests.html.

Fukuyama, F. (1992), *The End of History and the Last Man*, New York: Free Press.

Galbraith, J. K. (1979), *Annals of an Abiding Liberal*, New York: Houghton Mifflin.

Galbraith, J. K. (2012), *Inequality and Instability: A Study of the World Economy just before the Great Crisis*, Oxford: Oxford University Press.

Gallup, J. and J. Sachs (2000), 'Agriculture, climate, and technology: why are the tropics falling behind?', *American Journal of Agricultural Economics* 82 (3): 731–737.

Gallup, J., J. Sachs, and A. Mellinger (1999), 'Geography and economic development', *International Regional Science Review* 22 (2): 179–232.

Gapminder.org (2018), 'Number of people by income', accessed July 18, 2018 at https://www.gapminder.org/tools/#uipresentation:true;&chart-type=mountain.

Garrett, G. (2017), 'Do trade agreements lead to income inequality?', accessed November 11, 2018 at http://knowledge.wharton.upenn.edu/article/do-trade-agreements-lead-to-income-inequality/.

Gilens, M. (2009), *Why Americans Hate Welfare: Race, Media, and the Politics of Antipoverty Policy*, Chicago: University of Chicago Press.

Gilens, M. (2012), *Affluence and Influence*, Princeton, NJ: Princeton University Press.

Gilens, M. and B. Page (2014), 'Testing theories of American politics: elites, interest groups, and average citizens', *Perspectives on Politics* 12 (3): 564–581.

Glazerman, S., A. Protik, B. Teh, J. Bruch, and J. Max (2013), 'Transfer incentives for high performing teachers: final results from a multisite randomized experiment', US Department of Education, November, accessed November 19, 2018 at https://files.eric.ed.gov/fulltext/ED544269.pdf.

Gleik, J. (2011), *The Information: A History, A Theory, A Flood*, New York: Pantheon Books.

Goldberg, P. and N. Pavcnik (2016), 'The effects of trade policy', NBER Working Paper 21957, accessed November 11, 2018 at https://www.nber.org/papers/w21957.

Goldin, C. and C. Rouse (2000), 'Orchestrating impartiality: the impact of "blind" auditions on female musicians', *American Economic Review* 90 (4): 715–741.

Goldrick-Rab, S. (2016), *Paying the Price: College Costs, Financial Aid, and the Betrayal of the American Dream*, Chicago: University of Chicago Press.

Gonzalez, F., G. Marshall, and S. Naidu (2017), 'Start-up nation? Slave wealth and entrepreneurship in civil war Maryland', *Journal of Economic History* 77 (2): 373–405.

Greenwood, J., N. Guner, G. Kocharkov, and C. Santos (2014), 'Marry your like: assortative mating and income inequality', PSC Working Paper Series 53, accessed May 18, 2018 at http://repository.upenn.edu/psc_working_papers/53.

Hacker, J. and P. Pierson (2010), 'Winner-take-all politics: public policy, political organization, and the precipitous rise of top incomes in the United States', *Politics & Society* 38 (2): 152–204.

Hamilton, D. and W. Darity, Jr. (2010), 'Can "baby bonds" eliminate the racial wealth gap in putative post-racial America?', *Review of Black Political Economy* 37 (3–4): 207–216.

Hanlon, S. and S. Steinberg (2013), 'Loopholes in the estate tax show why revenue must be on the table', Center for American Progress, January 24, accessed May 15, 2018 at https://www.americanprogress.org/issues/economy/news/2013/01/24/50457/loopholes-in-the-estate-tax-show-why-revenue-must-be-on-the-table/.

Harari, Y. N. (2018), *21 Lessons for the 21st Century*, New York: Spiegel & Grau.

Haskel, J. and S. Westlake (2017), *Capitalism without Capital: The Rise of the Intangible Economy*, Princeton, NJ: Princeton University Press.

Hayek, F. (1944), *The Road to Serfdom*, Chicago: University of Chicago Press.

Heckman, J. (2012), 'Promoting social mobility', *Boston Review*, September 1, accessed April 7, 2018 at http://bostonreview.net/forum/promoting-social-mobility-james-heckman.

Hellebrandt, T. and P. Mauro (2015), 'The future of worldwide income distribution', Peterson Institute for International Economics Working Paper 15-7, accessed February 9, 2018 at https://papers.ssrn.com/sol3/papers.cfm?abstract_id=2593894.

Henrich, J., R. Boyd, S. Bowles, C. Camerer, E. Fehr, H. Gintis, and R. McElreath (2001), 'In search of homo economicus: behavioral experiments in 15 small-scale societies', *American Economic Review* 91 (2): 73–78.

Hlasny, V. and P. Verme (2019), 'The impact of top incomes biases on the measurement of inequality in the United States', Working Paper, accessed June 26, 2019 at http://www.ecineq.org/ecineq_paris19/papers_EcineqPSE/paper_465.pdf.

Hoff, K. and P. Pandey (2004), 'Belief systems and durable inequalities: an experimental investigation of Indian caste', World Bank Policy Research Working Papers, accessed June 6, 2018 at https://www.princeton.edu/rpds/seminars/pdfs/hoff_indiancaste.pdf.

Holmes, O. W. (1927), Dissenting opinion, US Supreme Court Case, *Compania General de Tabacos de Filipinas v. Collector*, 275 US 87, argued and submitted October 18, decided November 21, 1927.

Howard, P. and D. Sylvan (2015), 'Expert consensus on the economics of climate change', New York University Law School Institute for Policy Integrity, December, accessed January 26, 2019 at https://policyintegrity.org/files/publications/ExpertConsensusReport.pdf.

Howell, J. and J. Elliot (2017), 'Damages done: the longitudinal impacts of natural hazards on wealth inequality in the United States', *Social Problems*, accessed January 26, 2019 at https://academic.oup.com/socpro/advance-article/doi/10.1093/socpro/spy016/5074453.

Hoxby, C. and C. Avery (2013), 'The missing "one-offs": the hidden supply of high-achieving, low-income students', *Brookings Papers on Economic Activity* 2013 (1): 1–65.

Hoyes, H. and A. Patel (2015), 'Effective policy for reducing inequality? The earned income tax credit and the distribution of income', NBER Working Paper 21340, accessed November 18, 2018 at https://www.nber.org/papers/w21340.

Hsieh, C., E. Hurst, C. Jones, and P. Klenow (2018), 'The allocation of talent and US economic growth', Working Paper, August, accessed February 20, 2019 at http://klenow.com/HHJK.pdf.

Huggett, M., G. Ventura, and A. Yaron (2011), 'Sources of lifetime inequality', *American Economic Review* 101 (7): 2923–2954.

Hungerford, T. (2010), 'The redistributive effect of selected federal transfer and tax provisions', *Public Finance Review* 38 (4): 450–472.

Institut Français d'Opinion Publique (2010), 'Perception of inequalities: comparison of views in 12 countries', accessed February 8, 2018 at http://www.ifop.com/media/poll/1191-2-study_file.pdf.

International Monetary Fund (2017), 'Tackling inequality', *IMF Fiscal Monitor*, October, accessed November 11, 2018 at https://www.imf.org/en/Publications/FM/Issues/2017/10/05/fiscal-monitor-october-2017.

Islam, S. and J. Winkel (2017), 'Climate change and social inequality', United Nations/Department of Economics and Social Affairs Working Paper 152, accessed January 26, 2019 at https://www.un.org/esa/desa/papers/2017/wp152_2017.pdf.

Jargowsky, P. (2015), 'Architecture of segregation', The Century Foundation, August 7, accessed June 26, 2019 at https://tcf.org/content/report/architecture-of-segregation/?agreed=1.

Jaumotte, F. and C. Buitron (2015), 'Inequality and labor market institutions', IMF Staff Discussion Note SDN/15/14, July, accessed May 18, 2018 at https://www.imf.org/external/pubs/ft/sdn/2015/sdn1514.pdf.

Jayadev, A. and S. Bowles (2006), 'Guard labor', *Journal of Development Economics* 79 (2): 328–348.

Jefferson, T. (1813), *The Writings of Thomas Jefferson*, reprinted (1905), ed. A. A. Lipscomb and A. E. Bergh, Washington, DC: Thomas Jefferson Memorial Association.

Johnson, S. (2012), 'The internet? We built that', *New York Times*, September 21, accessed September 9, 2019 at https://www.nytimes.com/2012/09/23/magazine/the-internet-we-built-that.html.

Jones, C. (2015), 'Pareto and Piketty: the macroeconomics of top income and wealth inequality', *Journal of Economic Perspectives* 29 (1): 29–46.

Jordà, Ò., K. Knoll, D. Kuvshinov, M. Schularick, and A. Taylor (2017), 'The rate of return on everything, 1870–2015', NBER Working Paper 24112, accessed May 20, 2018 at http://www.nber.org/papers/w24112.

Jordahl, H. (2009), 'Economic inequality', in G. T. Svendsen and G. L. H. Svendsen (eds), *Handbook of Social Capital*, Cheltenham, UK and Northampton, MA, USA: Edward Elgar Publishing, pp. 323–336.

Kalma, A. (1991), 'Hierarchisation and dominance assessment at first glance', *European Journal of Social Psychology* 21 (2): 165–181.

Kaplan, G., E. Pamuk, J. Lynch, R. Cohen, and J. Balfour (1996), 'Inequality in income and mortality in the United States: analysis of mortality and potential pathways', *British Medical Journal* 312 (7037): 999–1003.

Kaplan, S. (2012), 'Executive compensation and corporate governance in the US: perceptions, facts and challenges', NBER Working Paper w18395, accessed April 10, 2018 at http://www.nber.org/papers/w18395.

Kaplan, S. and J. Rauh (2013), 'It's the market: the broad-based rise in the return to top talent', *Journal of Economic Perspectives* 27 (3): 35–56.

Karabarbounis, L. and B. Neiman (2014), 'The global decline of the labor share', *Quarterly Journal of Economics* 129 (1): 61–103.

Kawachi, I. and B. P. Kennedy (2002), *The Health of Nations*, New York: The New Press.

Kawachi, I., B. P. Kennedy, and R. Wilkinson (1999), 'Crime: social disorganization and relative deprivation', *Social Science & Medicine* 48 (6): 719–731.

Kena, G., L. Musa-Gillette, X. Wang, A. Rathbun, J. Zhang, S. Wilkinson-Flicker, A. Barmer, and E. Dunlop Valez (2015), 'The condition of education 2015', National Center for Education Statistics, accessed May 12, 2018 at http://nces.ed.gov/pubs2015/2015144.pdf.

Keynes, J. M. (1920), *The Economic Consequences of Peace*, New York: Harcourt, Brace.

Kiatpongsan, S. and M. Norton (2014), 'How much (more) should CEOs make? A universal desire for more equal pay', *Perspectives on Psychological Science* 9 (6): 587–593.

Kiszewski, A., A. Mellinger, A. Spielman, P. Malaney, S. Sachs, and J. Sachs (2004), 'A global index representing the stability of malaria transmission', *American Journal of Tropical Medicine and Hygiene* 70 (5): 486–498.

Klein, E. (2010), 'Where does the Laffer curve bend?', WashingtonPost.com blog, accessed March 24, 2018 at http://voices.washingtonpost.com/ezra-klein/2010/08/where_does_the_laffer_curve_be.html.

Knack, S. (2003), 'Groups, growth and trust: cross-country evidence on the Olson and Putnam hypotheses', *Public Choice* 117 (4): 341–355.

Knack, S. and P. Keefer (1997), 'Does social capital have an economic payoff? A cross-country investigation', *Quarterly Journal of Economics* 112 (4): 1251–1288.

Kohler, T., M. Smith, A. Bogaard, G. Feinman, C. Peterson, A. Betzenhauser, M. Pailes, E. Stone, A. Prentiss, T. Dennehy, L. Ellyson, L. Nicholas, R. Faulseit, A. Styring, J. Whitlam, M. Fochesato, T. Foor, and S. Bowles (2017), 'Greater post-Neolithic wealth disparities in Eurasia than in North America and Mesoamerica', *Nature* 551 (1): 619–622.

Kopczuk, W. (2015), 'What do we know about the evolution of the top wealth shares in the United States?', *Journal of Economic Perspectives* 29 (1): 47–66.

Korinek, A., J. Mistiaen, and M. Ravallion (2006), 'Survey nonresponse and the distribution of income', *The Journal of Income Inequality* 4 (1): 33–55.

Krosch, A. and D. Amodio (2014), 'Economic scarcity alters the perception of race', *Proceedings of the National Academy of Sciences* 111 (25): 299–307.

Krueger, A. (1999), 'Measuring labor's share', *American Economic Review* 89 (2): 45–51.

Krueger, A. (2012), 'The rise and consequences of inequality in the United States', speech to the WhiteHouse.Gov. Council of Economic Advisers, January 12, accessed February 8, 2018 at https://cdn.americanprogress.org/wp-content/uploads/events/2012/01/pdf/krueger.pdf.

Kuznets, S. (1955), 'Economic growth and income inequality', *American Economic Review* 65 (1): 1–28.

Lakner, C. (2017), 'Global inequality', in H. Boushey, J. B. DeLong, and M. Steinbaum (eds), *After Piketty: The Agenda for Economics and Inequality*, Cambridge, MA: Harvard University Press, pp. 259–279.

Lakner, C., G. Mahler, M. Negre, and E. Prydz (2019), 'How much does reducing inequality matter for global inequality?', Working Paper, accessed June 26, 2019 at http://www.ecineq.org/ecineq_paris19/papers_EcineqPSE/paper_412.pdf.

Lakner, C. and B. Milanovic (2013), 'Global income distribution: from the fall of the Berlin Wall to the Great Recession', World Bank Policy Research Working Paper 6719, accessed February 21, 2018 at http://documents.worldbank.org/curated/en/914431468162277879/pdf/WPS6719.pdf.

LaVito, A. (2017), 'Starbucks is opening a store in China every 15 hours', accessed May 14, 2018 at https://www.cnbc.com/2017/12/05/starbucks-is-opening-a-store-in -china-every-15-hours.html.

Leblang, D. (1996), 'Property rights, democracy and economic growth', *Political Research Quarterly* 49 (1): 5–26.

Lee, J. (2019), 'Rentier premium and wealth inequality', Working Paper, accessed June 26, 2019 at http://www.ecineq.org/ecineq_paris19/papers_EcineqPSE/paper_169 .pdf.

Lemieux, T., W. Macleod, and D. Parent (2009), 'Performance pay and wage inequality', *Quarterly Journal of Economics* 124 (1): 1–49.

Lindbeck, A. (1995), 'Hazardous welfare-state dynamics', *American Economic Review* 85 (4): 9–15.

Lindert, P. (2009), *Growing Public*, Cambridge: Cambridge University Press.

Lindert, P. and J. Williamson (2011), 'American incomes, 1774–1860', NBER Working Paper 19211, accessed May 12, 2018 at https://gpih.ucdavis.edu/files/w17211.pdf.

Lofstrom, M. and S. Raphael (2016), 'Crime, the criminal justice system, and socioeconomic inequality', *Journal of Economic Perspectives* 30 (2): 103–126.

Lucas, R. (2004), 'The industrial revolution: past and future', *The Region*, Annual Report of the Federal Reserve Bank of Minneapolis, May, pp. 5–20.

Lundberg, S., R. Pollak, and J. Stearns (2016), 'Family inequality: diverging patterns in marriage, cohabitation, and childbearing', *Journal of Economic Perspectives* 30 (2): 79–102.

Lusardi, A., D. Schneider, and P. Tufano (2011), 'Financially fragile households: evidence and implications', NBER Working Paper w17072, accessed March 24, 2018 at http://www.nber.org/papers/w17072.

Luxembourg Income Study Database (2019), accessed January 8, 2019 at https://www .lisdatacenter.org/.

Maddison Project (2018), 'Maddison historical statistics', accessed May 12, 2018 at https://www.rug.nl/ggdc/historicaldevelopment/maddison/.

Mankiw, N. (2013), 'Defending the one percent', *Journal of Economic Perspectives* 27 (3): 21–34.

Manyika, J., M. Chui, M. Miremadi, J. Bughin, K. George, P. Willmott, and M. Dewhurst (2017), 'A future that works: automation, employment and productivity', McKinsey Global Institute, accessed May 22, 2018 at https://www.mckinsey .com/~/media/McKinsey/Global%20Themes/Digital%20Disruption/Harnessing %20automation%20for%20a%20future%20that%20works/MGI-A-future-that -works-Executive-summary.ashx.

McCarty, N., K. Poole, and H. Rosenthal (2016), *Polarized America: The Dance of Ideology and Unequal Riches*, Cambridge, MA: MIT Press.

McClelland, R. and S. Mok (2012), 'A review of recent research on labor supply elasticities', Congressional Budget Office Working Paper 2012-12, accessed July 1, 2018 at https://www.cbo.gov/sites/default/files/cbofiles/attachments/10-25-2012 -Recent_Research_on_Labor_Supply_Elasticities.pdf.

McKernan, S., C. Ratcliffe, E. Steuerle, and S. Zhang (2013), 'Less than equal: disparities in wealth accumulation', Urban Institute, accessed February 8, 2018 at https://static1.squarespace.com/static/543c2809e4b00b9cbab96575/t/ 54c6ebb9e4b0762f61e19f9b/1422322617903/Urban.org+-+Less-Than-Equal -Racial-Disparities-in-Wealth-Accumulation.pdf.

McLanahan, S. (2004), 'Diverging destinies: how children are faring under the second demographic transition', *Demographics* 41 (4): 607–627.

McLanahan, S. and C. Jencks (2015), 'Was Moynihan right?', *Education Next* 15 (2): 14–20.

Meer, J. and J. West (2016), 'Effects of the minimum wage on employment dynamics', *Journal of Human Resources* 51 (2): 500–522.

Mencken, H. L. (1916), *A Book of Burlesques*, New York: John Land Co.

Milanovic, B. (2015), 'Global inequality of opportunity: how much of our income is determined by where we live?', *Review of Economics and Statistics* 97 (2): 452–460.

Milanovic, B. (2016), *Global Inequality: A New Approach for the Age of Globalization*, Cambridge, MA: Harvard University Press.

Mill, J. S. (1848), *Principles of Political Economy*, London: John W. Parker Publishing.

Miller, G. (1956), 'The magical number seven, plus or minus two: some limits on our capacity for processing information', *Psychological Review* 63 (2): 81–97.

Monty Python (1970), 'Tax on thingy', *Monty Python's Flying Circus*, accessed February 18, 2018 at http://www.montypython.net/scripts/taxthing.php.

Morelli, S. (2017), 'Rising inequality and economic stability', in H. Boushey, J. B. DeLong, and M. Steinbaum (eds), *After Piketty: The Agenda for Economics and Inequality*, Cambridge, MA: Harvard University Press, pp. 412–435.

Morelli, S. and A. Atkinson (2015), 'Inequality and crises revisited', *Economia Politica* 32 (1): 31–51.

Muñoz, M. (2019), 'Do European top earners respond to labor taxation through mobility?', Working Paper, accessed June 26, 2019 at http://www.ecineq.org/ecineq_paris19/papers_EcineqPSE/paper_274.pdf.

Naidu, S., E. Posner, and G. Weyl (2018), 'Antitrust remedies for labor market power', University of Chicago Public Law Working Paper 665, accessed November 11, 2018 at https://papers.ssrn.com/sol3/papers.cfm?abstract_id=3129221.

National Center for Education Statistics (2018), 'Preschool and kindergarten enrollment', accessed January 28, 2019 at https://nces.ed.gov/programs/coe/indicator_cfa.asp.

Naughton, B. (2017), 'Is China socialist?', *Journal of Economic Perspectives* 31 (1): 3–24.

Neumark, D. and W. Wascher (2007), 'Minimum wages and employment', *Foundations and Trends in Microeconomics* 3 (1): 1–182.

Nichols, A. and J. Rothstein (2015), 'The earned income tax credit (EITC)', NBER Working Paper 21211, accessed November 11, 2018 at http://www.nber.org/papers/w21211.pdf.

Norton, M. and D. Ariely (2011), 'Building a better America—one wealth quintile at a time', *Perspectives on Psychological Science* 6 (1): 9–12.

Nozick, R. (1974), *Anarchy, State, and Utopia*, New York: Basic Books.

OECD (2010), 'Developing countries set to account for nearly 60% of world GDP by 2030, according to new estimates', accessed February 9, 2018 at http://www.oecd.org/dev/pgd/economydevelopingcountriessettoaccountfornearly60ofworldgdpby2030accordingtonewestimates.htm.

OECD (2011), 'Divided we stand: why inequality keeps rising', accessed May 18, 2018 at https://www.oecd.org/social/soc/49170768.pdf.

OECD (2016), 'BEPS Project Explanatory Statement: 2015 Final Reports', OECD/G20 Base Erosion and Profit Shifting Project, accessed May 15, 2018 at http://dx.doi.org/10.1787/9789264263437-en.

Ostry, J., A. Berg, and C. Tsangarides (2014), 'Redistribution, inequality, and growth', IMF Staff Discussion Note, April, accessed April 14, 2018 at https://www.imf.org/external/pubs/ft/sdn/2014/sdn1402.pdf.

Oxfam (2018), 'Public good or private wealth', accessed January 20, 2019 at https://www.oxfamamerica.org/explore/research-publications/public-good-or-private-wealth/.

Page, B., L. Bartels, and J. Seawright (2013), 'Democracy and the policy preferences of wealthy Americans', *Perspectives on Politics* 11 (1): 51–73.

Pager, D. (2003), 'The mark of a criminal record', *American Journal of Sociology* 108 (5): 937–975.

Paine, T. (1797), *Agrarian Justice*, reprinted (2016) in *Thomas Paine: Collected Writings*, Seattle, WA: Stellar Classics.

Palomino, J., G. Marerro, B. Nolan, and J. Rodriguez (2019), 'The contribution of inheritances to wealth inequality in France, Spain, the UK, and the US', Working Paper, accessed June 26, 2019 at http://www.ecineq.org/ecineq_paris19/papers_EcineqPSE/paper_460.pdf.

Pavcnik, N. (2017), 'The impact of trade on inequality in developing countries', Dartmouth College Working Paper, accessed November 11, 2018 at https://www.dartmouth.edu/~npavcnik/docs/JH%20Inequality.pdf.

Payne, K. (2018), *The Broken Ladder: How Inequality Affects the Way We Think, Live, and Die*, New York: Viking.

Payne, K., J. Brown-Iannuzzi, and J. Hannay (2017), 'Inequality increases risk taking', *Proceedings of the National Academic of Sciences* 114 (18): 4643–4648.

Peltzman, S. (2009), 'Mortality inequality', *Journal of Economic Perspectives* 23 (4): 175–190.

Pew Economic Mobility Project (2011), 'Does America promote mobility as well as other nations?', November, accessed February 9, 2018 at http://www.pewtrusts.org/~/media/legacy/uploadedfiles/pcs_assets/2011/critafinal1pdf.pdf.

Pew Research Center (2011), 'Wealth gap grows between whites and minorities', accessed January 11, 2017 at http://www.pewresearch.org/fact-tank/2011/07/26/wealth-gap-grows-between-whites-and-minorities/.

Pew Research Center (2014a), 'January 2014 political survey', accessed February 8, 2018 at http://assets.pewresearch.org/wp-content/uploads/sites/5/legacy-questionnaires/1-23-14%20Poverty_Inequality%20topline%20for%20release.pdf.

Pew Research Center (2014b), 'Wealth inequality has widened along racial, ethnic lines since end of Great Recession', accessed January 11, 2018 at http://www.pewresearch.org/fact-tank/2014/12/12/racial-wealth-gaps-great-recession/.

Pew Research Center (2015), 'The American middle class is losing ground', accessed February 8, 2018 at http://www.pewsocialtrends.org/2015/12/09/the-american-middle-class-is-losing-ground/.

Philippon, T. and A. Reshef (2012), 'Wages and human capital in the US finance industry: 1909–2006', *Quarterly Journal of Economics* 127 (4): 1551–1609.

Phillips, M. (2011), 'Parenting, time use, and disparities in academic outcomes', in G. Duncan and R. Murnane (eds), *Whither Opportunity? Rising Inequality, Schools, and Children's Life Chances*, New York: Russell Sage Publishing, pp. 207–228.

Piketty, T. (2014), *Capital in the Twenty-First Century*, Cambridge, MA: Harvard University Press.

Piketty, T. (2018), 'Brahmin left vs merchant right: rising inequality and the changing nature of political conflict', WID.world Working Paper 2018/7, accessed July 10, 2019 at http://piketty.pse.ens.fr/files/Piketty2018.pdf.

Piketty, T., E. Saez, and G. Zucman (2018), 'Distributional national accounts: methods and estimates for the United States', *Quarterly Journal of Economics* 129 (3): 1–57.

Pinker, S. (2018), *Enlightenment Now: The Case for Reason, Science, Humanism, and Progress*, New York: Viking Press.

Pollack, E. and R. Thiess (2011), 'Taxes on the wealthy have gone down dramatically', Economic Policy Institute, April 14, accessed May 15, 2018 at https://www.epi.org/publication/taxes_on_the_wealthy_have_gone_down_dramatically/.

Posner, E. and E. G. Weyl (2014), 'A radical solution to global income inequality: make the US more like Qatar', *The New Republic*, November 6, accessed July 28, 2018 at https://newrepublic.com/article/120179/how-reduce-global-income-inequality-open-immigration-policies.

Posner, E. and E. G. Weyl (2018), *Radical Markets: Uprooting Capitalism and Democracy for a Just Society*, Princeton, NJ: Princeton University Press.

Psacharopoulos, G. and H. Patrinos (2018), 'Returns to investment in education: a decennial review of the global literature', Policy Research Working Paper WPS 8402, accessed May 12, 2018 at http://documents.worldbank.org/curated/en/442521523465644318/pdf/WPS8402.pdf.

Putnam, R. D. (2000), *Bowling Alone: The Collapse and Revival of American Community*, New York: Simon & Schuster.

Putnam, R. D. (2001), 'Social capital: measurement and consequences', *Canadian Journal of Policy Research* 2 (1): 41–51.

Putnam, R. D. (2015), *Our Kids: The American Dream in Crisis*, New York: Simon & Schuster.

Radelet, S. (2015), 'Prosperity rising', *Foreign Affairs* 95 (1): 35–45.

Rainer, H. and T. Siedler (2009), 'The role of social networks in determining migration and labour market outcomes', *Economics of Transition* 17 (4): 739–767.

Rank, M. (2004), *One Nation, Underprivileged: Why American Poverty Affects Us All*, New York: Oxford University Press.

Rasmussen Reports (2011), '11% think government should provide basic income grant for all', September, accessed January 25, 2019 at http://www.rasmussenreports.com/public_content/politics/general_politics/august_2011/11_think_government_should_provide_basic_income_grant_for_all.

Rawls, J. (1971), *A Theory of Justice*, Cambridge, MA: Harvard University Press.

Reardon, S. F. (2011), 'The widening academic achievement gap between the rich and the poor: new evidence and possible explanations', in G. J. Duncan and R. M. Murnane (eds), *Whither Opportunity? Rising Inequality, Schools, and Children's Life Chances*, New York: Russell Sage Foundation, pp. 91–116.

Reardon, S. F. and K. Bischoff (2011), 'Growth in the residential segregation of families by income, 1970–2009', USA2010 Project Report, accessed February 9, 2018 at https://s4.ad.brown.edu/Projects/Diversity/Data/Report/report111111.pdf.

Reeves, R. V. (2014), *Saving Horatio Alger: Equality, Opportunity, and the American Dream*, Washington, DC: Brookings Institution Press.

Reeves, R. V. (2017), *Dream Hoarders: How the American Upper Middle Class Is Leaving Everyone Else in the Dust, Why That Is a Problem, and What to Do About It*, Washington, DC: Brookings Institution Press.

Reeves, R. V. and K. Howard (2013), *The Glass Floor: Education, Downward Mobility, and Opportunity Hoarding*, Washington, DC: Brookings Institution Press.

Reeves, R. V. and D. Matthew (2016), '6 charts showing race gaps within the American middle class', Brookings Social Mobility Memos, accessed February 9, 2018 at https://www.brookings.edu/blog/social-mobility-memos/2016/10/21/6-charts-showing-race-gaps-within-the-american-middle-class/.

Reeves, R. V. and J. Venator (2014), 'Saving Horatio Alger: the data behind the words (and the Lego bricks)', August 21, Brookings Social Mobility Memos, accessed May 9, 2018 at https://www.brookings.edu/blog/social-mobility-memos/2014/08/21/saving-horatio-alger-the-data-behind-the-words-and-the-lego-bricks/.

Richter, B., K. Samphantharak, and J. Timmons (2009), 'Lobbying and taxes', *American Journal of Political Science* 53 (4): 893–909.

Robin, C. (2013), 'Nietzsche's marginal children: on Friedrich Hayek', *The Nation*, accessed March 23, 2018 at https://www.thenation.com/article/nietzsches-marginal-children-friedrich-hayek/.

Roosevelt, T. (1901), 'First annual message, December 3', accessed March 24, 2018 at http://www.presidency.ucsb.edu/ws/?pid=29542.

Rosen, S. (1981), 'The economics of superstars', *American Economic Review* 71 (5): 845–858.

Rosenfeld, J. (2014), *What Unions No Longer Do*, Cambridge, MA: Harvard University Press.

Roser, M. (2018), 'Global economic inequality', accessed July 30, 2018 at https://ourworldindata.org/global-economic-inequality.

Rothstein, B. and E. Uslaner (2005), 'All for all: equality, corruption, and social trust', *World Politics* 58 (1): 41–72.

Rothstein, J. (2010), 'Is the EITC as good as an NIT? Conditional cash transfers and tax incidence', *American Economic Journal: Economic Policy* 2 (1): 177–208.

Rothwell, J., J. Lobo, D. Strumsky, and M. Muro (2013), 'Patenting prosperity: invention and economic performance in the United States and its metropolitan areas', Metropolitan Policy Program at Brookings Institution report, February, accessed April 6, 2018 at https://www.brookings.edu/wp-content/uploads/2016/06/patenting-prosperity-rothwell.pdf.

Rouen, E. (2017), 'Rethinking measurement of pay disparity and its relation to firm performance', Harvard University Working Paper 18-007, accessed June 3, 2018 at https://www.hbs.edu/faculty/Publication%20Files/18-007_182aaa61-979e-4f84-ac61-d7e3837779d6.pdf.

Rousseau, J.-J. (1775), *A Discourse on Inequality*, reprinted (1985), New York: Penguin Books.

Ruef, M. (2002), 'Strong ties, weak ties and islands: structural and cultural predictors of organizational innovation', *Industrial and Corporate Change* 11 (3): 427–449.

Russell, B. (1930), *The Conquest of Happiness*, New York: Liveright.

Rycroft, R. (2009), *The Economics of Inequality, Discrimination, Poverty, and Mobility*, Abingdon: Routledge.

Saez, E. (2013), 'Striking it richer: the evolution of top incomes in the United States', University of Berkeley Working Paper, accessed February 8, 2018 at https://eml.berkeley.edu//~saez/saez-UStopincomes-2011.pdf.

Saez, E. and P. Diamond (2011), 'The case for a progressive tax from basic research to policy recommendations', *Journal of Economic Perspectives* 25 (4): 165–190.

Saez, E., J. Slemrod, and S. Giertz (2012), 'The elasticity of taxable income with respect to marginal tax rates: a critical review', *Journal of Economic Literature* 50 (1): 3–50.

Saez, E. and G. Zucman (2016), 'Wealth inequality in the United States since 1913: evidence from capitalized income tax data', *Quarterly Journal of Economics* 131 (2): 519–578.

Sandel, M. (2009), *Justice: What's the Right Thing to Do?*, New York: Farrar, Straus & Giroux.

Sandel, M. (2012), *What Money Can't Buy: The Moral Limits of Markets*, New York: Farrar, Straus & Giroux.

Scheidel, W. (2017), *The Great Leveler: Violence and the History of Inequality from the Stone Age to the Twenty-First Century*, Princeton, NJ: Princeton University Press.

Schlozman, K. L., S. Verba, and H. E. Brady (2012), *The Unheavenly Chorus: Unequal Political Voice and the Broken Promise of American Democracy*, Princeton, NJ: Princeton University Press.

Schmitt, J., H. Shierholz, and L. Mishel (2013), 'Don't blame the robots: assessing the job polarization explanation of growing wage inequality', Economic Policy Institute, November 19, accessed May 12, 2018 at https://www.epi.org/publication/technology-inequality-dont-blame-the-robots/.

Schumpeter, J. (1942), *Capitalism, Socialism, and Democracy*, New York: Harper & Brothers.

Schwartz, C. (2010), 'Earnings inequality and the changing association between spouses' earnings', *American Journal of Sociology* 115 (2): 1524–1557.

Sen, A. (1985), *Commodities and Capabilities*, Amsterdam: North-Holland.

Shapiro, C. and J. Stiglitz (1984), 'Equilibrium unemployment as a worker discipline device', *American Economic Review* 74 (3): 433–444.

Shapiro, T., T. Meschede, and S. Osoro (2014), 'The widening racial wealth gap: why wealth is not color blind', in R. Cramer and T. R. William Shanks (eds), *The Assets Perspectives: The Rise of Asset Building and its Impact on Social Policy*, New York: Springer, pp. 99–122.

Short, N. (2019), 'Antitrust deregulation and economic inequality in the United States', Working Paper, accessed June 26, 2019 at http://www.ecineq.org/ecineq_paris19/papers_EcineqPSE/paper_416.pdf.

Sinclair, U. (1994), *I, Candidate for Governor: How I got Licked*, Berkeley: University of California Press.

Singh-Manoux, A., N. Adler, and M. Marmot (2003), 'Subjective social status: its determinants and its association with measures of ill-health in the Whitehall II study', *Social Science & Medicine* 56 (6): 1321–1333.

Sitaraman, G. (2017), *The Crisis of the Middle-Class Constitution: Why Economic Inequality Threatens Our Republic*, New York: Knopf.

Smith, A. (1759), *The Theory of Moral Sentiments*, accessed April 10, 2018 at https://books.google.com/books/about/The_Theory_of_Moral_Sentiments.html?id=z1sAAAAAMAAJ&printsec=frontcover&source=kp_read_button#v=onepage&q&f=false.

Smith, A. (1776), *An Inquiry into the Nature and the Causes of the Wealth of Nations*, London: W. Strahan and T. Cadell.

Soares, S., R. Osório, F. Soares, M. Medeiros, and E. Zepeda (2007), 'Conditional cash transfers in Brazil, Chile and Mexico: impacts upon inequality', International Poverty Center Working Paper 35, accessed November 15, 2018 at http://www.ipc-undp.org/pub/IPCWorkingPaper35.pdf.

Solon, G. (2016), 'What we didn't know about multigenerational mobility', *Ethos* 14, February 20–24, accessed April 7, 2018 at https://www.csc.gov.sg/docs/default-source/ethos/ethos_issue14.pdf.

Solow, R. (2003), 'Dumb and dumber in macroeconomics', manuscript for a Festschrift in honor of Joseph Stiglitz, accessed September 9, 2019 at https://www.scribd.com/document/20594916/Dumb-and-Dumber-in-Macroeconomics-Robert-m-Solow-So-How.

Solow, R. (2008), 'The state of macroeconomics', *Journal of Economic Perspectives* 22 (1): 243–249.

Solt, F. (2016), 'The Standardized World Income Inequality Database', *Social Science Quarterly* 97 (1): 1267–1281.

Statista (2018), 'Number of international and United States Starbucks stores from 2005 to 2017', accessed May 14, 2018 at https://www.statista.com/statistics/218366/number-of-international-and-us-starbucks-stores/.

Stiglitz, J. (2011), 'Of the 1%, for the 1%, by the 1%', *Vanity Fair*, May, accessed April 16, 2018 at https://www.vanityfair.com/news/2011/05/top-one-percent-201105.

Stiglitz, J. (2012), *The Price of Inequality: How Today's Divided Society Endangers Our Future*, New York: W. W. Norton.

Swift, A. (2005), 'Justice, luck, and the family: the intergenerational transmission of economic advantage from a normative perspective', in S. Bowles, H. Gintis, and M. Osborne Groves (eds), *Unequal Chances: Family Background and Economic Success*, Princeton, NJ: Princeton University Press, pp. 256–276.

Taplin, J. (2017), 'Is it time to break up Google?', *New York Times*, April 22, accessed November 18, 2018 at https://www.nytimes.com/2017/04/22/opinion/sunday/is-it-time-to-break-up-google.html.

Taylor, J. (1814), *An Inquiry into the Principles and Policies of the Government of the United States*, London: Routledge & Kegan Paul.

Thaler, R. (1985), 'Mental accounting and consumer choice', *Marketing Science* 4 (1): 199–214.

Thiel, P. (2014), 'Competition is for losers', *Wall Street Journal*, September 12, accessed January 27, 2019 at https://www.wsj.com/articles/peter-thiel-competition-is-for-losers-1410535536.

Thurow, L. (1971), 'The income distribution as a pure public good', *Quarterly Journal of Economics* 85 (2): 327–336.

Tideman, N. (1994), 'Interview with Milton Friedman', in N. Tideman and M. Gaffney (eds), *Land and Taxation*, London: Shepheard-Walwyn, pp. 121–131.

Tinbergen, J. (1974), 'Substitution of graduate by other labour', *Kyklos* 27 (2): 217–226.

Traub, A., L. Sullivan, and T. Meschede (2017), *The Asset Value of White Privilege: Understanding the Racial Wealth Gap*, New York: Demos.

Treisman, D. (2000), 'The causes of corruption: a cross-national study', *Journal of Public Economics* 76 (3): 399–457.

Trounstine, J. (2015), 'Segregation and inequality in public goods', *American Journal of Political Science* 60 (3): 709–725.

Tyson, L. and M. Spence (2017), 'Exploring the effects of technology on income and wealth inequality', in H. Boushey, J. B. DeLong, and M. Steinbaum (eds), *After Piketty: The Agenda for Economics and Inequality*, Cambridge, MA: Harvard University Press, pp. 170–208.

University of Texas Inequality Project (2018), 'Tutorials', accessed July 10, 2018 at http://utip.lbj.utexas.edu/tutorials.html.

Urata, S. and D. Narjoko (2017), 'International trade and inequality', ADBI Working Paper 675, Asian Development Bank Institute, accessed July 17, 2018 at https://www.adb.org/publications/international-trade-and-inequality.

US Bureau of the Census (2015), 'Income, poverty, and health insurance coverage in the United States', accessed February 8, 2018 at https://www.census.gov/content/dam/Census/library/publications/2016/demo/p60-256.pdf.

US Bureau of the Census (2016), 'The majority of children live with two parents', Census Bureau Reports, accessed January 7, 2019 at https://www.census.gov/newsroom/press-releases/2016/cb16-192.html.

Van Parijs, P. and Y. Vanderborght (2017), *Basic Income: A Radical Proposal for a Free Society and a Sane Economy*, Cambridge, MA: Harvard University Press.

Veblen, T. (1899), *The Theory of the Leisure Class: An Economic Study of Institutions*, New York: Macmillan.

Wacziarg, R. and K. Welch (2008), 'Trade liberalization and growth: new evidence', *World Bank Economic Review* 22 (2): 187–231.

Waldfogen, J. and E. Washbrook (2011), 'Income related gaps in school readiness in the United States and United Kingdom', in T. Smeeding, R. Erikson, and M. Jantti (eds), *Persistence, Privilege, and Parenting: The Comparative Study of Intergenerational Mobility*, New York: Russell Sage Publishing, pp. 175–208.

Wall Street Journal (2019), 'Economists' statement on carbon dividends', accessed January 26, 2019 at https://www.wsj.com/articles/economists-statement-on-carbon-dividends-11547682910.

Walras, L. (2010), *Studies in Social Economics*, trans. J. Van Daal and D. Walker, London: Taylor & Francis.

Wang, W. (2014), 'Record share of wives are more educated than their husbands', Pew Research Center, February 12, accessed May 18, 2018 at http://www.pewresearch.org/fact-tank/2014/02/12/record-share-of-wives-are-more-educated-than-their-husbands/.

Wanli, Y. (2015), 'Rural–urban income gap grows', *China Daily*, April 22, accessed February 9, 2018 at http://www.chinadaily.com.cn/china/2015-04/22/content_20509439.htm.

Watkins, J. (2013), 'Gild the throne! Kanye West and Kim Kardashian flush nearly $1million on gold plated toilets for their new Bel Air mansion', *The Daily Mail*, July 24, accessed May 18, 2018 at http://www.dailymail.co.uk/tvshowbiz/article-2376311/Kanye-West-Kim-Kardashian-flush-nearly-1-million-gold-plated-toilets-new-Bel-Air-mansion.html.

Watson, T. (2009), 'Inequality and the measurement of residential segregation by income in American neighborhoods', *Review of Income and Wealth* 55 (3): 820–844.

Weil, D. (2017), 'Income inequality, wage determination, and the fissured workplace', in H. Boushey, J. B. DeLong, and M. Steinbaum (eds), *After Piketty: The Agenda for Economics and Inequality*, Cambridge, MA: Harvard University Press, pp. 209–231.

Western, B. and J. Rosenfeld (2011), 'Unions, norms, and the rise in US wage inequality', *American Sociological Review* 76 (4): 513–537.

Wheelan, C. (2010), *Naked Economics: Undressing the Dismal Science*, New York: W. W. Norton.

Wilkinson, R. and K. Pickett (2006), 'Income inequality and population health: a review and explanation of the evidence', *Social Science & Medicine* 62 (7): 1768–1784.

Wilkinson, R. and K. Pickett (2009), *The Spirit Level: Why Greater Equality Makes Societies Stronger*, New York: Bloomsbury Press.

Wilson, W. J. (1996), *When Work Disappears: The World of the New Urban Poor*, New York: Vintage Publishing.

Wolfers, J. (2015), 'Fewer women run big companies than men named John', *New York Times*, March 2, accessed May 18, 2018 at https://www.nytimes.com/2015/03/03/upshot/fewer-women-run-big-companies-than-men-named-john.html?abt=0002&abg=0&mtrref=www.buzzfeed.com&gwh=62F0AC7C02D491F87CC1DBDC4569F923&gwt=pay.

Wolff, E. N. (2014), 'Household wealth trends in the United States, 1962–2013: what happened over the Great Recession?', NBER Working Paper 20733, accessed April 14, 2018 at https://www.nber.org/papers/w20733.

Wolff, E. N. (2017), *A Century of Wealth in America*, Cambridge, MA: Harvard University Press.

Wolff, E. N. (2019), 'The decline of African-American and Hispanic wealth since the Great Recession', Working Paper, accessed June 26, 2019 at http://www.ecineq.org/ecineq_paris19/papers_EcineqPSE/paper_14.pdf.

World Bank (2015), 'Doing business 2015', accessed July 17, 2016 at http://www.doingbusiness.org/reports/global-reports/doing-business-2015.

World Bank (2016), 'Poverty overview', accessed February 9, 2018 at http://www.worldbank.org/en/topic/poverty/overview.

World Bank (2018), 'Poverty', accessed July 17, 2018 at http://www.worldbank.org/en/topic/poverty/overview.

World Health Organization (2010), 'World malaria report 2010', accessed February 15, 2019 at https://www.who.int/malaria/world_malaria_report_2010/en/.

Zak, P. and S. Knack (2001), 'Trust and growth', *Economic Journal* 111 (470): 295–321.

Zandi, M. (2017), 'What does rising inequality mean for the macroeconomy?', in H. Boushey, J. B. DeLong, and M. Steinbaum (eds), *After Piketty: The Agenda for Economics and Inequality*, Cambridge, MA: Harvard University Press, pp. 384–411.

Zucman, G. (2014), 'Taxing across borders: tracking personal wealth and corporate profits', *Journal of Economic Perspectives* 28 (4): 121–148.

Zwolinski, M. (2013), 'Why did Hayek support a basic income?', accessed January 17, 2019 at https://www.libertarianism.org/columns/why-did-hayek-support-basic-income.

Index